Doing Field Projects: Methods and Practice for Social and Anthropological Research

John Forrest with Katie Nelson

WILEY Blackwell

This edition first published 2022
© 2022 John Wiley & Sons, Inc.

All rights reserved. No part of this publication may be reproduced, stored in a retrieval system, or transmitted, in any form or by any means, electronic, mechanical, photocopying, recording or otherwise, except as permitted by law. Advice on how to obtain permission to reuse material from this title is available at http://www.wiley.com/go/permissions.

The right of John Forrest to be identified as the author of this work has been asserted in accordance with law.

Registered Office
John Wiley & Sons, Inc., 111 River Street, Hoboken, NJ 07030, USA

Editorial Office
9600 Garsington Road, Oxford, OX4 2DQ, UK

For details of our global editorial offices, customer services, and more information about Wiley products visit us at www.wiley.com.

Wiley also publishes its books in a variety of electronic formats and by print-on-demand. Some content that appears in standard print versions of this book may not be available in other formats.

Limit of Liability/Disclaimer of Warranty
The contents of this work are intended to further general scientific research, understanding, and discussion only and are not intended and should not be relied upon as recommending or promoting scientific method, diagnosis, or treatment by physicians for any particular patient. In view of ongoing research, equipment modifications, changes in governmental regulations, and the constant flow of information relating to the use of medicines, equipment, and devices, the reader is urged to review and evaluate the information provided in the package insert or instructions for each medicine, equipment, or device for, among other things, any changes in the instructions or indication of usage and for added warnings and precautions. While the publisher and authors have used their best efforts in preparing this work, they make no representations or warranties with respect to the accuracy or completeness of the contents of this work and specifically disclaim all warranties, including without limitation any implied warranties of merchantability or fitness for a particular purpose. No warranty may be created or extended by sales representatives, written sales materials or promotional statements for this work. The fact that an organization, website, or product is referred to in this work as a citation and/or potential source of further information does not mean that the publisher and authors endorse the information or services the organization, website, or product may provide or recommendations it may make. This work is sold with the understanding that the publisher is not engaged in rendering professional services. The advice and strategies contained herein may not be suitable for your situation. You should consult with a specialist where appropriate. Further, readers should be aware that websites listed in this work may have changed or disappeared between when this work was written and when it is read. Neither the publisher nor authors shall be liable for any loss of profit or any other commercial damages, including but not limited to special, incidental, consequential, or other damages.

Library of Congress Cataloging-in-Publication Data
Names: Forrest, John, 1951- author.
Title: Doing field projects : methods and practice for social and
   anthropological research / John Forrest with Katie Nelson.
Description: Hoboken, NJ : John Wiley & Sons, 2022. | Includes
   bibliographical references and index.
Identifiers: LCCN 2021061401 (print) | LCCN 2021061402 (ebook) | ISBN
   9781119734611 (paperback) | ISBN 9781119734604 (pdf) | ISBN
   9781119734628 (epub)
Subjects: LCSH: Ethnology--Fieldwork. | Sociology--Research. |
   Anthropology--Research.
Classification: LCC GN346 .F67 2022 (print) | LCC GN346 (ebook) | DDC
   305.80072/3--dc23/eng/20220120
LC record available at https://lccn.loc.gov/2021061401
LC ebook record available at https://lccn.loc.gov/2021061402

Cover image: Courtesy of John Forrest
Cover design by Wiley

Set in 9.5/12.5pt STIXTwoText by Integra Software Services Pvt. Ltd, Pondicherry, India

I dedicate this work to my son Badger Forrest-Blincoe who, despite dad's wishes for him otherwise, became an anthropologist. He is a champion fieldworker whose progress I monitor with high regard.

Contents

Preface (Including a Word to Instructors) *vi*
Foreword (Including a Word to Student Readers) *ix*

1 Introduction *1*
2 Getting Started *22*
3 Ethics of Fieldwork *27*
4 Research Design *33*
5 Self-Study *39*
6 Proxemics *52*
7 Mapping *59*
8 Recorded Interviews *77*
9 Participant Observation *94*
10 Engaged Anthropology *100*
11 Process Documentation *111*
12 Visual Anthropology *117*
13 Sensory Observation *129*
14 Performance *138*
15 Life Histories (and Oral History) *147*
16 Charting Kinship *158*
17 Digital Ethnography (1) Social Media *167*
18 Digital Ethnography (2) Online Gaming *182*
19 Digital Ethnography (3) Human–Computer Interaction *186*
20 Digital Ethnography (4) Online Meetings/Classes *192*
21 Winding Down and Gearing Up *197*

References Cited *205*
Index *212*

Preface (Including a Word to Instructors)

Most of the projects in this book were originally designed for undergraduate majors in anthropology, and they have been thoroughly tested over more than 20 years of teaching them. However, they may also be useful to anyone with an interest in qualitative methods, including postgraduate students in anthropology as well as researchers in related fields. Prior to the 1980s, there was precious little interest in teaching fieldwork methods to undergraduates, especially in the United States. There were some individual instructors who took it upon themselves to teach and supervise fieldwork projects, but no overall institutional expectation that undergraduates need be trained as fieldworkers, and, in fact, there was a significant contingent within the discipline that was actively hostile to the idea of undergraduates conducting fieldwork. There was not even a uniform interest in teaching field methods to doctoral candidates in those days. Eventually seminars and field schools, such as the one created by H. Russell Bernard, set about ensuring that professional fieldworkers had a solid methodological grounding before embarking on sustained fieldwork. Such seminars produced invaluable written resources for the novice fieldworker, and they continue to proliferate. These resources are, however, geared to a level of professionalism that is unnecessary for many undergraduate projects.

Undergraduate student needs are highly varied, but, no matter what their personal and professional goals in life are, they can all benefit from having some grounding in anthropological methods. While it is typical for a biology or chemistry course to have a lab component, it is less common for cultural anthropology courses to have a methods course. This is true for a number of reasons. First, anthropological fieldwork does not happen in a self-contained laboratory. Therefore, it is not easy to supervise. Second, fieldwork can take considerable amounts of time (with much of it unproductive). Third, there are numerous ethical concerns about dealing with human subjects that have to be monitored carefully. Fourth, setting up the kind of fieldwork projects that undergraduates can productively engage in is a challenge. The last issue is the reason for this book. Undergraduate fieldwork is similar to graduate work in some ways, but not identical by any means, and should really be handled differently. Hence the projects in this volume.

This book is the product both of my own intensive professional experience as a fieldworker over a period of 40 years in the swamps of the Tidewater of North Carolina, the pueblos and Hispano villages of New Mexico, Buenos Aires and surrounds (my birthplace), and urban Cambodia (where I currently live), as well as smaller projects in England, Ukraine, Mari-El in the Russian Federation, and northern Italy, and of my experience designing and teaching a fieldwork methods course for undergraduates, which ran annually for over 20 years. I also introduced fieldwork methods into my Introduction to Anthropology course, not as a full-blown lab section akin to bio or chem lab, but as a paper requirement in the second half of the semester, where students could pick one assignment to pursue. Many examples in this book can be used in this way.

This book is designed to be a self-contained text for undergraduate instruction, but, if you are an instructor considering using these projects for your classes, either as individual exercises, or strung together as a full-blown course, you should realize that, despite the personal details and the specificity, there is a great deal of flexibility built into each exercise, and you should feel free to add and modify as you see fit. In certain spheres, such as the development of research design, it is expected that you will have your own needs and ideas, and you should treat the suggestions here as a rough template only. Most of the projects can be used on their own, although some of the later ones build on skills acquired in earlier ones, and several require the kind of planning that is, perhaps, impractical for a stand-alone exercise in a course for which a field project is only an adjunct.

Although this text is designed for use in undergraduate courses in anthropology, it is not limited to that audience. Postgraduate students may also use it to gain insight into qualitative fieldwork as a method, particularly at the beginning of their studies. Trainees in a variety of disciplines from sociology and social psychology to market research and hotel management can also use relevant projects to apply qualitative methods of investigation to their own specialties. These days, there is a common popular belief that if social data under investigation are quantified, the resultant "study" is somehow more rigorous (that is, more "scientific") than a qualitative one. This perception may sometimes be reasonable, but it does not have to be. Qualitative investigations can be designed in a thoroughly rigorous manner, and may yield results that are more nuanced and insightful (and, therefore, more "useful"), than a strictly quantitative one. In that regard, the methods outlined in this text can be used by anyone interested in facets of social research, so that the projects can be tailored for use by people in human resources, public relations, political campaigns, workplace efficiency, and the like, where a deeper understanding of various components of the social landscape can be beneficial.

My goals as a teacher of anthropology have been student-centered from the outset. To this end, I have always valued an approach to teaching anthropological theory that addresses the crucial question of where our raw information comes from, what it looks like, and how it is used to generate theory. When undergraduates engage in fieldwork for themselves, they gain an understanding of both the strengths and weaknesses of the anthropological method. They also start to gain practical insight into explanatory modeling and theory building, which helps in their critical reading of classic texts in anthropology.

The projects in this text can be used individually as assignments in a variety of anthropology courses (including Intro to General or Social/Cultural Anthropology), or chosen units can be pieced together to form an entire qualitative methods course – for undergraduate majors in anthropology, or in allied fields where such fieldwork is applicable. There are too many projects described here for a methods class covering a

12- to 15-week term, or even a whole academic year, so a certain amount of selection is necessary. Furthermore, a number of the projects deal with topics that are not pertinent to the needs and interests of all instructors and can be omitted. My purpose is to open up as many choices as possible and leave it up to individual instructors to determine how to make use of the projects independently or woven together.

Both because the world is now dominated by digital technology and because the COVID-19 pandemic beginning in 2019 forced many universities to switch to online resources for teaching, there are a number of ways to use this book in a socially distanced manner. There are four chapters devoted exclusively to digital ethnography (17–20) and many projects, such as those that involve interviews, contain suggestions for carrying them out online rather than in person. There is enough such material presented here that the book can be used exclusively as an online tool if the need arises.

Chapters both before and after the projects themselves analyze the history of fieldwork in anthropology in Europe and North America, pointing out the pros and cons of the method, as well as underlining certain pitfalls and biases that can easily (and unwittingly) creep in. These chapters also investigate the complex process of writing field notes themselves, as well as problematizing the numerous ways – good and bad – that field notes have been, and can be, converted into finished ethnographic writing. My intention in these chapters, as well as in the projects themselves, is to give instructors scope for further discussion with their students concerning the importance of the fieldwork method in anthropology, along with consideration of the numerous debates that continue to surface regarding its reliability and utility.

Throughout the projects presented here there is an awareness that the fieldworker is the instrument of field study, in the same way that a telescope is the instrument of astronomy or the microscope of microbiology, and I have made an effort to incorporate self-analysis and self-reflection on the part of the novice fieldworker in the process of data collection whenever possible. Such self-awareness is also reflected periodically in some of my project descriptions by way of highlighting how critical it is for the accurate interpretation of the results of fieldwork to understand the personal biases and interests of the person gathering the data. To that end, I often include my own field notes and project data as examples, as well as those of my former students, as I do when I am teaching. I hope these examples can be used as springboards for instructors to incorporate their own experiences into their teaching of these projects, rather than as replacements.

I would like to thank a number of colleagues for insightful comments during the preparation of this manuscript, including Shaka McGlotten, who helped with the chapters on digital ethnography, as well as Alasdair Clayre of UNIMAS Kuching, James Peacock, UNC Chapel Hill, and former students Janette Yarwood, and Elisabeth Jackson. I would like to give special thanks to all the anonymous reviewers of the many versions of the manuscript over the years who have helped enormously in shaping the work into what it is today. Their help has been invaluable.

Foreword (Including a Word to Student Readers)

When I was first asked to join this book as a supporting author, I was delighted to have the opportunity to contribute to such an innovative text. I had already reviewed a draft of the book and was impressed by the variety of field projects it contains as well as the depth by which each exercise is presented. I have been a college anthropology instructor for over 15 years and have written about qualitative methods and teaching and learning in anthropology textbooks and through my work as a founding member and Associate Editor of the *Teaching and Learning Anthropology Journal*. John (whom I personally refer to as Juan Alejandro – his birth name) is a number of years my senior and has the experience of a full life and career as an anthropologist and professor behind him. His own research background is varied and rich. His depth of knowledge and experience complements my passion for pedagogical accessibility and relevance. You will find that the exercises in this volume likewise represent these qualities. They are comprehensively classroom-tested and are engaging.

There are a number of fieldwork books in print, but none quite like this one. This text is designed for students, or others, with an interest in learning qualitative anthropological fieldwork methods, regardless of whether they intend to pursue a career in the social sciences. Through straightforward introductory exercises to more complex research approaches, you will learn step by step how to craft and execute research using qualitative fieldwork in a professional manner. Regardless of whether you have previous fieldwork experience or are new to qualitative research, you can gain valuable skills through these projects.

As you will learn, conducting ethnographic fieldwork at the undergraduate level has not always been supported historically within cultural anthropology. For many years, faculty were discouraged from teaching research methods, in part because they feared ethnographic research could not be conducted well without extensive advanced training. Yet in the past 20–30 years this trend has begun to change. Juan and I firmly believe learning to conduct fieldwork early in one's academic career is extremely important. By learning fieldwork skills, you will likely gain far more than the ability to operationalize research techniques. You will learn, for instance, to use your senses of bodily perception to notice, observe, describe, and analyze a wide range of social and cultural phenomena around you. You will come to appreciate what you uniquely bring to fieldwork and other social contexts. You will recognize the ways that people interact with the space and objects around them in their physical environment. You will learn how to interview others and find meaning in their narration. You will learn from others by participating in the same activities they do. You will use numerical data, digital environments, and performances as ways to see seemingly ordinary activities in extraordinarily different ways. In sum, you will learn to think like an anthropologist.

I suspect you will carry many of the skills and perspectives you learn through the projects in this book with you throughout your future career and life. As I tell my students, anthropology is one of the few disciplines that intersect with nearly every other field of study or area of practice. Whether you study business, become a lawyer, go to medical school, work in construction, or take a job as a stockbroker or deep sea diver, you will find ways that fieldwork can help you in your work.

The work of being a human embedded in a cultural environment studying other humans and cultures can be challenging. But mostly, it is exciting. Best of luck to you on your fieldwork journey!

Katie Nelson, PhD

1

Introduction

Part I A Brief History of Fieldwork

Why Fieldwork?

Ethnographic fieldwork is the hallmark research approach of sociocultural anthropology. Its centrality has not waned since its inception more than a century ago, yet the variety of questions that fieldwork answers has expanded greatly. For instance, anthropologist Olga Lidia Olivia Hernandez studies Aztec dance collectives in multiple sites in Baja California, Mexico; and California, USA. She conducts fieldwork to understand why Aztec dance emerged as a form of ethnicity on the US-Mexico border among non-indigenous participants, and how national, political, religious, and bodily processes are involved in the reappropriation of Aztec dancing (Olivas 2018). Taking a more multidisciplinary approach in her fieldwork among Orangutan care workers in Borneo, anthropologist Juno Salazar Parreñas draws on anthropology, primatology, Southeast Asian history, gender studies, queer theory, and science and technology studies. She explores the violence care workers and Orangutans experience. She asks if conservation biology can turn away from violent techniques to ensure Orangutan population growth and embrace a feminist sense of welfare (Parreñas 2018). Anthony Kwame Harrison conducts fieldwork in San Francisco among the underground hip-hop scene. Harrison interviewed area hip-hop artists and also performed as the emcee "Mad Squirrel." His immersion in the subculture allowed him a unique vantage point to examine the changing nature of race among young North Americans, as well as issues of ethnic and racial identification, and how different ethnic groups engage hip-hop in different ways as a means to claim racial and establish subcultural authenticity (Harrison 2009).

Fieldwork is an extraordinarily flexible and expansive methodology, allowing researchers to ask challenging questions and uncover deep, nuanced, and contextualized answers that are rarely self-evident. The purpose of this book is to guide you step by step as you learn ethnographic techniques. Ultimately, I hope you will use them to answer the types of questions you are most passionate about. However, in order to gain competence in ethnographic fieldwork techniques, it is important to understand what ethnographic fieldwork is, what makes it special, and how it evolved into the preeminent research approach in cultural anthropology

Doing Field Projects: Methods and Practice for Social and Anthropological Research, First Edition. John Forrest.
© 2022 John Wiley & Sons, Inc. Published 2022 by John Wiley & Sons, Inc.

Armchair Anthropology

Before ethnographic fieldwork became the well-established and rigorous research tool it is today, it went through a number of significant changes. In the nineteenth century, a very few (primarily North American) anthropologists traveled away from the comforts of their hometowns to study "others," while the majority of them preferred to stay at home and gather their data by consulting the records of travelers instead. By the start of the twentieth century, the balance had shifted, with the great majority venturing out from their homes. At that time (and later), the seemingly self-evident divide between sociology and anthropology was that sociologists studied "us," whereas anthropologists studied "them." Otherwise, both disciplines were interested in how societies/cultures worked.

In the nineteenth century, influential anthropologists such as E.B. Tylor, and James George Frazer developed highly generalized analyses of cultures. They tended to view small scale societies as if they were isolated from one another and from the impact of global forces, such as colonialism, which most certainly had a major impact on their internal social structures and belief systems, yet were largely ignored. These anthropologists, who dominated the field in Europe, did not conduct fieldwork at all, but, instead, sought cross-cultural information from the seclusion of their library armchairs. They drew their grand conclusions about the evolution of culture around the world from diverse sources without any systematic concern for the reliability of the materials they used nor the context in which they were written. Their goal was to show that under the incredible diversity of cultural practices there was a bedrock unity.

A classic example of this approach is Frazer's multivolume *Golden Bough* (Frazer 1890), which was one of the towering centerpieces of anthropological theorizing in the nineteenth century, well into the twentieth. He took data from any and all available sources – travelers' journals, newspaper articles, historical archives, etc. – with no clear assessment of the truth or validity of the information, nor was he concerned with contextualizing the data culturally because overarching theorizing about religion worldwide was the ultimate goal. Thus, finding common patterns globally took precedence over the specialized analysis of fine-grained cultural details.

The weakness of Frazer's method is that without cultural context, cross-cultural comparison of specific symbols is meaningless. For example, take the image of a snake. What a snake means in different cultures varies tremendously, in no small part because snakes are themselves enormously varied, both within geographic regions and between them. Some snakes are small and harmless, some are large and terrifying, some are fatally poisonous, some have domestic uses, and so on. When snakes are a main component of tales globally they can take on myriad meanings. It is simply impossible to gather together all the tales and images of snakes worldwide and meld them into a unified theory of the meaning of snakes to humans. They are forces for good or for evil, protectors or destroyers, creators or demolishers, healers or killers, wise teachers or treacherous betrayers, etc. etc. But if you gather together a group of tales from around the world without paying attention to such cultural details, as Frazer did, you can weave fantastical theories concerning the meaning of the snake in human culture. Ethnographic fieldwork that paid attention to fine-grained details and cultural context put an end to that kind of theorizing.

At the turn of the twentieth century, scholars such as Émile Durkheim and Max Weber were interested in how modern European cultures functioned and evolved, but they did not limit themselves to that sphere alone. They wrote about Pacific Rim cultures at great length as well, including indigenous Australian and traditional Chinese and Indian religious beliefs and practices. Both assumed that, at some level, all humans operated according to certain fundamental, discoverable principles. In other words, they were searching for human universals, rather than exploring what made people diverse. Like anthropologists of the nineteenth century, their data were second-hand. They did no fieldwork for themselves. As social science matured in the early twentieth century the split between sociology and anthropology opened up, with anthropologists carving out intensive, long-term fieldwork projects with peoples well outside of Europe and North America as their domain – in large part, supported by, and promoted by, colonialist governments for their own ends. In this context, getting out of their armchairs and getting to grips with the pragmatics of rigorous, "scientific" (that is, grounded and verifiable) fieldwork in foreign places was a major breakthrough in the development of anthropology as a discipline.

The Evolution Century

In many ways we can think of the nineteenth century as the "evolution century." The notion that things evolve according to scientifically discoverable principles became the mantra across the board in academia. Wilhelm and Jacob Grimm, famous for their folktale collections, were significant linguists who documented in detail how languages evolved, Charles Lyell suggested that rocks and the physical landscape evolved according to discoverable scientific principles, Mary Anning found fossil evidence of change in lifeforms over time, and Charles Darwin (as well as Alfred Russel Wallace) argued that species evolve via the process of natural selection. Evolution seemed like the perfect paradigm to cover all branches of inquiry, and the study of human cultures looked as if it could easily fit under the umbrella of evolution along with the others. E. B. Tylor in Britain (Tylor 1871) and Lewis Henry Morgan (Morgan 1877) in North America developed complementary paradigms of universal sociocultural evolution that became normative in anthropology until the early twentieth century. Both Tylor and Morgan argued that the movement through various stages – which Morgan labeled savagery, barbarism, and civilization – was controlled by discoverable scientific principles akin to the three-age system which is still in use (in considerably modified form) in many branches of Old World archeology.

The three-age system, or the movement from Stone Age to Bronze Age to Iron Age, was once seen as an obvious and inevitable sequential progression. There is a simple, although flawed, logic which governs the three-stage progression, as follows. The first humans used rocks to make their tools for cutting, mashing, scraping, and killing because rocks and muscle power were all they had at the outset. They would have used wood, bones, and vines also, of course, but stone tools are what remain in the archeological record, so the era was dubbed the Stone Age. This era saw numerous innovations, including the domestication of plants and animals. Thus, it was eventually divided into the Old Stone Age (or Paleolithic), the period before domestication, and the New Stone Age (or Neolithic), the period after domestication. Domestication of plants led to sedentism because people had to stay in one place to cultivate their crops. Sedentary peoples could build permanent structures which migratory or nomadic foragers could not. These included ovens for baking that could also be used for firing pottery. Subsequently, these peoples could control heat sufficiently to smelt metals. Copper and tin were smelted first because they have low melting points. Thus, they could produce bronze (an alloy of copper and tin) to make tools which are superior to stone tools ... and so it goes.

Archeologists now see that the three-age system is neither applicable to all cultures worldwide nor as logical a series of steps as once appeared obvious. Some cultures never developed metallurgy indigenously, yet they managed to evolve in complex ways sociopolitically. Some cultures had a distinct copper-using era (the Chalcolithic) in between their Stone and Bronze Ages. Some cultures skipped over the Bronze Age entirely and moved directly from stone tools to iron ones. The possibilities are seemingly endless, and what was once presumed to be a series of inevitable advancements taken in logical steps is now seen to be a much more fluid and malleable process, influenced by a variety of variables including geography and contact with other cultures. In the nineteenth century, however, such nuances were less well known because both archeological methods and ethnographic fieldwork were in their infancy. Reliable data were scarce.

While the 1870s were productive in North America in some spheres of ethnographic fieldwork, such as Morgan's extensive collection of kinship data, first from the Iroquois (Morgan 1851), and later from the Winnebago, Crow, Yankton, Kaw, Blackfeet, Omaha, and others (Morgan 1871), there were two significant problems with the research. First, Morgan relied almost exclusively on interviews, which meant that the information which he collected had no cultural context with which to frame it and, hence, make sense of it, and, second, because there was a physical and intellectual separation between museum departments, which were engaged in field expeditions, and university teaching departments of anthropology, which might have been bastions of ethnographic theory but were virtually nonexistent. Consequently, field data did not translate into theory within a university environment. Morgan never held an academic position but, almost by default (there being no rivals in academia), his paradigm of universal cultural evolution held center stage, and was heavily relied upon by all manner of theorists, from Karl Marx to Sigmund Freud, to buttress their own theories of social development.

The three-age system of archeology, and hence cultural evolution, has the concept of *progress* built into it. Evolution in other academic spheres does not imply that the processes under study which are evolving are also progressing. For example, Modern English is not better than Middle English or Old English in any absolute sense. Each form of the language suits the needs of the people using them in their respective eras. Likewise, marble is not better than limestone even though it is the metamorphosed form of limestone. Both rocks serve their purposes. The verbs "evolve" and "change" in these contexts are almost exact synonyms, and the scholars in biology, geology, and linguistics understood this idea. Unfortunately, the three-age system of Old World archeology, when transformed into a full-blown theory of cultural evolution, can carry with it the notion that cultures advance or improve as they move through the stages.

Not surprisingly, in the nineteenth century the idea of "progress" in both archeology and sociocultural anthropology was equated with technological advancements, as befits a world that was rapidly changing ("advancing" in their terms) under the powerful thrust of the Industrial Revolution, thus placing technology at the center of cultural analysis in anthropology.

The nineteenth century also saw the pinnacle of European colonialism across the globe. This colonialism was fueled by greed, and supported by racist assumptions that colonized peoples were inferior to their colonial masters and, therefore, could be exploited with impunity. To be profitable, industries in Europe, especially Britain, needed cheap raw materials and cheap labor, which colonialism provided in abundance. Slavery was an outgrowth of the colonial system, justified by a stance that non-European peoples were inferior, racially and culturally to Europeans. Civilizing them was the "White man's burden." The anthropology that developed in Europe in the early twentieth century was profoundly shaped by this colonialist mentality in complex ways, especially within the imperial holdings of European nations.

Off the Verandah and into the Colonies

At the beginning of the twentieth century, British anthropologists started to emulate their colleagues in North America by journeying well away from home to conduct fieldwork. The turning point for British anthropology was the Torres Straits expedition of 1898 led by psychologist-turned-anthropologist, W.H.R. Rivers, and including C.G. Seligman, who later taught Bronislaw Malinowski, E.E. Evans-Pritchard, and Meyer Fortes. The Torres Straits lie between the northern tip of Queensland in Australia and the southeastern shores of Papua New Guinea, and their indigenous island peoples are culturally and linguistically distinct from either, and from each other.

The six members of the expedition were an assortment of psychologists, linguists, and ethnologists, and their preferred method of fieldwork was interviewing as well as taking physical measurements. In the process, Rivers discovered that the people he interviewed had the same visual abilities as Europeans, yet had no word for the color blue, and used the same word for blue things as for black things. Likewise, they did not have words to distinguish biological siblings and cousins. Inspired by his work in the Torres Straits, Rivers spent several months in 1901–2 among the Todas of the Nilgiri Hills of southern India.

At the time the Todas numbered about 700 individuals living in relative seclusion from other south Indian cultures. They were a **polyandrous** (one woman with multiple husbands) society divided into **moieties** who lived primarily on buffalo pastoralism and dairying – which involved a number of complex religious ceremonies, all meticulously noted by Rivers and eventually published in *The Todas* (1906). In the preface he writes that his work is "not merely the record of the customs and beliefs of a people, but also the demonstration of anthropological method" (Rivers 1906: v). The first 11 chapters are an extremely detailed description of the dairy cult and its priests among the Todas, but then it trails off into generalities concerning gods, magic, kinship, clanship, crime, and so on, and does not integrate these descriptions with his analysis of pastoralism. Furthermore, he failed to document the existence of matrilineal clans alongside the patrilineal ones. The problem was that he had to use an interpreter to communicate with the Todas, and he lived in a hotel the entire time – leading to what is sometimes called "verandah ethnography" – the replacement for armchair anthropology. That is, anthropologists now journeyed away from their cloistered libraries to far-flung locations and peoples, but then interviewed them on hotel verandahs rather than living with them in their own villages, one-to-one. Bronislaw Malinowski changed all of that.

According to Malinowski's later recounting of the story of how he developed **participant-observation** fieldwork, his inspiration began while attending Jagiellonian University in Kraków in Poland, pursuing a doctorate in physics and mathematics. He became bedridden with an illness, and during his convalescence he began to read Frazer's *Golden Bough*. Taken by the ideas in the work, he abandoned his current track (after the doctorate) and went to the University of Leipzig in Germany, where he studied economics and psychology, and then in 1910 went to England to study anthropology at the London School of Economics under C.G. Seligman.

Malinowski was in Australia attending a conference in 1914 when World War I broke out, which left him in a precarious position because he was an Austro-Hungarian citizen and, therefore, an enemy noncombatant alien as far as the British were concerned. The Australian government was sympathetic to his plight, however, and gave him funds first to do fieldwork on Mailu Island in Papua, and then in the Trobriand Islands. The particulars are a little obscure, but the received wisdom (based in part on his diary) is that Malinowski was not comfortable with his first placement in Papua. He did not speak the local languages and did not have the ability to live with the people he was investigating, so he felt limited in his ability to understand the culture. What is a little perplexing in hindsight is why these early attempts at fieldwork seemed so limiting to him. What Malinowski was undertaking at first in Papua – verandah fieldwork – was the norm for social anthropology at the time. Thus, in June 1915 he started again in the Trobriand Islands off the northeast coast of New Guinea and continued, off and on, for several years, this time living among the Trobrianders and learning about their culture by being thoroughly immersed in it, in isolation, for long periods.

Malinowski's contribution to anthropological data collecting cannot be underestimated, and the range of his subject matter is astounding. His method is sometimes referred to now as an "off the verandah" technique, meaning that he broke with the custom of interviewing indigenous people on a hotel verandah, and, instead, lived and worked with them in their local villages – learning the local language rather than relying on an interpreter. The methodological point that Malinowski stresses in *Argonauts of the Western Pacific*, his best-selling, compendious account of island to island exchange (kula ring) and ocean-going canoe travel in Melanesia, is that the participant observer is both intimately involved in the culture under study while, at the same time, scientifically detached. For example, at one point he writes that the goal of the ethnographer in the field is "to grasp the native's point of view, his relation to life, to realize his vision of his world" (Malinowski 1961 [1922]:25).

Today, anthropologists often use the term **"emic"** to denote discussion of social situations in local terms (Malinowski's "native's point of view") and **"etic"** to refer to the anthropologist's perspective. These terms are derived from Kenneth Pike's analysis of language. In his *Language in Relation to a Unified Theory of the Structure of Human Behavior* (Pike [1954, 1955, 1960] 1967), Pike draws a technical distinction between a "phonetic" and a "phonemic" analysis of the sounds of a language. Phonetic differences are any differences in the sound of a word that can be detected, and phonemic differences are *differences that make a difference* to the semantic meaning of the word in that language. For example, English speakers can detect the difference between an aspirated and unaspirated /p/ when it is pointed out to them (phonetic difference), but the difference makes no difference to the meanings of words in English (phonemic difference). If you hold your hand close to your mouth and say the word "paper," you should feel a puff of air on the first /p/ and not on the second. The first /p/ is aspirated, the second is not. You can experiment to make them both aspirated or both unaspirated, but the meaning of the word does not change whichever way you say it. Linguists say that there is a phonetic difference (you can detect the difference), but not a phonemic difference (the meaning of the word does not change). In languages such as Khmer, aspirated and unaspirated /p/ are both phonetically *and* phonemically different. Using one versus the other changes the meanings of words.

Strip off the /phon/ component of Pike's terminology ("phone" = "sound") and you have "etic" and "emic." You can add new prefixes to get such concepts as "proxemics" – documenting the use of interpersonal space to infer what different distances mean locally (see Chapter 6) – or "aesthemics" (as opposed to "aesthetics") – understanding value judgments concerning beauty in indigenous terms. Or, you can simply use the suffixes "emic" and "etic" as analytic words in their own right (pronounced /eemic/ (long e) and /etic/ (short e) – same is in "phonemic" and "phonetic").The emic/etic distinction is of considerable importance in anthropology in general and in fieldwork methodology in particular. It often, simplistically, gets translated into: ways of viewing things from an "insider" (emic) versus "outsider" (etic) perspective in anthropological discourse, but such a translation is rather misleading, although not entirely inaccurate.[1] Pike, as a linguist, frequently used the phrase "differences that make a difference" to describe an emic approach, which I can illustrate with a simple example.

In Cambodia it is considered disrespectful, as a general rule, to show bare skin on shoulders or knees in public. Some men get away with going shirtless if the weather is hot and they are involved in heavy labor, but otherwise everyone is expected to cover their shoulders. This rule is rigidly enforced in sacred places, such as pagodas. People are denied entry if their bare shoulders are visible. But, covering one's shoulders is not straightforward. One cannot simply drape a scarf, shawl, or other loose piece of cloth over bare shoulders and expect to be admitted to a pagoda. In European terms, shoulders with skin visible are bare, but shoulders covered with a shawl are not bare. The emics of Khmer culture are different. For your shoulders to be considered "covered" you must be wearing a fitted garment that has sleeves, such as a shirt or jacket, so that the skin on your shoulders is not visible. That is, simple visibility is not the issue. *How* the skin on your shoulders is covered matters. In Khmer emics: shoulders with skin showing and shoulders covered by loose material = bare; shoulders covered with a fitted garment = not bare. In this case, bare skin versus shawl on skin is a difference that does *not* make a difference. That is, it is an etic difference, not an emic one, to Khmer people.

---

1 See https://www.researchgate.net/publication/246054591_Emics_and_Etics_The_InsiderOutsider_Debate for further details.

Malinowski valued probing Trobriand Islanders' emic view of the world, but he was also interested in an etic approach. He writes:

> Not even the most intelligent native has any clear idea of the Kula as a big, organised social construction, still less of its sociological function and implications ... The integration of all the details observed, the achievement of a sociological synthesis of all the various, relevant symptoms, is the task of the Ethnographer ... the Ethnographer has to construct the picture of the big institution, very much as the physicist constructs his theory from the experimental data, which always have been within reach of everybody, but needed a consistent interpretation.
>
> (Malinowski 1961 [1922]: 83–84)

Malinowski's early history as a physicist is clear here, and his comments raise questions about fieldwork methods and their ultimate purpose. Here he is saying that fieldwork data are akin to experimental data in physical science in that in both cases the observer gathers the welter of observations together and is able to abstract overarching principles from all the myriad details. This is a point of view that we must ponder very carefully. Is it the goal of ethnographer as social *scientist* to take a mass of field observations and reduce them down to social laws in the way that Isaac Newton took a mass of experimental observations and reduced them to the laws of motion, or is there a different goal in anthropology? This debate has swung back and forth for some time with no clear answers, although at present the overwhelming majority of cultural anthropologists reject the scientific model (see Part II).

Post-Colonial Anthropology

The step from hotel verandah to village hut was a major leap forward for ethnographic fieldwork, but it contained some baggage that was rarely acknowledged. No matter how much Malinowski wanted to be a "participant" in local activities, he was always going to be perceived as an outsider, and, as importantly, he was going to be categorized as a member of the colonial elite. This status cannot avoid coloring the relationship between ethnographer and people being recorded. Whether in interviews, participant-observation, or both, there always exists a power dynamic informed by the status of the parties involved.

It is not an accident that all prewar ethnographic fieldwork conducted by British social anthropologists took place among peoples who had been colonized and become part of the British empire. Nor is it a coincidence that many of their works, such as *African Political Systems*, edited by Meyer Fortes and E.E. Evans-Pritchard (1940), and *Political Systems of Highland Burma* by Edmund Leach (1954), spoke directly to the political organization of subject populations. Colonial offices in Britain funded such research because they wanted to devise strategies for controlling local people by using their own power structures rather than simply imposing British law arbitrarily. Whether consciously or unconsciously, such a situation inevitably leads to a skewed power dynamic between ethnographer and people being analyzed.

During the mid-twentieth century, many European colonies, particularly those controlled by Britain and France, pushed for independence. When that independence was achieved, European anthropologists no longer had easy access to what many previously saw as their "natural laboratories" – especially in Africa and Asia. Once the colonial powers gave way to indigenously controlled governments, the continued role of anthropology came under scrutiny both in the former colonies and at home in anthropology departments. This time period is now conventionally thought of within anthropology as "post-colonialist" with a mindset which seeks to redress the long-standing imbalance of power and authority between the person conducting fieldwork and the people being analyzed. Post-colonial anthropology also seeks to change the very framework of investigation, including the continuing assessment of the relative value of various lines of inquiry both for the inquirer and for the community in the spotlight. It also includes the restructuring of inquiry so that the people under analysis are able to conduct the analysis themselves.

The process of transforming ethnography from an outsider enterprise to an insider one meant that both methods and theory came under deep examination and were forced to change because of it. On the one hand, if a member of a group of people whose cultural history lies well outside of mainstream Euro-American practices takes on the job of ethnographic inquiry, the intellectual norms of Euro-American anthropology get imported into that inquiry (including its goals as well as its procedures). Thus, the insider may (perhaps unwittingly) take on the role of an outsider. On the other hand, an indigenous ethnographer may have the desire, and ability, to change the methods and analysis of anthropology to suit local needs and expectations, although such changes bring their own problems (see, for example, Hannoum 2011; Hurston 1935; Mingming 2002).

The underlying colonialist sympathies of anthropologists such as Malinowski and Evans-Pritchard are now reasonably well understood, although their implications are still being explored and debated. In Malinowski's case, his private diaries confirm his many ethnic and gender biases explicitly. It is just as easy to identify inherent prejudices in the fieldwork of the earliest practitioners, even in the absence of confidential personal data. We should also acknowledge attempts by anthropologists, from the mid-twentieth century on, to reflect on the nature of their own fieldwork and its inherent limitations (e.g. Briggs 1970; Dumont 1978; Marriott 1953; Powdermaker 1967, Rabinow 1977 (& 2007). In light of this complicated history of the development of anthropological fieldwork, today, it is ever more important for fieldworkers to be hyper-vigilant concerning the power dynamics that exist between the ethnographer and the people providing ethnographic information (e.g. Ayi et al. 2007; Bester et al. 2003; Cerwonka and Malkki 2007; Gardner 2006; Siegel 2011); I will discuss this issue in more detail throughout this book, beginning with Self-Study (Chapter 5).

Another change in anthropology during the post-colonial era is an increasing emphasis on the need for fieldwork to do *something* beyond the collecting and analysis of field data for pure research purposes only. This had led to the development of the specialty of **applied anthropology**, including **medical anthropology** (see in particular Kedia and Van Willigen 2005). Applied anthropology required that anthropologists become more directly engaged with the people under investigation (see e.g. Albro et al. 2011; Armbruster and Laerke 2008; Price 2004; Sanford and Angel-Ajani 2006), such that activism and **engaged anthropology** became field methodologies in their own right and are now mainstream within the discipline (see Chapter 10). Today, applied anthropologists work in a myriad of areas, including in business, IT, healthcare, environmental science, archaeology, and other fields. There are numerous benefits, as well as drawbacks, involved in applied and **activist anthropology**, including ethical concerns created by the deliberate intervention with communities. These issues are directly addressed in relevant chapters.

In the process of coming of age, qualitative fieldwork went through a great deal of methodological and philosophical soul searching concerning the nature of the data being collected and the ways they were analyzed and presented, as anthropologists became more and more skeptical about the validity of the ethnographies of the past. Could field data ever be considered objective, and, even if such a goal was possible, was it desirable? Should fieldwork follow the basic models of hypothesis testing that dominate the physical sciences? How do we ensure that qualitative methods are legitimately rigorous? These, and many other, questions were posed repeatedly, beginning in the postwar years and they continue to this day. Therefore, before beginning actual projects we need to take a step back and review some key methodological issues to bear in mind when embarking on fieldwork.

Part II Analytic Strategies

Fieldwork Vs Ethnography (or Ethnology)

Analytically, there is a difference between doing fieldwork and writing ethnography (or "doing" sociocultural anthropology), although the edges between the two are fuzzy. Rather loosely, we can think of fieldwork as the process of data collection, and ethnography as the next step: writing up field notes into finished form that analyzes the field data. But things are not that simple. There is a necessary synergy between data collection and its analysis. Etymologically, "ethnography" is a blend of two Greek roots (ethnos = a people + graphein = to write). The older, more generic, term for the study of cultures was **"ethnology"** where the suffix logos (= knowledge) was preferred – akin to biology (life knowledge), geology (earth knowledge), theology (god knowledge), and anthropology (humankind knowledge). Today, "ethnology" is considered a somewhat dated term, although it is still used, and the notion that we are *writing* about a culture seems to sit better philosophically with anthropologists than the thought that we definitively *know* something about them. After all, writing about cultures always entails analysis even if only implicitly. There is no such thing as a simple description of a culture without some kind of analysis. The bias of the observer is inevitable.

Terminology aside, curiosity about "other" cultures has a long history (see e.g. Malefijt 1974; Honigmann 1976). Not only did ancient and medieval scholars, such as Plutarch and Ibn Khaldun, describe the cultures of other lands, they also developed theories concerning why people in those lands behaved in the ways that they did. These classical theorists had numerous insights, some of which we can still debate today (does climate affect personality and/or behavior, for example), but they lacked rigorous fieldwork methodologies. Well-designed fieldwork is what sets apart the modern study of ethnography from these older sources. But "rigor" in the context of qualitative analysis is a thorny issue. Controlled experiments are not ethically viable in sociocultural anthropology, although certain kinds of quantitative analysis used in anthropology (such as studies of nutrition or life expectancy cross-culturally) are able to borrow rigorous methodologies in emulation of physical science. This point raises the objective versus subjective dilemma within social science.

Objective Vs Subjective (and Anti-Objective)

The distinction between objective and subjective data (which is sometimes used to distinguish between the physical sciences and the humanities – with the social sciences hovering somewhere in the middle) is popularly believed to be an easily defined dichotomy. Often, people view objective reality as being independent of any observer, whereas subjective reality is filtered through the biases of a human spectator. For instance, "This coffee is 95°C" (objective) versus "This coffee is too hot" (subjective). This commonsense dichotomy has been under scrutiny by scholars for centuries because it is deeply problematic when held up to the light. Can there be a physical "objective" reality that is independent of the senses needed to appreciate its composition? **Postmodern** philosophers have further questioned the seemingly "obvious" distinction between objective and subjective realities and led anthropologists to question whether objectivity (however defined) is possible at all – especially in the social sciences. Can a fieldworker *objectively* study a social situation? Should they even try?

The critique of objectivity in anthropology began in the postwar years, reaching one kind of climax in the essays in Dell Hymes's collection *Reinventing Anthropology* (Hymes 1972). The last two sections of this anthology focus on different facets of this critique (see especially Jay 1972; Scholte 1972; Diamond 1972). Since then, the forces of philosophical opposition to objectivity in anthropology have shaped into well-known main currents in the discipline, such as the movements toward reflexivity and humanism (see e.g. Clifford and Marcus 1986; Dwyer 1999; Geertz 1990, Goodall 2000; Hertz 1997; Herzfeld 1987; Marcus 1998; Richardson 1990; Robben and Sluka 2012).

While the critique of objectivity in the social sciences has taken many forms, what one should carefully consider before embarking on fieldwork is less the notion that the data obtained through fieldwork are *un*objective, or incapable of being made objective, but rather the idea that they can be deliberately conceived of as *anti*-objective; that is, they can stand in conscious *opposition* to objectifiable data. In the case of life histories, for example, certain parts of them may be objectified (in the conventional sense) when it comes to certain kinds of facts, but that is not their point. Personal meanings are inscribed deeply within them, and these are not matters of objectifiable fact at all, but, rather, what certain incidents or events *mean* to the individual in question (see Linde 1993; Rosenwald and Ochberg 1992; Zeitlyn 2008). Such meanings cannot, by their very nature, be made "objective."

It may be that this anti-objective approach to field data always requires some kind of conversion experience on the part of the fieldworker mediated by the people they are engaged with in the field. An illustration of this concept comes from my dissertation fieldwork in Tidewater, North Carolina, which I discuss in greater detail in Chapters 7 and 16. The experience helped me move away from attempting to objectify the data that constituted the daily lives of my research participants, but it was a tough lesson to learn (Forrest 1988a; Forrest and Blincoe 1995). The following exchange took place in my very first interview in the town where I conducted my doctoral fieldwork in 1978. I was sitting in FI's[2] living room and she had a quilt on her lap that was a prized family heirloom. Because as a brand-new fieldworker I was eagerly intent on getting the "facts" (objectively) I asked:

JF: So when was it made?"
FI: Well let me see … it was made by Lizzy Brown, my daddy's granddaddy's second wife when they were first married. I think he was around 42 or 3 at the time. Now he died when I was five and he was 93, and I was born in 1902, so you work it out.
JF: OK, He must have died in 1907 at the age of 93, so he was born in 1814, which would have made him 42 in 1856. That means it's about 120 years old [in 1978].
FI: Uh-huh.

It took me over six years of listening to this recording and other interviews again and again, before the penny dropped and I realized the degree to which FI and I were pursuing radically different agendas. Of course, it is possible to objectify certain facts about the quilt, such as its date of manufacture (or its age), but such objective facts are outside FI's value system – as it relates to the quilt. Two responses in FI's discourse make this clear. The first is the command, "… so you work it out." In essence, what she is really (politely) saying is something like the following: "I will tell you what I know about the quilt's chronology in terms that matter to me or are significant to me, and you can convert them into your value system if you want to – I don't want to and I am not going to."

Having then finished that part of our conversation, and being proud of my mental skills, and, indeed, beginning to see the "value" of the quilt in *my* terms (i.e. "my gosh, 120 years old"), FI brushed aside my interest with the noncommittal "Uh-huh" which stops short of being impolite, but could be translated as "if you say so, but so what?" Her tone and facial expression indicated that she had heard what I had said, but was not interested. *Her* value terms in relation to the quilt were:

1. the maker's *name*
2. her **affinal** relationship to the maker
3. her **consanguineal** relationship to the maker's husband
4. chronological information associated with rites of passage:
    a. the maker's husband's age at *marriage*
    b. the maker's husband's age at *death*
    c. FI's age at the maker's husband's *death*
    d. FI's year of *birth*

---

2 I identified each of the people I interviewed with a pair of capital letters that kept their identity hidden from outsiders, but used a simple algorithm for me to be able to identify them easily. Meanwhile, in my transcriptions I used JF for myself.

What I later discovered was that for FI, affines get *named* when discussing them, but consanguineal kin are referred to almost exclusively by *kin terms*. Furthermore, even though an affine made the quilt, its history is linked to the chronological details of a blood relative. Having made this discovery, I was then able to go back to other interviews with FI and note that she always said "my daddy made ... "or "my mama did ..." but never "my husband worked ..."; always "Lem worked ..."

I was too far removed from the value system of the community at the time of these interviews to be able to be instructed in anything other than a kind of objectified way. It was not just a simple matter of me being a foreigner geographically (born in Argentina, raised in Australia and England); I was a cognitive stranger as well. The sad truth is that I would have related to them in their own terms a lot quicker than I did if I had never taken anthropology courses, because the discipline had inclined me to *study* them (that is, observe), rather than to *learn* from them (that is, engage). They tried their best to include me in their value system, but my training resolutely resisted their efforts. I get it now – too late, of course. What is critically important to understand, though, is that no matter how bad a pupil I was, our interviews always had an instructional purpose, and that what I thought I was trying to discover was less important in the minds of the people in the community than what they thought I ought to know. That is, they rejected my attempts at etic analysis in favor of their own emic approach, which they considered to be more important. And, of equal importance, I recorded all the interviews, and therefore have been able to return to them year after year, deepening my understanding of the community. *Field notes are a permanent record.*

What I did not understand at the time was that interviewing as a fieldwork method can be surprisingly deceptive in that the material being produced may contain multiple layers of meaning that are not evident at the time that the interview is being conducted. One benefit of recording interviews is that you can return to them repeatedly and continually reassess what you have recorded, as in the example above. In fact, this kind of reassessment can begin almost immediately as you are transcribing, and can continue for years. Recorded interviews, by their very nature, are artificial events in the life of a community you are studying, but another significant benefit is that they are one method of entering into the subjective reality of the people you are working with. In this book there are numerous projects that employ interviews in part or as the whole exercise. Keep in mind that *different methods of investigation produce different kinds of data*. Not only is interviewing only one method of data collecting, the way that you approach recorded interviews determines the kind of data you receive. Most anthropologists today prefer to record interviews in *partnership* with the person being interviewed as opposed to seeing the interviewee as an object to be studied. Indeed, this approach is useful in multiple methods; not just interviews.

While the objective/subjective distinction can still serve a purpose in a generalized, **heuristic** manner, the best we can accomplish is what we can call "objectifiable" information, that is, collecting certain kinds of information in ways that allow them to be measured in standardized or quantized ways (see Thapan 1998). Certain objectifiable facts are always going to have their uses. When dealing with issues such as economics or nutrition or medicine, one might, of necessity, need to gather objectifiable data, such as the calorific value of foods commonly eaten or the analgesic properties of locally made teas. But even such objectifiable data are only usable within a context which will inevitably be subjective. What the facts are, is objectifiable; why they matter (and which ones are important), is always subjective.

Idiographic Vs Nomothetic Approaches

Right from the start of the twentieth century, the status of anthropology as a science (even when qualified as a "social" science) was a topic of debate. Both Boas and Malinowski had pursued advanced degrees in the physical sciences before becoming anthropologists and undertaking ethnographic fieldwork and, therefore, brought an element of scientific inquiry to their fieldwork. Meanwhile, Boas' student, Alfred Kroeber, characterized anthropology as "the most humanistic of the sciences and the most scientific of the humanities," which was his way of softening the sense that ethnographic inquiry was a scientific endeavor akin to physics or chemistry, yet it was still a science.

We commonly call the methods of physical scientists, such as Galileo and Newton, "**reductionist**" because they take the complexity of observable reality and *reduce* all the details to simple principles that ultimately govern the seemingly endless details. The observer stands outside of what is being observed in order to uncover its mysteries. The philosopher Wilhelm Windelband (1848–1915) called this approach "**nomothetic**" and contrasted it with the "**idiographic**" approach of the humanities. The humanistic approach is the diametric opposite of reductionism because it is interested in exploring the rich contexts and diversity of cultural phenomena, rather than stripping them away in order to hypothesize simple, unifying principles.

For example, if you like romantic comedies, you will not be stopped from watching a new Netflix release by a friend telling you that the main characters in the movie fall in love near the beginning, face a difficulty that pulls them apart, but then find a way, by some twist of fate or other plot device, to be together in the end. You know this structure: *you like it*. You take this structure as a given, and you go to the movie because you want to see the *specifics*: the exact character of the principles, the jokes, the absurd misunderstandings, and so forth. It is the particulars that attract you, not the generalities (which you assume). We call the focus on the particulars of a situation, over the desire to reduce its specifics to general rules, an **idiographic approach**, and it is the hallmark of interpretive analysis in ethnography. This book takes the position that ethnographic analysis sits somewhere between the nomothetic and the idiographic. Through the projects in this book you will have ample opportunity to explore both approaches.

Undergraduate Fieldwork

One of the prime motivations in producing this text is to teach fieldwork methods to undergraduates (as well as other novice researchers). Yet undergraduate research has not always been encouraged. Since Malinowski pioneered the gathering of data through participant observation in the Trobriand Islands, fieldwork has been entrenched within the discipline and viewed as a "sacred" activity (see Sluka and Robben 2012). Indeed, nearly all PhD programs in cultural anthropology today require a student to produce a dissertation based on intensive fieldwork (of a year or more). There are outliers who have managed to graduate without doing fieldwork, but they are rare indeed. Fieldwork is considered the quintessential rite of passage for entering the profession.

Allowing undergraduates into the sacred rites of the profession was at one time viewed with extreme caution, yet increasingly it is seen as an important, if not essential, experience for students (see Ingold 1991; Sharma 1989; Sharma and Wright 1989; Thorn and Wright 1990; Watson 1995). Starting in the 1980s and 1990s, many social and cultural anthropology programs in Britain and the United States embraced undergraduate fieldwork as a core curricular component, but this trend met with loud resistance in some quarters. The chief objections to undergraduate fieldwork are that the positive benefits are limited and do not outweigh the harm that can be caused by inexperienced researchers both to themselves and to those they are working with. Without getting knee deep in this debate I would simply say that adequate advanced preparation and constant supervision by trained faculty mitigate the potential dangers that can arise, and that, in my experience, the value of undergraduate projects has been immense. If it were not, I would not be writing this text. Now, field methods requirements for undergraduates are relatively common, and quite popular because of the enduring effects it has on the students. Fieldwork is like that. It changes you.

While not getting bogged down in the intense quarrels within the discipline concerning the validity of our field research, you should familiarize yourself at some point with the continued re-evaluation of the overarching legitimacy of our methods. I recommend dipping into some of the following:

Anthropological Practice: Fieldwork and the Ethnographic Method by J. Okely
(Berg Publishers, 2006)

Ethnographic Fieldwork: An Anthropological Reader Edited by C.G. Antonius, M. Robben and Jeffrey A. Sulka
(Wiley-Blackwell, 2006)

Being There: Fieldwork in Anthropology (Anthropology, Culture and Society) by C. W. Watson,
(Pluto Press, 1999)

Fieldwork Is Not What It Used to Be: Learning Anthropology's Method in a Time of Transition by James D. Faubion and George E. Marcus eds.,
(Cornell UP 2009)

Ethnography: Understanding Qualitative Research by Anthony Kwame Harrison.,
(Oxford University Press, 2009)

You might also want to look at how fieldwork on communities that interest you is conducted by anthropologists who have a particular/personal slant on their data, and how this work gets translated into ethnography. Instead of pretending to be presenting "objective" data about individuals and communities, or to being "objective" about their research findings, ethnographers now routinely embrace their own cultural identities, as well as their sympathies with marginalized and oppressed peoples, and use those identities to encourage nuanced or multifaceted ways of writing ethnography. The following is a small example of the types of ethnography that explore marginalized identities. You should review at least one such ethnography to get a sense of ways in which you can move away from traditional, objectified writing. Your instructor can help you find more.

The Body Silent: The Different World of the Disabled by Robert F. Murphy (Holt 1987)

A Coincidence of Desires: Anthropology, Queer Studies, Indonesia by Tom Boellstorff (Duke University Press, 2007)

Veiled sentiments: honor and poetry in a Bedouin society, by Lila Abu-Lughod. (University of California Press 1986).

High Tech and High Heels: Women, Work, and Pink-Collar Identities in the Caribbean by Carla Freeman. (Duke University Press, 2000).

Encounters with Aging: mythologies of menopause in Japan and North America. Margaret Lock. (University of California Press 1993)

Citizen Outsider Children of North African Immigrants in France by Jean Beaman (University of California Press 2017)

Burning at Europe's Borders: An Ethnography on the African Migrant Experience in Morocco by Isabella Alexander-Nathani. (Oxford University Press 2021)

Borders of Belonging: Struggle and Solidarity in Mixed-Status Immigrant Families by Heidi Catañeda. (Stanford University Press: 2019)

Decolonizing Extinction: The Work of Care in Orangutan Rehabilitation by Juno Salazar Parreñas (Duke University Press 2018)

Out of roughly 3,000 students I have taught fieldwork to (including some 400 anthropology majors), only 4 have pursued postgraduate training in anthropology. The rest are employed as social workers, activists, doctors, lawyers, and professionals of various stripes. But, nearly all retain a strong sense of the anthropological method, and look back to their fieldwork classes as turning points in their understanding of key concepts: how to listen well, how to attend to authentic voice, how to situate meaning in cultural context, and so forth.

Many of my former students mentioned their experience with the various skills learned in fieldwork in job applications and interviews, and some of them continue to use these skills in their work environment. Qualitative research methods are poorly understood by the general public, as well as by employers. Nonetheless, savvy employers can be convinced of the benefits of hiring someone with field methods skills. I won't go so far as to say that having field methods skills will land you a job, but having them is another arrow in your quiver.

At minimum, training in anthropological field methods develops a way of observing and interacting with the world in general – all the time. Of course, it will be up to you to assimilate the lessons learned in field methods into your life as a whole. This process should not be difficult because intensive and analytic engagement with people is potentially life altering anyway. On the other side of the coin, it is important to bear in mind – always – that intense engagement with people carries a moral and ethical burden. I take up this issue in a subsequent chapter on ethics which is mandatory reading before you begin any of the projects (Chapter 3).

Most of the projects in this book are self-contained, but a few rely on methods developed in others, and, where this is the case, I cross-reference the projects. I will be giving examples of projects that my students developed to give you ideas; you might find some of them worth emulating. But I also encourage you to be creative in your choice of field situations. When I taught a methods course I always had one class per project that was a practicum in which I walked my students through an example project, and usually involved them in some form of observation and documentation so that they had a little practical experience of the method before they embarked on their own projects. From time to time in the project instructions in this book I discuss salient practicums I used as additional aids in your learning process. Your instructors will undoubtedly have experiences of their own to share with you in a similar vein. You should use their knowledge as you proceed, and be guided by their preferences for the precise execution of projects and their presentation. The projects proposed here may be used as is, or they can be tailored to various instructional needs. Fieldwork is, by nature, a disciplined process that, while rigorous, allows for spontaneous flexibility.

Vocabulary and Writing

Ethnographic writing is its own species of writing, and has come under critical scrutiny in recent decades for its capacity to mislead and misrepresent people. *How* you write about people is as important as *what* you say about them, and it is possible to offend the people you are writing about, or to give the wrong impression about them, by using inappropriate vocabulary or phrasing. This is a topic that you should discuss at length with your instructor; here I will simply point out a few cautions to bear in mind when presenting your data.

Anthropologists have been sensitive for some time to the fact that groups of people are commonly identified in multiple ways – the term(s) that outsiders use to name them, and the term(s) they use to name themselves. "Eskimo," for example, is an outsider term, whereas "Inuit" (and variants) is an insider term. In reasonably straightforward cases, anthropologists opt for using the insider term. But things are not always straightforward. Take the case of people from predominantly Spanish-speaking countries in North, Central, and South America (and the Caribbean) living in the United States. What do you call them as a group? Are they a definable group? Do they have an insider term?

The problem with finding a term for Spanish-speaking peoples from the Americas living in the United States is that this is a multicultural demographic when viewed from the inside, but homogeneous when considered by outsiders. Any single term that identifies them as a group is going to entail treating them with some sense of unity as an "other" group (other than dominant, white, US culture). That is, the supposed unity of the group exists only in the minds of outsiders. It is common to hear Spanish-speaking immigrants in the United States being called "Mexicans" regardless of their country of origin, and in this case "Mexican" is often used as a derogatory term. The desire for such people to adopt a collective term for themselves is an overt admission that they form a group in the eyes of an oppressing class and that they need a collective term to use in their struggle to fight back against oppression.

The problem with finding a collective term is that every one of them carries negative connotations for some or all of the people. "La Raza" had a currency for decades – originating in political struggles in Mexico in the 1920s. The problem is that "raza" is a loaded, potentially racial/racist, term that has, among other things, the implication not just of being non-white, but of being actively anti-white. In Argentina we have a specific classification, "rubio/a," meaning something like the English term "white" and includes a substantial percentage of the population in urban areas. Rubios of Argentine origin (myself included) have major issues with being lumped into the general category of La Raza (which defaults in our minds to what we call "moreno/a" (brown) or "mestizo/a" (mixed) – also heavily loaded terms). In the 1960s, "Chicano" had widespread popularity among some groups but not with others. It had originally been a derogatory outsider term, but, as is quite common with such slurs, was picked up by insiders and used as a badge of honor. In turn, "Hispano/a," "Latino/a," etc. have all been adopted and discarded.

One of the additional problems with Spanish is that many words have genders. The suffix "-o" is typically masculine, and the suffix -a is feminine When you have an unidentified group of people who could be male or female or both, the traditional linguistic convention has been to use the masculine plural. This usage is now changing. For example, "Latino/a" where gender is unclear or generic, or, more commonly nowadays, "Latinx" where the "x" indicates an undefined gender. In English, similar problems have been addressed in an analogous manner. At one time, the correct usage would have been to default to the masculine for pronouns, as in the sentence, "When a doctor is unsure of a diagnosis, he will …" Nowadays there are two choices to replace "he" in that sentence: one being the composite "s/he" (or he/she) and the other being to use the plural "they" – which is becoming more common usage. Gendered terms for occupations, such as "actress," "poetess," and "sculptress," have all but disappeared from contemporary discourse.

There are numerous adjectives and nouns in common use in English that can be classified as dead metaphors (that is, words that carry metaphorical meanings either etymologically or historically, but no longer do so in contemporary speech) which can be culturally offensive even though their historic meanings have long since passed away. Anthropologists try to err on the side of caution in this regard. Take, for example, the old British slang word "clodhopper" (sometimes shortened to "clod") meaning someone who is either physically or mentally clumsy. A "clod" refers to a lump of dirt such as you would find on a farm or in rural areas, so a clodhopper, that is, someone who has to hop over clods of dirt, is a farmer or rural person in general, implying that a clumsy person is like a (stupid) farmer. The word "clown" has exactly the same history. In the sixteenth century it was a term for a rustic or peasant, shifting in meaning over time to mean anyone whose actions were foolish. Where can we draw the line? Is it acceptable to call an argument "myopic" when the term refers specifically to a visual impairment? Probably not, even though the word is in common usage. Caution is always needed.

Terms such as "philistine," which are derived from ethnic slurs, raise the issue of how to refer to ethnic and geographic designations. It is impossible to refer neutrally to the region of the world that was once the homeland of a group of Semitic peoples that became known Biblically as the Israelites, because any term you use for the region as a whole – Palestine, Israel, Canaan, Levant, et al. – will offend someone. Political designations have shifted over time, but whichever one you choose, it is a **hegemonic** label and, therefore, problematic. By that same token, "American" as an adjective for people and things that originate in the United States is offensive to me as it is to many people from Argentina, and much of South and Central America as a whole. Aren't we Americans? In Spanish we use the term "estadounidense" (person or thing from the United States) or, more generally, "norteamericano" (North American) as adjectives in place of "americano" (American) which is too broad. But if you were born and raised in the United States you probably use "American" as a self-designation without thinking. The American Anthropological Association does. It can be challenging, but eye-opening, to examine your language usage critically.

Even terms that were at one time in common usage in anthropology, such as "tribe," have come under suspicion even though they may have insider approval (as in parts of the first nations of the United States). Such terms tend to get lumped into the category of colonialist terminology, and are, indeed, vague when applied indiscriminately. But sometimes the alternate choices are either confusing or unhelpful. Take, for example, the adjective "indigenous." It comes from Latin and its original meaning was "born in (a place)," but this meaning has been supplanted by a meaning of "original peoples" (synonymous with "aborigine" – that is, "ab origine" meaning "from the beginning"). In contemporary usage, however, "indigenous" is generally used to mean "the people who were living in a place when European colonists arrived." You cannot legitimately refer to the Lenape as the *original* inhabitants of New York or the Inca as the *original* inhabitants of Peru. Peoples came and went continuously before Europeans arrived. But, the arrival of European colonists in a region put a timestamp on who was there when they arrived. Thus, even "indigenous" is a colonial term (meaning "descendants of people who were here at the time that the first colonists arrived"). There is no clear solution, but it is common in ethnographic writing nowadays to designate a group using the term for them that they use in their local language for themselves. Thus, for example, "Navajo" was the name given by Spanish missionaries to a group of people living in North America. They refer to themselves as *Diné* ("the people"), which is how anthropologists typically refer to them now.

At one time, anthropologists were in the habit of using the term "informant" to describe a person giving information to the ethnographer. The term has a rather dark undertone, as in "police informant," but its more general usage in anthropology has habitually been less sinister: an informant "informs" the fieldworker, but thereby implies a certain kind of distance between speaker and listener. Because of the negative connotations of the term, contemporary anthropologists are more inclined to work with either more neutral or more indicative (and inclusive) terms such as "participant," "interlocutor," "partner," or "interviewee." Sometimes, however, using "informant" is the generic choice that fits best. Not all fieldwork situations are partnerships or symmetrical relationships by any means, and it can be misleading to represent them with vocabulary suggesting that they are.

Likewise, I am mindful that even the "field" and "fieldwork" can be loaded terms. When you interview someone in his/her home, are you "in the field"? Yes and no. The "field," once conceived of as an "other" place where the "other" were studied, is now no longer a viable term, and certainly not when it comes to the projects in this book which are likely going to be conducted in situations with which you are reasonably familiar (even though some components will necessarily be new to you). The term "fieldwork" is somewhat less troublesome. Fieldwork is the process of gathering ethnographic data. Doing fieldwork has more to do with a certain mindset rather than with the people or places involved. That mindset has different facets, but it is always more than simply looking on or even "being there" as fieldwork is sometimes described (Watson 1999; Bradburd 1998).

Even if you go to live in a country that is alien to you, for a year or more, so that you are forced to learn a new language, meet new people, engage in forms of daily life that are foreign to you, and participate in strange customs, you are not necessarily doing fieldwork – even though some of the behaviors overlap. If you move to a strange location, your primary interest in learning about the place is likely to be pragmatic – where to live, how to get food, where to work, and so forth. Fieldworkers have to learn these things also, but they are not primary. Fieldwork has an ethnographic purpose as its focus, and, therefore, you must always maintain an ethnographic mindset, even if that mindset is not always front and center.

The purpose of fieldwork is to gather data to write ethnography. Therefore, you are "in the field" whenever you are gathering ethnographic data. The "field" is not a place, it is an attitude (or group of attitudes), or what we can call a mindset. The best way to establish this point is to think of a variety of people who are gathering data and what their purposes are: detective, tourist, journalist, and fieldworker. They are all concerned with useful data, but what can be considered "useful" is determined by the purposes for which the data are gathered, and how they will be used subsequently.

So, what is an ethnographic mindset? There is no easy answer to that question, and the exercises in this book provide a hands-on approach to grasping what it is that fieldworkers do. It is not one thing. Sometimes they observe, sometimes they engage, sometimes they participate, sometimes they take action. Sometimes they take notes, or make voice recordings, or take photographs, or make videos, or draw maps, or play computer games, or combinations of all of these and more. After you have done some of the exercises here we can return to the question, and I have some additional thoughts in my concluding chapter. Meanwhile, you can keep the salient question in the back of your mind, "What am I seeking to achieve?" Fieldwork is never a passive enterprise; it must always be actively reflective and reflexive (at some level).

Likewise, instruction in fieldwork can also be reflexive. This book is a fair example in places. In many projects I introduce instructions and suggestions in a reflexive manner. That is, I reflect on the kinds of practices that worked well in my classes, and also on what I might have done to improve them. This practice developed out of my general desire to see teaching as a *partnership* with my students. When I was a classroom lecturer, there came a point in most classes when I would talk directly about my life, beginning with the observation that I had a life outside the classroom. I told my students that I had a wife and son, I owned a house, had bills to pay, had heartaches and joys, just like everyone else. I did not just magically appear for 90 minutes twice a week, dispense objective information, and then disappear into some nameless void. In that sense, teaching anthropology is not like teaching chemistry (not for me, at least).

I have taught chemistry without injecting myself into my lessons; I have never taught anthropology that way.

My students often used the expression "the real world" to describe life outside the university, and I frequently pointed out to them that the expression implied that the university was not real. It is real. It is part of the world. You can talk about the office world or the factory world or the university world, but one is not more or less real than any other. They all have their rules and they all have their rewards and punishments. What matters is how well you know the rules (which is one of the issues to be delved ethnographically). I am embedded in many chapters in this book to show you how I derived my methods, and you (and your instructor) are free to question them, and alter them, instead of treating them as absolute instructions to be obeyed without demur. What I do works for me (usually); it may not work for you. All I can do is tell you *why* my methods work for me. That is why the book is (minimally) reflexive.

This is a book about learning how to do fieldwork and how to present your findings to your instructor or some other relatively self-contained, or private, audience. You are not being asked to create a polished finished product to be widely disseminated. That enterprise is a step beyond what is required of you here. Organizing your field data and presenting it to your instructor is an intermediate step between gathering the data in the first place, and honing it into professional-level output. That final step is not within the purview of this book. If you have an interest in pursuing this subject more, specifically as it relates to both the gathering of data and the conversion of data to output for public consumption, you can consult the anthology, *Fieldnotes, The Makings of Anthropology* edited by Roger Sanjek (1990) or *Writing Ethnographic Fieldnotes* by Robert Emerson et al. (2011). The latter book is primarily concerned with how you go about taking notes during fieldwork and should also be consulted in this regard, because the process is not as obvious as may seem at first, and there are many wrinkles that you may not have thought of. Although in its second edition, the book is somewhat dated given the technologies now available to fieldworkers. When I present the individual projects in this book, I give different strategies for note taking depending on the nature of the project.

Individual projects in this book offer a wide array of methods for presenting your data including standard written reports, PowerPoint slide shows, videos, blogs, and so on, and which one you choose will depend on the parameters of the project, your instructor's requirements, and your own preferences.

2

Getting Started

You cannot simply dive into fieldwork unprepared. Not only do you need certain basic equipment, which will vary from project to project, you also need to have a firm grasp from the beginning on how to carry out and execute a project from start to finish. We can take these procedures step by step.

Equipment

Smartphone

Your smartphone can replace many of the traditional tools of the fieldworker including notepad, camera, and voice recorder, and can be used as such from time to time. There are, however, several dangers in using your smartphone for all your fieldwork needs. First and foremost, there are multiple ways that your phone can fail, including damage, battery failure, and loss of signal. Thus, even if you are comfortable multitasking on your phone, you should always have a backup system for everything (notes, photos, voice recording) – *always*. In any event, it is much more functional if you can have separate, dedicated equipment for voice recording, photography, and note taking. Imagine trying to hold an interview concerning a skilled process, take photos, and keep notes all at the same time using a smartphone only.

One major problem with a smartphone is that it is a phone. You do not want to be in the middle of an interview only to have a text message or a phone call come through. You can silence these options, of course, and you should during fieldwork even when you have other devices with you. On the whole, though, it is a much simpler option to have separate equipment with you dedicated to voice recording and photography, as needed. With many smartphones you also have to contend with memory issues. If your phone is packed with selfies and holiday pix, you may run into memory shortages at critical junctures. This problem is especially acute when it comes to lengthy voice recordings. You do not want to be halfway through an interview and run out of memory. You could also run into battery issues with voice or video recording.

Technology has the bad habit of failing on you at the worst possible time, meaning that you can miss opportunities, some of which may be gone forever. Therefore, redundancy is always important. Not only will you be grateful for having a notebook and voice recorder with you when your smartphone battery dies, but you will also be relieved of having to use your phone for every fieldwork function. On the other hand, if your voice recorder or camera malfunctions, you will be glad that your smartphone can pick up the slack (especially if you carry a portable power pack with you for instant recharging). REDUNDANCY!!!

Notebook

Even in this digital age, a small notebook and pen are still important tools for doing fieldwork. I say this, not because I was trained in the 1970s and am stuck in my ways, but because notebook and pen are invaluable adjuncts to other equipment. For example, when you are recording an interview, you can jot down questions that come up, but which are inconvenient to ask at that moment. When I am doing fieldwork, I usually have with me my camera bag containing my 35 mm DSLR (digital single lens reflex) camera (which is also a video camera), spare lenses, extra batteries, and a sound recorder. It is a small unobtrusive bag that anyone might carry around with their daily essentials. It also has a front pocket where I keep my smartphone and my notebook and pens (plural – always have a spare). "Always have a spare" should be your mantra. Running out of ink or battery power should never be a problem.

The most basic point about fieldwork, whether you are working with one person, or you are in a crowded situation, is that you should not draw unnecessary attention to yourself. You are aiming for people to act naturally around you; otherwise, your data can be unduly compromised. As it is, our presence as a fieldworker changes the situation, but you want to minimize this effect as much as you can, or, at the very least, take your presence into account. Unshipping a giant video camera and tripod or pulling out a professional laptop, not only draws attention to yourself, it also alters the way that people categorize you and respond to you. Furthermore, it is not just big pieces of fancy equipment that can get people uncomfortable. Even a full-sized notepad or a clipboard is intrusive. How many times have you seen a person standing on a street carrying a clipboard and you have wanted to walk in the other direction or duck for cover? A little pocket-sized notebook is far less threatening. You don't even need a bag to carry it in. You can show up for a session in your normal clothes with it in a pocket, and you can start talking or observing before you even take out your notebook. You want to be unobtrusive, but not secretive. It is unethical to document people without their knowledge and informed consent. We will get into specifics in individual projects because there are major differences between public events and private interviews. Just keep the basic principle in the forefront of your mind.

I did the great bulk of my PhD dissertation fieldwork carrying only a small, pocket-sized notepad and pen into the field during the day. I had much larger notebooks in my room for writing up my formal notes each evening, and I kept my finished notes in orderly file folders. But my small notepad was my constant companion. Keep in mind though that you need to get into the habit of taking notes at a regular pace when you are using a notebook, so that the people you are working with do not start to believe that the things you write down are more important than the things you do not. They are not anyway, but you do not want to give that impression.

If you are skilled at taking notes quickly and accurately using the notepad app on your smartphone, then use it. Typically, however, people have a hard job taking notes as fast on a smartphone as with notebook and pen. Experiment if you are unsure. Type the following notes (or something equivalent) on your smartphone and then write them in a notebook, and figure out which method is easier, more comfortable, and quicker for you:

> Meet at the coffee shop near Hamid the baker's at 5 p.m. Thursday 12th.
> Mrs. Carranza worked in a butcher's shop in the 1950s in Brooklyn.
> Remember to ask her about work conditions, pay, hours, etc.

With either notebook or smartphone you will have your own shorthand for being able to take notes speedily, and you may develop more tricks as you progress with these projects. For now the task is to find the most convenient way to jot notes as you go.

Voice Recorder

Apart from your notebook, a voice recorder is your most valuable fieldwork tool, so choose one with care. Digital voice recorders come in all price ranges from around $30 to well over $1,000. The fact that modern recorders are small and can record long sessions without checking on them is a great blessing. You do, however, need to pay attention to a number of features when considering which recorder to buy – and you should buy your own. Other equipment you can borrow if necessary, but you need to own a voice recorder.

Of critical importance in choosing a recorder is its range and clarity of recording. Recorders come with built-in microphones of varying quality. Very expensive models can record music in stereo with extraordinary precision. This is overkill for regular fieldwork. For a typical interview you need a recorder that you can place on a table between you and your interviewee, and it will pick up all that both of you say – clearly. Do not buy a recorder online. Go to a store and test out their products. Sit in a simulated interview situation with the salesperson and test out the floor models. Make sure that when you play back the recording, you can hear the voices plainly, and they are not unduly muddied by ambient noise in the environment.

You will find that a number of recorders pick up voices adequately, so then you must turn your attention to other features. You need a recorder that will allow you to keep interviews separate in labeled files, and you must be able to pinpoint precise moments in each interview via a counter or timer. It is important to have all of your field data properly filed and indexed, so that when you are writing notes or a paper, you can jump immediately to that spot in an interview where, say, Arjun talked about fracturing his pelvis in a skiing accident. It's not good enough to know that he talked about it at some point in an interview last Thursday. Good indexing is vital, which means that your recorder must facilitate this process without complications. More details on indexing and filing are laid out in the relevant projects.

Some recorders use replaceable batteries, some rechargeable. If it has a rechargeable battery, buy a spare, and keep it charged. If it uses replaceable batteries, keep spares with you at all times. Batteries have a bad habit of dying at inconvenient moments.

Also make sure that data on the recorder is easily transferable to other media. Ideally it should have a memory card that allows you to make backup copies of interviews on your laptop or other device. Backup copies are essential. *Never rely on a single copy.* You may also consider backing up your data on a cloud storage service.

Camera

For routine field photography, you can use the camera in your smartphone provided that it is up to the task. Many of the latest models can take excellent photos, but they can be memory and battery hogs. Make sure that whenever you set out to complete a project you have space in memory for the number of photos you are likely to take, and that you have some device with you for a quick recharge if the need arises. Otherwise, you may decide that for field photography a dedicated camera is your best option.

This point leads me to an important issue about fieldwork photography in general, namely, that your purpose is not to take photos that are aesthetically pleasing, although it does not hurt if they are. First and foremost, you are recording data. A photo for fieldwork needs to record relevant information, but it does not have to be composed artistically. You do have to be concerned with not getting too close or too far away from your subject matter, but it does not matter if there are extraneous details in your shot. There is more on this subject in relevant projects.

Cameras come in all price ranges with all manner of attachments. How much you want to spend will be determined by your abilities with a camera (and your wallet). A DSLR camera is the optimum choice because the viewfinder (or monitor) shows you exactly what the lens is seeing, and, therefore, the image that you frame will be the image that is captured. For fieldwork, a camera with point-and-shoot ability is ideal, that is, a camera that automatically adjusts focus, shutter speed, and aperture size, so that all you have to worry about is what to point at. Even with plenty of experience operating a camera manually it is best not to have to concern yourself with changing settings when you are recording data. The less attention you have to give to your equipment when conducting fieldwork, the better. Having decent zoom capacity for close-ups is useful, as is having the ability to capture wide-angle shots. Currently I use an 18/400 lens, which covers most bases and is not desperately unwieldy (although it is noticeable). In the past I used an 18/55 lens, which was perfectly adequate for documentation most of the time and did not take up much space. Expense may be your critical criterion here.

Most digital cameras nowadays can also take video, but they are limited in this respect. The built-in microphones are usually of poor quality, and video gobbles up memory and battery. They also tend to have time limits on recordings to prevent filling the memory card. If you have ambitions of making field videos of any length, you will need a dedicated video camera with an adequate external microphone.

Computing

A number of projects in this volume are designed to be completed online, or they have an online option. Most of these projects are best completed using a laptop or desktop computer with an ample monitor and a webcam (either built in or external), although many are also designed with a smartphone in mind. For projects that involve heavy visuals, a desktop or laptop is the better option rather than a smartphone. Smartphone cameras are limited and their screens are too small to capture much other than a single person, whereas a laptop or desktop monitor can display a wide field of vision, or multiple people, at the same time. You will also need *reliable* high-speed internet access – emphasis on reliable. Before you begin any online projects, thoroughly test your internet service to be sure that heavy usage for an hour or more is not likely to result in dropped links or frozen screens. There can be no certainty in this regard, but you need to take all necessary precautions to limit the chances of failure.

Keeping a Journal

If you are doing a number of these projects for some kind of course of study or training, I strongly advise you to keep a personal journal (in the spirit of Malinowski's *Diary*). A journal has several functions. The projects themselves have a built-in self-critical component, and this is an important part of each exercise. A journal has a somewhat different purpose, although self-critical analysis needs to be in there. It is crucial to realize that a journal is not a public document; it is your private space for ruminations. It is for your eyes only. You can note down anything in a journal that comes to your mind at the time – including what you had for lunch or if it was raining on the way to an interview. You should not spend much time thinking about what is and is not relevant as a journal entry. It is a written version of your inner monolog, so that anything and everything are relevant.

Reflexivity (pp 20–21) is not a necessary component of many of the projects in this book, but an assessment of your successes and failures each time is essential. Personal ruminations on how well you think you are doing, what things you can do differently, fears you have, and the like are part of the ongoing process of maturing as a fieldworker and should be recorded. The individual entries can serve as a guide concerning your personal motivations, for example, when you are writing up the results of each project, but the journal also has the long-term benefit of being a permanent record of your inner workings as a fieldworker, and can be consulted long after your training has finished.

3

Ethics of Fieldwork

Because fieldwork is the study of people, following ethical principles is especially important. I address specific ethical issues as they arise in relation to the projects in this book and in each case I give detailed instructions and caveats. Here I want to underscore general ethical guidelines that are *always* applicable. These guidelines are in place both for the protection of the people you interact with, and for your own protection. First, consider the ethical guidelines established by the American Anthropological Association. The full text of the latest (2012) *Principles of Professional Responsibility* can be found here: http://ethics.americananthro.org/category/statement. This Statement is divided into sections that are self-explanatory and should be read in detail. Each section has a list of citations (with links) that you can also consult.

1. Do No Harm
2. Be Open and Honest Regarding Your Work.
3. Obtain Informed Consent and Necessary Permissions.
4. Weigh Competing Ethical Obligations Due Collaborators and Affected Parties.
5. Make Your Results Accessible.
6. Protect and Preserve Your Records.
7. Maintain Respectful and Professional Relationships.

You may also consult: *Ethics and Anthropology: Ideas and Practice* by Carolyn Fluehr-Lobban (Lanham, Maryland: AltaMira Press, 2013)

Not all the ethical points raised in the AAA's *Statement* are germane to the projects in this book; they cover the full range of professional fieldwork endeavors. The following is a discussion of some of the key points that are most relevant to the projects in this book.

Do No Harm

The promise to "Do No Harm" comes from the Hippocratic Oath for physicians, but it equally applies to ethnography. Physicians have their own ethical dilemmas to contend with, but yours are somewhat similar, somewhat different. When physicians want to suggest a risky or experimental procedure that might potentially cause harm, they are ethically obligated to discuss the procedure with their patients. An analogous situation can occur during fieldwork. All information is power, and that information has the potential to do harm. Fieldworkers are obliged to protect their informants and themselves from physical, psychological, and other types of harm.

Imagine, for example, you want to map the layout of supermarket shelves, and, having obtained the requisite informed consent of the manager or owner, you proceed to gather data. In the course of your investigations you determine that product placement on the shelves is directly linked to the store's profitability. Items with the highest profit margin for the store are placed at eye level within easy reach, whereas those with the lowest profit margin are harder to access. You map the store with this research question in mind, and then produce a finished map. Such "insight" is not exactly breaking news, but its dissemination is potentially damaging to the store's bottom line. You have to consider your ethical obligations in this regard. If you are open with the manager, and he/she agrees that you may proceed, you have fulfilled your ethical obligation, but you must still decide whether the conclusions that you reach outweigh the potential harm caused by their dissemination. That equation must always be in your mind.

Take, for example, a situation that occurred to Katie Nelson when she worked with a group of 10 undocumented Mexican immigrant college students in Minnesota, USA, for 13 months. She was studying this population as part of her doctoral research looking at identity formation and contestation among undocumented youth in the context of national discourses and labels that tend to dehumanize, marginalize, and discriminate against them. As part of her research strategy she collected detailed life history interviews of each of her primary informants. After her fieldwork period came to an end, Nelson included the life histories in her 250-page dissertation, which she planned to publish. After consulting with her academic advisors and other colleagues she came to the decision that in order to protect her informants from any harm the publication of her work might cause, she would use pseudonyms to obscure their true names and identities.

After completing the dissertation, she shared the completed draft with her informants for their feedback. On the whole they were pleased with the way Nelson portrayed them in her work, yet one informant didn't want to be represented using a pseudonym. Instead, he asked Nelson to use his true name in the written document. In the time since Nelson had interviewed him, this young man had become an outspoken local activist for the rights of the undocumented in Minnesota and U.S. society. He wanted his true name to be used so his activism work would be documented and substantiated by Nelson's research. Additionally, a new executive action initiative established by President Obama had taken place, which had shifted the political landscape. After discussing the issue with him further, Nelson's informant felt the Deferred Action measure provided him some protection from future deportation and thus a pseudonym was not necessary. Nelson, however, still had some doubts. She knew the Deferred Action could be reversed in future when another U.S. president took power. This would put her informant at risk for discovery and possible deportation. She wanted to protect all her informants from harm, but also wanted to meet her informant's wishes.

More problematic in the admonition to Do No Harm is the possibility that the fieldwork situation may harm *you*. Here the Self Study can be critically useful. Before embarking on fieldwork I recommend you first carry out the Self Study project (Chapter 5).

One of the objectives of this project is to identify what activities could potentially harm you. The types of harm can be wide-ranging For instance, if you decide to be a participant observer in a rock climbing group, the dangers and safety measures will be spelled out by your leader, and you will be able to make a sensible decision as to whether to proceed. Participating in a political protest is another matter entirely. Even if the other participants are expressly nonviolent, there may yet be violent encounters – with counter-protesters or the police, for example. As a general rule, you should not be involved in any activities in which you run the risk of physical harm.

The potential for emotional or psychological harm to yourself is harder to assess. For example, a woman conducting an interview with a man, which seems at the outset to be innocuous, may devolve into sexual harassment or abuse. Your normal, common-sense radar should be able to alert you to such situations, and you should not shut your usual defenses off just because you are conducting fieldwork. If this kind of situation occurs, you should end the fieldwork *immediately*. Data gathering should never supersede personal safety.

Somewhat more abstract psychological dangers may turn up, and here is where the Self Study project is most important. We all have emotional triggers, and you may have memories of past traumas that trouble you. Addressing these issues is the domain of therapy, and if you have been in therapy you will be aware of them. I am not proposing that you engage in intense therapy before beginning fieldwork, but you must always have a degree of self-awareness, and you must always conclude a fieldwork session with a modicum of self-analysis and self-criticism. You must not expose yourself to psychological harm in the course of fieldwork, in the same way that you must avoid harming others. My general rule of thumb is not to embark on any fieldwork exercise that makes you uncomfortable in a significant way.

Institutional Approval

At minimum, all fieldwork conducted by undergraduates (and university students in general) must be approved by a university's Human Subjects Committee, Internal Review Board, or similar committee. *DO NOT START WORK ON PROJECTS IN THIS BOOK WITHOUT INSTITUTIONAL APPROVAL*. This is a hard-and-fast rule with no exceptions. If you are doing these projects for a field methods class, it is possible that the class has blanket approval for its students. My field methods course had general approval from my university on the condition that I monitor each project, and that I submit an annual report to the committee. Check with your instructor if you are using these projects for a class. If you are pursuing them alone, or as part of a larger research project, check with the head of your department, dean, or supervisor.

Having standards for the ethical use of human subjects in experimentation has long been an issue when it comes to testing drugs, inducing clinical problems for trial purposes, and the like. But by the 1960s there was an increasing awareness that using human subjects in sociology, anthropology, or experimental psychology could also potentially inflict harm, either personal or social, and safeguards needed to be put in place to minimize risk. Hence, every university has a committee devoted to assessing the potential for danger in using human subjects for research, and either approving that research, or not. At first blush you might think that interviewing people about their lives would carry few, if any, risks, however, unfortunately, that is not the case. Historically, anthropological fieldwork is littered with examples of people who have been harmed by information they have communicated to anthropologists. This point leads to the next ones.

Informed Consent

All fieldwork requires the informed consent (in some form or other) of the participants. The actual form of the consent, and the method to obtain it, vary from project to project, but the basic principles are always the same: people with whom you are working as ethnographic subjects must be aware of your purposes in using them for information, and how you intend to use the data obtained from them. However, the type of informed consent required can vary significantly from situation to situation. For instance, if you are documenting a public event, there is no need to obtain consent from everyone involved when collecting generalized data because the public has been invited expressly to be actively engaged with the event (in some sort of participant capacity – even if only as a consumer/audience member). When you begin talking to individuals about their experiences at such public events, you do need some kind of informal, informed consent, but this need not be much more than a simple question (preferably recorded) such as, "I am writing a paper for a college class on _____ (whatever kind of event it is). Is it all right to ask you some questions?" Scheduled, one-on-one fieldwork, such as life history interviews, requires more in the way of informed consent.

Let us unpack the word "informed." Clinical trials for medications require that the participants be made aware of the risks involved in taking the medication, and also of the protocols (such as whether there will be control groups not taking the medication, and what the chances are that a participant will be in the control group or not). Experimental psychology research trials usually require that the participants be made aware of protocols, including whether deception is going to be employed, and that adequate debriefing after the trials is built into the procedures so that participants are eventually fully informed about procedures (and will have access to the results eventually).

Being informed and giving consent is much simpler for participants in qualitative anthropological fieldwork, partly because such research does not involve controlled experimentation, and partly because deception is not ethically permissible (see below). Quantitative fieldwork is a somewhat different matter, but the projects in this volume are all qualitative. In the projects in this volume that require informed consent (mostly interviews), "informed" means making sure that your interviewee knows your purpose in conducting the fieldwork, and what you will do with the information once you have collected it. The simplest way to accomplish this is to start a recording with something like:

> My name is _____ and I am here with _____ talking about _____. I am going to be using part of the interview for _____. Before we start, may I ask you if this is acceptable to you?

If at some later stage you have the good fortune to publish parts of the fieldwork, you may need to return to get a signed consent from the informant. This will depend on the requirements of the publisher. It is also advisable at the beginning of the recording to tell your interviewee that it is perfectly acceptable for them to stop the interview at any point, for any reason.

Finally, I will point out that minors are not legally capable of giving informed consent. Therefore, by usual ethical standards, fieldwork with children is not advisable. Technically, a parent or guardian can give consent on behalf of a minor, but it is simplest to just avoid children altogether. That way you are never in jeopardy.

Openness

I usually had at least one student each year in my methods class who wanted to hide recording equipment from participant-observer events to capture the "real thing," or take photos without permission. Such practices are always unethical. There is a bit of a grey area here when it comes to public events, but the guidelines are straightforward. I err on the side of caution. That is, I never take a person's photograph without their approval (whether I am going to disseminate it or not). In this case, you are not looking for formal informed consent, you are just asking something like, "Is it all right to take your photo." You may be surprised at the percentage of people who refuse – for whatever reason. After all, it is intrusive to take a stranger's photograph.

In public settings it can be acceptable to take group photos, especially if other participants are doing the same. But publishing such photos may still land you in ethical trouble. Publishers may refuse to use a photo if the people in it are identifiable (and you do not have informed consent from them). I ran into this problem when picking cover photos for one of my books. The photo was of a baptism by full immersion in a local body of water which I thought was remarkably engaging, but my publisher would not allow it. Even though the event was in the open and fully accessible to the public at large, it was not ethical to publish the photo.

When you are dealing with events that are open to the public, you must be careful. Take, for example, a Sunday church service or Friday prayers at the local Mosque. You are likely freely invited to attend, but your motives for attending may not be clear to all in attendance. In general, it is not ethical to make recordings at such events, and photography is likely forbidden. You can speak to the imam or pastor before the service, and/or you can speak to participants to discover what is and is not permissible. You can also simply look around. Are other participants taking notes or photos? If not, you should not either. Apart from being good ethical practice, this injunction is also good fieldwork practice in general: you do not want to draw attention to yourself unnecessarily.

Events that have their own internal ethical guidelines prohibiting reportage must be strictly avoided. These include the likes of 12-step meetings, Masonic rituals, fraternity initiations, and so forth. They are quite intentionally secret affairs, so that even if you are eligible to attend them, you may not report on them. No exceptions.

Anonymity/Confidentiality

Routinely, fieldworkers preserve the anonymity of the people they are engaging with and the places where they have conducted fieldwork when they present their findings. Likewise, you should use pseudonyms for all the people and places involved in your fieldwork. There are special cases where anonymity is next to impossible, but you must make a good faith effort. There are also many cases where anonymity may seem to be absurd. Suppose, for example, you are documenting how your granny makes the chicken soup that has been a family favorite for generations. Using her real name may not seem to be problematic to you, and chances are that it is not. Nonetheless, it is always best to start with pseudonyms. You can use real names later if the need arises, but you cannot hide a real name with a pseudonym after you have revealed it.

Getting into the habit of disguising people and places in your notes and presented materials is also a solidly good practice that you should get used to from the outset. It should end up being second nature to you. Professionals acknowledge that attempts at preserving anonymity are not cast-iron secure. Anyone who is really intent on finding out where (precisely) I have conducted fieldwork and with whom I have worked should be able to discover exact details without too much difficulty. But doing so will take effort, and casually prying minds will be excluded. Likewise, do not share your fieldwork details with others without safeguards in place.

4

Research Design

Good research design lies at the heart of all good field research, and you should, in close consultation with your instructor, give careful consideration to how exactly you are going to carry out each project before you get too deeply into it. Each of the projects in this book has some introductory material on how to approach it, and there are many different strategies depending on the nature of the project. Choosing someone to interview in order to record a life history is a completely different matter from finding a space to map, and the methods used to carry out these projects are fundamentally different also. There is no one-size-fits-all model for research design in qualitative fieldwork. Nevertheless, there are certain guidelines that apply to most situations. To begin, field research must be driven by a research question. How to arrive at a research question is often a complicated matter, as is the nature of research questions themselves, but going into a fieldwork project, large or small, without some kind of research question, even a vague one, is potentially a recipe for disaster.

No matter how simple or rough your research design is, you should start a field project with a reason that is more than "I'd like to know something about this." Certainly, that kind of loose pondering can be your initial jumping off point, but you have to make your purpose for inquiry much more explicit before you commence your actual fieldwork on a specific project.

Formulating a Research Question

The first step to formulating a research question is to locate your topic of interest, in general terms. Let's say that you are interested in learning about tai chi. You see an advertisement for one free tai chi lesson in your neighborhood. You can certainly go along to a lesson with no other thought in mind than to check out what it is all about. You can take the lesson, talk to the instructor and other participants, get a feel for the physical location, and generally assess the situation. Then you have to begin to narrow your focus to formulate a research question. Developing a research question at the start of a project can be challenging. Without enough basic context it is difficult or perhaps impossible to formulate an incisive or insightful research question, yet without a finely tuned research question it is difficult to gather focused data. That is the chicken-and-egg problem of all field research: the more you learn, the sharper your

Doing Field Projects: Methods and Practice for Social and Anthropological Research, First Edition.
John Forrest.
© 2022 John Wiley & Sons, Inc. Published 2022 by John Wiley & Sons, Inc.

questions, and the sharper your questions the more focused your data. Therefore, fieldwork is an inherently **iterative** process. That is, you ask questions to arrive at answers, and these in turn provoke new questions and so on. Eventually you reach a point at which your questions become refined enough and your answers are full and contextualized.

To narrow your focus you need to move beyond simple curiosity and key in on elements that stand out to you. You must start to ask Why? questions. For instance, after your first tai chi lesson you might ask: Why do people practice tai chi? Why do some people choose to teach tai chi? Do people have different motivations, and why? Such questions can provide the initial framework for fieldwork, but they are only a beginning. These questions are still much too general by themselves to provide more than general answers, and, in many cases, the answers will be obvious. Your job is to dig deeper than the obvious. Some people do tai chi for health and fitness reasons, some because they like the calm atmosphere, some because their friends do it, and so on. There may not be a single thread uniting everyone. In such a case, you may have to cast a wider net, or develop an entirely new question. Here is where the iterative process kicks in.

After the first lesson and initial questions to participants and the instructor, you might return home and do some independent research on the history and philosophy of tai chi. You may be surprised to discover that tai chi is considered a martial art, even though what you saw at your lesson was not aggressive at all (very slow and graceful), and that the practice has a large number of forms in the modern world, including genuine sparring with partners. You may also learn that tai chi incorporates components of Taoist, Confucian, and Buddhist philosophies. Armed with this information you can formulate some new questions: "What worldviews, if any, do students share, and what are they? Why?" "Are participants more interested in the health benefits or spiritual aspects of tai chi? Why?" Are there other factors that motivate participation, such as cultural expectations, power dynamics, ethnic identity, political persuasion etc.? Why? Are participants with certain ethnic or religious identities more likely to participate than others? Why or why not? These questions provide new answers which, in turn, prompt new questions.

The key to writing good research questions is to ask them in such a way as to get to a deeper and deeper understanding of the roots of social and cultural phenomena than is evident on the surface. A simple exercise you might carry out is similar to a common questioning game that many young children ask of their parents or other adults. The child asks: "Why do I have to go to bed?" The adult responds: "Because it is bedtime." "But *why*?" "Because it is night time and we go to bed at night." "Why?" "Because if you don't sleep, your body won't work well during the day. "But *why*?" "Because humans, like all animals, need sleep for their bodies to work well. And, like dogs and chickens, and many other animals, we prefer to be awake when the sun is out and we get tired and sleepy when the sun goes down." "Why?" "Because that is how we evolved over many hundreds of thousands of years to evade predators and get enough food to reproduce. Now, go to bed." You can keep going deeper with your research question until the possible answers to your questioning become absurd or venture too far outside of the realm of cultural anthropology, for instance, into the fields of physics, astrobiology, or basic chemistry, to be useful to a strictly anthropological inquiry.

It is important to note, however, that even seemingly excellent research questions may need to be modified throughout the course of fieldwork. All manner of things can go wrong with your research questions once you get into a project. Indeed, many professional anthropologists are likely to admit that their research questions, posed in the comfort of their universities before embarking on fieldwork, satisfied their doctoral committees, or got them research grants, but had to be revised or scrapped completely when they got into the nitty-gritty of fieldwork. This certainly was the case for me and many others I know. The point is that your research question opens the very beginning of a path through what can be a jungle of data.

In the physical sciences, hypothesis formation is the common standard for advancing research beyond simple curiosity because these sciences are generally founded on what is called the **"hypothetico-deductive model"** – at least, in theory. In very general terms, this approach involves surveying the data that already exists, asking why it is the way that it is (especially if there is a discernible pattern), formulating a working hypothesis to explain the data, coming up with predictions based on the hypothesis, conducting experiments to test the predictions, modifying the hypothesis if necessary based on experimental results, and so on.

Qualitative fieldwork is not an experimental science, so the model is not fully applicable, and it has its flaws and critics, even within experimental science. Development of the kind of hypothesis found in the natural sciences is not usually relevant for qualitative research because cultural anthropologists don't build hypotheses in order to rigorously test them to derive grand, generalizable theories. Cultural anthropology today is not a predictive science in this way. Instead, cultural anthropologists seek to understand the larger political, economic, historical, cultural factors that shape microsocial phenomena by looking for patterns in social life. Nevertheless, elements of the model are useful when it comes to developing a research design.

If we think of "hypothesis" in a looser way, as an interpretation or an explanation of the data derived from a research question, then the iterative process of asking a research question, seeing if there are any patterns or regularities, refining the question, and so on, resembles the scientific method in some respects. This is because cultural anthropologists do not simply gather information randomly: we have a purpose in mind. Thus, when you ask a research question, at the outset you can consider what kinds of answers you might expect, and if the answers that you ultimately receive are quite different from what you expected, then you can consider why this is the case.

Identifying a Unit of Analysis

One of the variables that will affect the kinds of questions that you ask is the **unit of analysis** of your project. That is, will you be looking at large-scale patterns within a society, phenomena that occur within subcultures, or patterns within the course of an individual's life? Your research questions have to be tailored to the situation. In the case of a life history interview, you are concerned with documenting an individual's experience, so that your initial question to the person being interviewed is likely to be some version of, "What happened?" Your research question can be something like, "Does the experience of this person match or contradict the public perception of this event?" or "In what ways do the fine-grained details of personal experience add a dimension to generic descriptions of an event?" or "How did this person's individual choices shape their life course or experiences?" Whereas, when observing, let's say, a wedding, your research questions are likely to focus on collective behaviors, such as, formalized movements and deportment, language, and dress codes: "Are there features of a wedding or a wedding between two men or two women that are distinctive in comparison with one between one woman and one man?" If it is between two women, do both/neither wear white?" "How does family income affect the choices of food served, and what do those choices mean? How do the couple's ethnicity or ethnicities shape the event? What are the formal and informal expectations for behavior for guests and the bride(s) and groom(s)?

Somewhere in the mix has to be a consideration of the cultural influences on what you are observing, but "culture" is a complex variable that is neither easy to define nor readily identified in your data. Start with the immediate group that you are investigating and then move outward. You will see when you get to the mapping project (Chapter 7) that I give examples of the layout of kitchens in two different countries. A kitchen in Italy looks very much like one you would find in the United States or in England, but in Morocco, for instance they are quite different. Why? Some of the answers to that question can be found in the differing cooking styles of the two regions, in terms of both what is expected of a meal and what cooking fuels are available. In Italy a "proper" meal consists minimally of a first course of soup or pasta and a second course of meat and vegetables, plus a dessert. In Morocco, everything is served at once (except for desert – usually fruit), and the main dish is often cooked in one large cone-shaped ceramic pot (called a Tajin). It is served on one single large plate and eaten by everyone together with bread. In Italy it is normal to have an oven for roasting and baking; in Morocco ovens are not as common because roasting and baking are inconvenient due to the year-round heat. If you want roast meat, or baked goods such as bread, cakes, or pastries, people typically buy them from vendors who have large commercial ovens. We can consider these to be cultural variables, but there are individual choices also.

In both Italy and Morocco, family income plays a major part in how a kitchen is designed and organized. In Italy, family income affects mainly the size and layout of the kitchen, including the amount of work and storage space. In Morocco the variation based on finances is much greater. The poorer households have a single heat source, usually wood or charcoal, located outside the house, whereas more well-to-do families cook over bottled propane, commonly with two burners, inside the house.

Or, I might ask the simplest of questions: Why are there virtually no accommodations for people in wheelchairs in Phnom Penh? Some major hotels have ramps as well as steps leading into them (and elevators internally), but very few other public or private buildings have any help for wheelchair-bound people, and the public streets are difficult to negotiate. The sidewalks are often clogged with parked cars, so that pedestrians have to walk in the road to bypass them – but, the curbs are high with few breaks in them to allow easy passage on and off in a wheelchair. Why has the government invested substantial funds to upgrade sidewalks so that now in heavily trafficked areas there are paving stones set in the center of the sidewalks to be used as guides for blind people walking with canes, but they have done nothing to change the curbs for wheelchairs? What do you notice about accommodations for people with disabilities where you live and why are they the way that they are? What are the cultural implications of such government decisions? These types of observations and insights are the kind that will help advance your research design.

Choosing locations and people to investigate go hand in hand with formulating research questions. There is nothing wrong with choosing events to study, or people to interview, out of simple interest or curiosity, and some of the projects in this book, such as the life history, rely primarily on interest more than on a targeted research question. Without doubt, you should not conduct a project that does not interest you – ever – although such a danger always exists when you are carrying out an exercise for training purposes. Sometimes, a field situation is not your first choice. You, or the situation you want to study, may have time constraints that are unworkable, or the like, so you may have to go with a second choice that is more convenient. Given that the projects here are for instructional purposes, such situations may arise out of necessity. Nonetheless, choosing a field location for no other reason than that it is handy is a mistake. You must have some interest in the site as well. At this point you are learning certain skills, so that your research will likely not be earth shattering. But your lack of interest in a project will be overtly and directly reflected in the work you produce.

When I first began teaching field methods, I used to insist that all fieldwork projects had to be conducted off campus, preferably in locations that were new to the student, but I relented on that requirement after several years. It is true that participating in events that are completely new to you can produce data experienced through fresh eyes, but it is also possible to see well-known situations in a new light if you are creative in developing a research question. The pitfall is that if you know a situation very well you can end up with a research question that you already know the answer to, or, you may have trouble formulating a question at all, because nothing seems unusual or noteworthy.

We all spend significant portions of our day on auto-pilot. This state of affairs is normal and efficient, but has to be overcome when carrying out fieldwork. There is a difference between seeing and observing or hearing and listening. The first verb in each pair describes the act of sensory data entering your body, and the second verb concerns *paying attention* to the meaning and content of that sensory data. Fieldwork, unlike normal, everyday life, is all about paying attention, or what I call "radical paying attention." You have to get into the habit of asking questions that you do not normally ask, and keep a note of things you observe: Why do the input keys on a drive-up ATM have braille numbers on them (blind people cannot drive up)? Why is the bride's side of the church the left-hand side as you enter? Why are deodorant, shampoo, and body soap marketed toward men and women differently, whereas hand soap and dish soap are not typically gendered? Why does the color red classically signify a warning (stop sign, red light) and green means you can proceed, yet when it comes to natural fruits many of them are ready to eat when they are red, but are unripe, and one should exercise caution, when they are green? In fact, "green" is used as a general metaphor for someone or something that is not ready to go.

As you prepare for the projects in this book you need to start radically paying attention to your world, observing and listening instead of merely seeing and hearing, and asking, "Why?" all the time. You will find that this stance is exhausting, which explains why we do not normally do it. Nonetheless, it is an important habit to cultivate as you are learning to conduct ethnographic fieldwork

Presenting Your Data

After you have done the fieldwork for a project, you will then prepare your data and results for presentation. Presenting your results may take many forms, and each project in this book has specific guidelines on how to do so. You should not see these guidelines as hard-and-fast rules, but as suggestions which you can modify to suit your own needs and skills. Your instructor may want you to use PowerPoint or some other software for oral, written, or video presentations.

In general terms, I recommend breaking your presentation into three parts: setup, data, and conclusions. Your instructor may have different, or more specific, guidelines, but these components will be in the mix somehow. Presenting your material clearly is as important as conducting fieldwork effectively.

Part 1. Setup

Here you present details concerning how you got started on the project. Lay out what interested you about it, how you fixed on specific places and/or people, and what your initial research question and hypothesis were (if hypothesis formation is appropriate). Also explain any preconceptions or concerns you had before beginning the project, and describe any missteps, such as canceled events, and other things that forced you to change plans.

Part 2. Data

Lay out your data in an appropriate manner. Methods of presentation of data are driven by the nature of the project. Sometimes you will have voice recordings, sometimes photos, sometimes plain written notes. Each chapter here will have specific advice about the presentation of data as well as advice on adding explanatory notes. As needed, get in the habit of using pseudonyms as well as disguising the location of events (wherever possible) to preserve confidentiality.

Part 3. Analysis and Conclusions

This section is much more than a simple declaration of whether your conclusions matched your expectations at the start of the project or not. This part of your presentation lets you delve freely into an analysis of your data as well as draw a variety of conclusions. These conclusions may take many forms. Sometimes you discover that your original research question was misguided or posed badly. Sometimes your intention was to establish a hypothesis in order to show it was false (the null hypothesis). Or, maybe you discovered that hypothesis formation was unnecessary or unhelpful. Sometimes your research design was badly conceived or your data are muddled. There are a thousand and one ways in which what you intended to do in a project and what you actually did do not coincide. This part of the presentation is your opportunity to critique yourself as well as to offer your formal conclusions.

5
Self-Study

In this chapter, you will engage in one or two introductory exercises designed to sharpen your observational skills and better understand your individual strengths as a fieldworker. While all people live in social worlds and observe things around them, doing so ethnographically is a distinct skill set. Knowing what to look for, recalling the important details, and describing and documenting phenomena accurately and contextually are foundational ethnographic skills introduced in this chapter. Equally important is knowing what you as an individual bring to the field. Because you *are the instrument used in ethnographic observation, it's important to appreciate the lens through which you interpret things and how you are interpreted by others.*

Learning Goals

1. *Explore your potential strengths and weaknesses as a fieldworker.*
2. *Develop observational and descriptive writing skills.*
3. *Consider problems that you might encounter during fieldwork based on a variety of personal factors, such as, age, gender, ethnicity, or other significant sociocultural factors about yourself.*

This starting set of projects, which you can choose between (or do both), involves exploring yourself and developing observational and descriptive skills as the necessary preliminary steps before conducting fieldwork. If you were a biology student learning to use a new kind of microscope or an astrophysics student using a new kind of telescope, you would not get involved in observations until you knew how your equipment worked – with some sense of its strengths and limitations. So it is with fieldwork. *You* are the instrument being used in investigations. You experience the world through your senses and interpret these inputs uniquely based on your life experiences and who you are as a person. Sure, you have technical equipment also, such as a voice recorder and camera, which you need to be able to use effectively, but you yourself are the most vital part of the toolkit. You need to know your strengths and weaknesses before you start, and you need to keep track of what you are bringing to each project on an ongoing basis. You need to be aware of your biases, in particular, because, as discussed in the introductory chapters, your data are not intrinsically neutral or objective. You bring yourself into

Doing Field Projects: Methods and Practice for Social and Anthropological Research, First Edition.
John Forrest.
© 2022 John Wiley & Sons, Inc. Published 2022 by John Wiley & Sons, Inc.

all your projects. Unfortunately, uncovering your biases is not a simple or straightforward process. It takes time and considerable self-reflection. Explicit bias is relatively easy to identify and redress. This type of bias is the traditional conceptualization of bias in that individuals are aware of their prejudices, preferences, and attitudes toward certain groups. Overt racism, misogyny, and xenophobia are examples. However, implicit bias is shaped by your culture in difficult to articulate ways and by definition operates on a subconscious level. That is, even if one does not intend to, their implicit biases can shape how they respond, interact with, and interpret people, events and things they encounter. One surprisingly revealing way to begin the process of uncovering your social biases is to take the Harvard Implicit Associations Test (IAT) https://implicit.harvard.edu/implicit/takeatest.html, which gives you scores based on the ways you group and define groups of people. The test instructions begin:

> The IAT measures the strength of associations between concepts (e.g., black people, gay people) and evaluations (e.g., good, bad) or stereotypes (e.g., athletic, clumsy). The main idea is that making a response is easier when closely related items share the same response key.

In taking the test, many find they hold surprising biases they were not fully aware of. It's a valuable first step to identifying stereotypes and assumptions of others you may have developed through your socialization process. The self-study projects in this chapter have two primary objectives. One is to hone your skills at observing and documenting in detail. The other is to examine what you bring to your projects. Carefully observing critical detail is not something people tend to be accustomed to in daily life, because a host of personal interests and distractions seep in all the time. Fieldwork requires focused attention to detail, and you will improve in this regard as you proceed. These first projects get you started. As well as critically examining others, you also need to examine yourself. There was a time in the history of anthropological fieldwork when the fieldworker was absent from reports. Such reports were essentially saying, "This is what happened; my presence was not relevant or important." Of course, this is simply not the case. The fieldworker's presence and personality are always important to the data produced.

There is now a whole area of research and writing known as reflexive anthropology that pointedly recognizes that the presence of the fieldworker matters. I suggest looking at Renato Rosaldo's "From the Door of His Tent: The Fieldworker and the Inquisitor" (Rosaldo 1986) for a critique of old habits in ethnography before reflexivity became important. There is further discussion in the concluding chapter, "Winding Down and Gearing Up" (chapter 21). At the very least, be aware that you are embedded in the data you record, and remember that it is a good idea to keep a journal whilst actively engaged in fieldwork (p 26). This practice makes self-study an ongoing process within your fieldwork.

Project #1: Seven-Day Sensory Diary

Seeing, hearing, and feeling are basic human senses (see chapter 13 for more details) that are at the heart of ethnographic research, yet most people pay little attention to them on a day-to-day basis. Recall that *you* are the tool through which you conduct ethnographic research. You will observe and hear and feel, and these sensations will be filtered through your life experiences and interpreted in particular ways. Because most people take these senses for granted and use them regularly, seeing, feeling and hearing may appear to be deceptively simple activities. However, seeing, hearing and feeling ethnographically are distinct activities and they require practice. The purpose of this exercise is for you to practice observing and describing your everyday life, recalling detail and reflecting on your interpretations in order to develop your ethnographic sensibilities.

Instructions

For this exercise you will keep a seven-day journal. For a period of no more than 20 minutes each day, you will document everything that you can recall that you saw, heard, and felt. You will also reflect on how your life experiences may have shaped your perspectives and memory. At the outset, you may think that your day-to-day life is rather boring and uneventful (trust me, it is not), or you may find it difficult at first to remember the things you saw and heard. However, after a few days, you will notice a change in your abilities to perceive, what you notice, and how you remember. You will be more present to the details in your environment and better able to draw insight from them. These sit at the heart of good ethnography.

1. Prepare your journal paper

Divide a piece of 8.5 × 11 inch paper into four quadrants. At the very top of the paper, write the date, time, and location where you are writing (the room, the city, etc.). In the top-left quadrant you will write what you saw that day. In the top-right quadrant you will write what you heard that day. In the bottom-left quadrant you will write what you felt in a bodily or tactile sense – this can include smells or tastes. At the bottom-right quadrant you jot down reflections on how your life experiences have shaped your perceptions that day. Your notes do not need to be in full sentences, and they can be in list form. You might even wish to draw a diagram or chart.

2. Make your observations

It is important to begin this exercise when you are able to commit 20 minutes each day to filling out your journal. Do not do it out of order. It is essential to write for seven days in sequence without any breaks between. This is the best way to develop your observational skills gradually. If you do miss one day, you will need to start over again (don't cheat!). Begin later in the day when most of the day's activities have come to a close. Set aside a space that is quiet and where you are by yourself. Spend five minutes writing down everything you recall for each quadrant. Be sure to spend no more than five minutes per quadrant. It is a good idea to use a timer so you do not go over time. Do your best to include as much detail as you can. For instance, what color was the coffee you poured that morning? Was the mug hot or cold? Was her voice raspy or high pitched? Did the fact that you once worked as a restaurant server help you recognize and appreciate the server's activities?

3. Prepare your presentation

Once you have completed seven days worth of journals, compile them and review each one in sequence. Note any changes in your observations as you progressed through the week Consider what was difficult about this exercise, and what went well

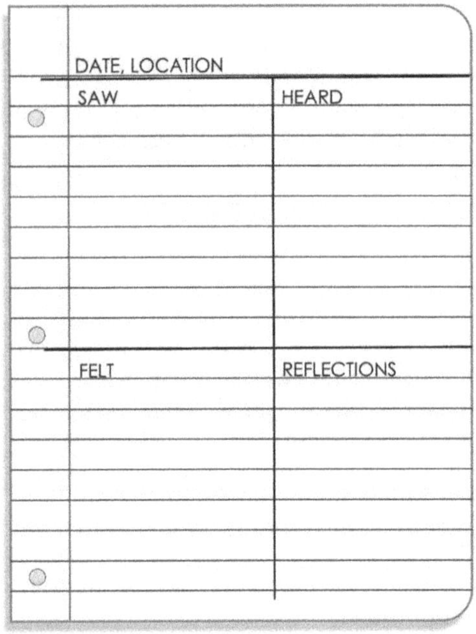

Figure 5.1 Blank Journal Page

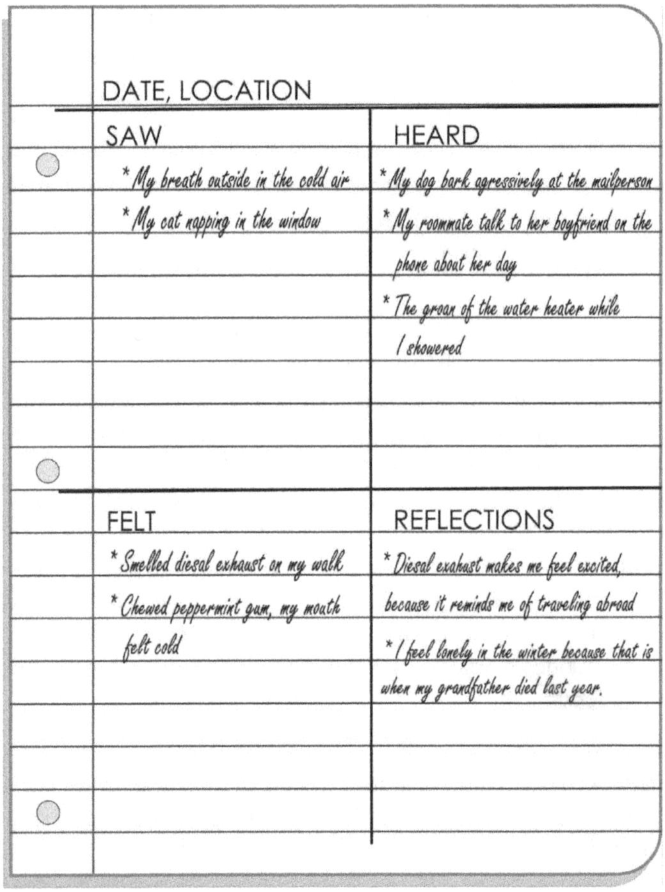

Figure 5.2 Sample Journal Page

Presenting this and the following essay project differs slightly from presenting strictly ethnographic ones in that your research question(s) is/are already established: "What are my strengths and weaknesses as an ethnographer?" and so forth. Submit your seven-day notes as raw data, and then articulate clearly what the exercise has revealed about your abilities as a fieldworker, noting which areas you need to work on.

Project #2: Personal Essay

Instructions

1. Select an incident

Begin this project by thinking of an incident in your life that stands out clearly in your memory as special. Maybe it was a trip abroad you took, or the time you broke your leg tree climbing, or something that happened on your first day in college. Do not slip into generalities. Do not talk about the whole of your summer trip to Greece, for example. Instead, describe a single meal with a family, or a chance meeting with a local. Be as *specific* as possible and as *detailed* as possible. When you have written the description, answer the following questions as your conclusion:

- Based on the experiences described in this essay, what personal strengths will you bring to fieldwork?
- What personal weaknesses do you think you will have to overcome?
- What attributes do you bring to fieldwork based on your various social statuses (age, ethnicity, gender, etc.) that will influence your ability to conduct fieldwork?

You may also write about anything else your narrative reveals about you. Maybe your story will help explain why you were drawn to anthropology. For example, I was born in Buenos Aires, and Argentino is the cultural identity I most directly relate to. However, my family moved to England from Argentina a while after Eva Perón died (because of political unrest), and I started infant school (first two grades) there when I was five years old. When I was seven, my family emigrated to South Australia and I began primary school (grades 3 to 7) there, in what was then a rural town north of Adelaide. Once, for a demonstration practicum for this assignment, I described my first day of school in South Australia. That day was a monumental challenge for me – etched in memory. I did not know anything about Australian culture, nor the school rules (written and unwritten), so I was completely lost and intimidated. I was also a year younger than all of the other students in my class, and I was small for my age. Learning how to assimilate into this new, and scary, culture was, in hindsight, one of the experiences – one of many – that set me on the track of becoming an anthropologist.

We have all had experiences in our lives that made a huge impact on us. The incident you choose does not have to be world shattering or of major significance to others. It can be a quite trivial event when viewed from the outside. It also does not have to be the *most important* event in your life. It only has to be an event that helps explore who you are, and what your strengths and weaknesses as a fieldworker are likely to be. It can be a recent event, or one from long ago in childhood. The important thing is that you are able to describe the event *in detail*. Detail is absolutely vital to successful fieldwork.

My students have covered a whole range of topics in their self-study essays. Here are some examples:

- Getting stopped by a traffic cop.
- Being suspected of shoplifting.
- The birth of a younger brother.
- Waiting for the plane at the airport for a first trip abroad.
- Getting a broken pelvis while skiing.

It does not have to be an incident that occurs on one day only, but it must be a sharply focused event. The following essay from one of my classes describes a trip from New York to Seattle by Greyhound bus which took place over four days. It does cover multiple days, admittedly, but it is focused on one thing: the anticipation of arrival during the trip and the emotions involved, as well as the ways she used to channel those emotions. I have reproduced the essay verbatim with absolutely no editorial changes from me. Islay (pseudonym) was, at the time, a photography major in the Visual Arts Conservatory at my university. She took the course to help her work on her skills as a documentary photographer, and she went on to be a professional photographer.

Self-Study: Islay Hill

It's a Monday afternoon early in the month of July. I'm twenty years old and I have no direction in my life. I completed my first two years at college and I don't have a job. I don't know what the future holds.

The Syracuse bus station is dark, lonely and quiet. People coming and going, straggling in and out, saying hellos and good-byes. I'm anxiously waiting; nervous, excited, scared. My luggage securely held at my side. My mother sits with me, also awaiting my departure, unapproving, although supportive. Two weeks I will be gone, away from everything; familiar faces, atmospheres. It's the longest consecutive length of time spent away from the only home I've ever known. My mother and I talk quietly amongst ourselves, keeping it light. We don't want the depth of our pain and sadness to surface, making it harder. It's easier and more comfortable to hide.

My excitement grows as the announcement is made; echoing its way throughout the walls of the building and through my frozen mind. A knowing glance is exchanged between us as we scuffle our way to the end of the line. Slowly, we approach the mouth of the Greyhound; its powerful structure, loud humming breath ready to devour me. I give my mother a lingering long hug and promising words to call soon. When I feel our release separating, I hand over my ticket to the driver and I take my first step onto the bus. I quickly scope the fully loaded seats, working my way to the back. The faces stare at me; empty, numb, distant. I take my seat in the back next to an older man wearing a cowboy hat. I am glad to be seated, finally; the pressure dulled, attention taken from me and onto other things, other thoughts ...

Roger was a boy I met in high school when I was sixteen years old. He immediately caught and stole my attention. He still had it, kept it hidden for four long years.

I am leaving Syracuse on a Greyhound. My final destination will be Seattle, Washington; a three and a half day ride with strangers. Some will accompany me the whole way, some will find their destination sooner, others will enter at the middle. I know some names, make friends, conversations, learn about lives so much different from my own. Others come and go; barely enough time to really see them, to open my eyes, like ghosts. Stops come often; ten minute smoke breaks, breakfast, lunch, and dinner always at McDonald's which doesn't help me out much being a vegetarian. We stop at almost every bus station, sometimes to pick up or let off, other times to switch a bus or driver. There are instances when we are stuck; delayed for hours at a time with nowhere to go, nothing around to see; deserted in a place never seen and never to be seen again. While the bus is in motion I read books, listen to music on headphones, and sleep in a fetal position using a sweater for a pillow. But most of the time is spent taking everything in; the beautiful mountains passing by, the clouds, the gapping masses of land opening up, penetrating my thoughts.

The fall was hard and fervent for Roger. He had been the love of my life at that time and I soon became the pawn in his chaotic little world. He gave me unbelievable love and pain, hope then misery, comfort to carnage. It was a roller coaster, unpredictable, the highs so high, and the lows held company with the dead. The first unraveling of our blithe days together was when the news came to me through his mouth on that sunny day turned cold. The news of his mother's permanent move to Seattle, Washington. A move in which he would also follow. The gloom was cast around me, hopeless, our love would rend, emaciate my life. I saw death, blood, boundless malady, suffocating losses.

That was four years ago. I've changed a lot, he probably has as well. I cannot help but wonder in what ways; if we still have our once unspoken connection.

Already so many miles have passed, so many hours and now days without anything remotely familiar, without the comfort of a bed to sleep. Still wearing the same clothes, no shower, only the endless stops into public restrooms.

Something is driving me, willing me forward. The past, my devotion, a longing happiness? I'm not sure what I'll find in the rainy city of Seattle; but I have to know, to find out if this will be my destiny. This is the last attempt at resolving my inner nightmare which haunts me, gnaws away at the image I have made; and come to love and hate. I had to know; to stay or leave, to forget or remember, to live or die.

By the third day I am able to make a few friends; one in particular. I think we've connected more so than the others because he too will be in for the long haul. His last stop, Seattle. He is a man in his mid-thirties; tall, heavy build, with only one eye. We talk for miles. He tells me he is picking up his life and simply moving on, going to look for work on a boat; no family or friends to speak of. Listening to his words of complete freedom, I am in awe of his will. He just decided one day to change his life and now he is on his way without the help of anyone. He is overtly friendly, extremely nice, perhaps even a little concerned for me; a stranger. I start to feel sick from the lack of nutrition in my body and offers me a peanut butter sandwich and locates a store close by that sells fruit.

I begin to notice how certain types of people begin to cultivate and stay together. Some remain mute, and the rest friendly; speaking with everyone.

It is late Thursday night when the bus finally rolls its way into Seattle, Washington. I finish It*, a Stephen King horror novel, beneath the reading light at the back of the bus. My excitement grows and I am overwhelmed to hear the driver's angelic voice over the loudspeaker announcing the last stop. It has already been one trying experience and yet it is really only just the beginning. My usual quiet demeanor is now exuding effulgence, a* luminal expression. I was finally going to exit this bus, finally going to see that face I dreamed about for so many brooding nights. The face I couldn't seem to abandon.

Stepping off the bus onto the pavement is wonderful; the air welcomes my presence, cool, crisp. Beckoning its way through my lungs. Strengthening, exhilarating. I've made it. The wonder still lies ahead; closer now. I could feel it, feel alive, enough to continue my own private journey.

I don't recognize him at first. He sits, at a distance on the front of his car, waiting. Slowly I start to make my way over, cautious; my eyes trying to focus. The recognition growing closer, more familiar, germinating, as we float toward each other. I'm lifted, smearing crispations, movement. Holding, grasping, meshing voices, wordless signals.

Six days we had ahead of us. Six days to discover what we've meant to each other. It is somewhat strange, a little awkward, but incredibly peaceful; a rush of grappling emotion straining and fighting to be known. To be heard. To be honest. The love is still there. Very evident, obvious, strong, like it never left.

There is talking; updates, laughter. A relief. This is something I had wanted for so long and so intensely that I was made blind. Ignorant. Such a hopeless romantic, I refused to see the gray, the problems, the fear.

I have what I thought I wanted. It is real, but not complete. Something is missing. I think I had known all along, but I couldn't just assume anything, I couldn't make assumptions. I had to go the extra length and prove it to myself, to prove that this was not meant to be. To put this man, this ghost, this memory to rest. It is probably one of the hardest realizations I will ever have to grip, because it means that I had to let a little of myself die, and then mourn the death.

I will remember this day; the day we both come to terms that we cannot be together. We understand that there are too many obstacles blocking this vision we have built. There is plenty of tears and sadness as I pack my bags. We try to erase, to numb the impact by telling jokes, shaken laughter mixing with sorrow.

It is early Thursday morning. We're driving to the bus station in the rain, the only day of rain throughout my stay. He hands me two packs of cigarettes and proceeds to carry my luggage inside. After I purchase my ticket, we quickly embrace; nothing drawn out, no words are passed. We are machines trying to fight off the immense pain and emotion that is twirling and screaming inside. There is no good-bye. He just walks away from me, opens the glass door, and looking back at me holds this frozen, intense stare, then lets it go. He let me go. He left our past and future floating in that bus station.

I have a four hour wait until the first bus and another three and a half days on the Greyhound back home. The ride back is quite a different experience than the first trip to the West. This time I'm not searching for anything, I'm not looking for an adventure; that part is over. Now all I want is to be in familiar territory, talk to my friends, sleep in my own bed. Most importantly, I want to heal. I have already begun that process. I am forced to, being truly alone with my inner thoughts, with nowhere to go. At first the pain brings apathy, to be put aside for later when the shock has gone. I try not to think too much. I entertain my mind by burying myself in the false lives of others. I read books and keep to myself.

I am home. To be here is a thrill in itself. It is like I've discovered a new self. I have a new start. I am once again, alive.

Those two weeks were very precious to me and I learned a lot about myself. I will always go the distance if I'm drawn, compelled toward something meaningful. I'll always gravitate and follow my pain, my love, to whatever it is that makes me feel. I won't rationalize, weighing the pros and cons. If it's that powerful, nothing will hold me down. I'm devoted, compassionate, forgiving. I'll hold onto thoughts and feelings. I can be very passionate and romantic. I have an extreme need to be loved. I don't like to give up or prove myself wrong. I'm generally a quiet person lacking confidence around unknown people. I will usually wait to be spoken to first. Rarely am I the one who tries to submerge into a conversation with others. I will always respond in a friendly manner. It took a few days to start to have regular relations with strangers on the bus. I didn't feel quite comfortable until I familiarized myself with the routine bus tactics, and when I felt accepted by the other passengers. The fact that we all had something in common, had some story to tell, made it easier for me to relate and have interest in their lives.

The two trips across the country were fairly different. All depending on my mood, emotional status, different and newer faces, physical and psychological exhaustion, the need for stability and comfort, the need to be home and to be living on a "normal" schedule. The trip back East seemed to pass by at a quicker rate. I wasn't as anxious, I was no longer driven by passionate reveries. I was no longer dwelling, wishing or hoping, but settled, calm, and willingly distracted.

This experience certainly relates on many levels, possibly negative and positive in constructing fieldwork. On a larger scale, and first and foremost, I feel uncomfortable being in non-familiar situations. I usually will need a warm-up span of time to get a feel for where my place will be, how I will blend or most easily survive. However, the positive aspect is that I dislike this quality about myself, so I tend to make a concerted effort to overcome this fear. And once I do become comfortable I have a great interest in learning about and analyzing other people's lives. However, it is difficult to be inquisitive when I feel that my own life is a mess. Which was proven on the trip back. I was sheltered, reticent, inert.

Good fieldwork techniques shown throughout my journey include devotion, passion, strong will, and the need to find the truth.

This is not a perfect essay as literature, or even as ethnography. . Yet, it tells me in rich ways what kinds of fieldwork, especially life histories, she will do a good job with, and what problems she expects to encounter. The story itself is thickly graphic. It is also strongly illustrative of the themes I want her to explore as a new fieldworker. She likes others to speak to her first, she is happy to let others talk while she listens, she can listen deeply when she feels a common bond with someone, she is passionate and seeks truth, but she is not a good listener when her own house is not in order.

Your essay need not be about a personal relationship, of course, but it should contain the same kind of attention to detail and the same kind of insight into what motivates you. Be as honest as possible. Do not limit yourself to personality traits, even though these are highly significant. You must also consider the external features you have that will be evident to people you want to investigate, and which will have an immediate bearing on your interactions. How will strangers classify you? Ethnicity? Gender? Age? How do you think these factors will influence your choices of field site, and, based on past experience, how people will interact with you at first? There is a complex power dynamic involved in the ethnographic investigation of others which is informed by the way people sum up the fieldworker, in terms of ease of communication between both parties, but also concerning the initial evaluation of the fieldworker's purpose and motivations. The ethnographic relationship has to be one of trust to be fully useful, but there are multiple hindrances to building such trust. Be sure to specify in your essay your ==inherent advantages and disadvantages in building trust with strangers, based both on how you see yourself and how others see you.==

At the time of writing, I am 70 years old and I live in Phnom Penh, capital of Cambodia. Those two factors are enough to give you some clues as to how I can and cannot relate to local Khmer people, although you would need to know more about the country to be able to infer greater detail. I am immediately identifiable to locals as a foreigner because of my eye shape and color, my skin color, my facial hair, my hair style, and other physical features. People have to ask me where I am from exactly if I talk to them because I look like what they generically classify as "European." When people who do not know me have to talk to me – shopkeepers, for example – they invariably use English, if they know any, to begin with even though I could just as well be French or German or Russian. Some Khmer people in the service sector are accustomed to talking to foreigners, but the majority are not, and tend to be extremely reticent in communication with me (in any language).

I lived on a small street in Phnom Penh for over two years, and, even though everyone on the street knew who I was, no one ever spoke to me or acknowledged my presence with more than a simple nod. This distance has partly to do with my age, partly to do with me being a foreigner, partly to do with my perceived social status, and partly to do with the fact that Khmer people are typically reserved in their interactions on the street with people who are not intimates (and usually with intimates also). Because of my age and my position as a university professor, from their perspective it would have been considered highly disrespectful to talk to me, even if I had wished for it.

If I had wanted to begin fieldwork on my old street I would have had to have borne these factors in mind in planning my strategy. There is one feature of Cambodia that interests me greatly: the long-term effects of the rule of Pol Pot and the Khmer Rouge (1975–79). During the Pol Pot, era around 24% of the population of Cambodia died through a combination of murder/execution, forced labor, and starvation. In addition, virtually the entire population was dislocated, with whole urban centers being emptied into rural areas, and farming families being relocated in the cities. All monks, people with an education, and people not considered to be ethnically pure Khmer were murdered. Even wearing glasses was enough to have someone taken to the killing fields on suspicion of being educated. As an anthropologist I want to know what the long-term effects of such cultural disruption are. How do I devise a plan for answering that question?

I am not going to give you an answer, but I want you to consider my conundrum when thinking about your own plans for fieldwork in relation to who you are as a person, how others see you, and what areas you would like to investigate. Maybe you have a specific interest in the treatment of immigrants or gender inequality in the workplace or police brutality or homophobia or sexual harassment. How will your personal qualities affect such investigations, positively and negatively? In what ways do your personal qualities attract you to, or repel you from, certain kinds of research?

Keep your self-study essay as a permanent reminder throughout the projects in this book. Turn to it repeatedly when you have finished a project, and see which insights you had at the outset that were correct, and which ones were mistaken or misleading (or not nuanced sufficiently). Self-study is a continuous process.

Autoethnography

Your self-study essay is a rudimentary form of what is called autoethnography. The term "autoethnography" can be used in general terms to describe self-reflective and autobiographical writing in the context of ethnographic fieldwork (Maréchal 2010), although what counts as autoethnography has changed considerably in the past 50 years. In the 1970s, autoethnography was used as a term for "insider" ethnography, that is, the ethnographic study of a culture of which the fieldworker was a member (Hayano 1979). More recently, Carolyn Ellis, who is noted for her autoethnographic work, defines it as "research, writing, story, and method that connect the autobiographical and personal to the cultural, social, and political" (2004: xix). According to Adams, Jones, and Ellis in *Autoethnography: Understanding Qualitative Research*,

> Autoethnography is a research method that: Uses a researcher's personal experience to describe and critique cultural beliefs, practices, and experiences. Acknowledges and values a researcher's relationships with others. Shows 'people in the process of figuring out what to do, how to live, and the meaning of their struggles' … . Social life is messy, uncertain, and emotional. If our desire to research social life, then we must embrace a research method that, to the best of its/our ability, acknowledges and accommodates mess and chaos, uncertainty and emotion.
>
> (Adams et al 2021)

To get a sense of the richness and complexity of autoethnography, specifically as it relates to your own self-study, you can consult any of the Further Reading references.

For now you should keep in mind the possibilities for autoethnography in a number of the projects outlined in later chapters, although you should consult your instructor concerning the advisability of taking this approach. The participant-observation project (chapter 9), for example, is designed specifically to familiarize you with a classic method, but with the necessary changes it could be conducted autoethnographically. The inherent problem with working in this way is that you lose the experience of the classic method, which has its values and is still widely used. A compromise would be to conduct one exercise using classic methods and then a second using autoethnographic methods, and then comparing the strengths and weaknesses of each.

Reflexivity

Somewhat related to autoethnographic writing is the practice of reflexive ethnography. In his Introduction to a section on Reflexive Fieldwork in *Ethnographic Fieldwork*, Antonius Robben writes:

> Reflexive anthropology arose from a critique of existing fieldwork practices and forms of textual representation. Bronislaw Malinowski ... had turned participant observation into the queen of anthropological field methods, and pioneered a combination of empathy and detachment, allowing an ethnographer to alternate the native's point of view with an objective stance. However, behind this seemingly controlled insider-outsider dialectic, there was continuous negotiation between fieldworker and informants about cultural representation which was shielded from readers by the ethnographer's rhetorical authority. Anthropologists did not pay attention to the power relation between fieldworker and informant, the intersubjective construction of fieldnotes, and the translation of experience and dialogue into authoritative texts.
>
> (Robben and Sluka 2012: 513)

It is now widely acknowledged within the discipline that all knowledge is power, and that there is always a power dynamic between the fieldworker and the people being investigated. In the early twentieth century, the power dynamic was implicit and largely unchallenged, whereas 100 years later we realize that the power dynamic exists, but it is not at all monolithic. The main function of reflexive ethnography is to unpack the complexities of the fieldwork process by having the fieldworker conduct a rigorous self-examination in the context of doing fieldwork.

Two Types of Reflexivity
Within anthropology, the term "reflexivity" is used in two, rather different ways. The first involves anthropology's more general self-critique concerning how people in classic ethnographies were represented, especially under feminist and anti-colonial challenges to these sources' authority (as well as more general concerns about knowledge production as expressed by Michel Foucault). Treating people as *objects* of study has largely been rejected in favor of more collaborative or cooperative approaches that engage the values and interests of the people under investigation.

The second kind of reflexivity practiced by anthropologists involves various modes of self-reference in which ethnographers call attention to themselves and their practices in the process of writing their ethnographies, as well as to the often self-reflective nature of people who are engaged in openly community activities. As such, reflexivity has often been used in studies of performance, public events, and rituals, but can also be seen in the analysis of acts or things held up for commentary or reflexive consideration by the practitioners themselves, making it clear that self-reflection is more than an academic tool of analysis. Everyone is capable of self-reflection.

It is important to stress that no matter which method you use, whether it be classic forms of ethnographic fieldwork, or some combination of reflexive ethnography and autoethnography (both of which break down the traditional insider/outsider dichotomy), you are always an *observer* at some level. You are always selecting from the kaleidoscope of events occurring around you what to notice, and, in turn, selecting from that sample what to record. The central issue is not whether you are observing, but, rather, the degree to which you are *detached* from these events that you are observing – or not. Whether you are talking to a close friend or a complete stranger you are relating to that person based on what you are seeing (that is, observing), and reacting (perhaps unconsciously) based on those observations.

Further Reading

Autoethnography

Adams, T., Holman Jones, S., and Ellis, C. (2021). *Handbook of Autoethnography*, 2nd ed. Routledge.

Ellis, C., and Bochner, A. (2000). Autoethnography, Personal Narrative, Reflexivity: Researcher as Subject. In: *The Handbook of Qualitative Research*, 2nd ed (eds. N. Denzin and Y. Lincoln), 733–768. Sage.

Ellis, C. (2001). With Mother/With Child: A True Story. *Qualitative Inquiry* 7 (5): 598–616.

Ellis, Carolyn. (2004). *The Ethnographic I: A Methodological Novel about Autoethnography*. Walnut Creek: AltaMira Press.

Ellis, C. (2009). *Revision: Autoethnographic Reflections on Life and Work*. Left Coast Press.

Ellis, C. and Rawicki, J. (2013). "Collaborative Witnessing of Survival during the Holocaust: An Exemplar of Relational Autoethnography." *Qualitative Inquiry*, 19/5: 366–380.

Ellingson, L.L. and Ellis, C. (2008). "Autoethnography as constructionist project." In *Handbook of constructionist research* (eds. J.A. Holstein and J.F. Gubrium), 445–466. Guilford Press.

Reflexivity

Archer, M.S. (2007). *Making our Way through the World: Human Reflexivity and Social Mobility*. Cambridge U. P.

Bartlett, S. and Suber, P. (eds.) (1987). *Self-Reference: Reflections on Reflexivity*. Springer.

Zenker, O. and Kumoll, K. (eds.) (2010). *Beyond Writing Culture: Current Intersections of Epistemologies and Representational Practices*. Berghahn

The following websites also contain valuable insights into the reflexive method:

https://rar.expressions.syr.edu/wp-content/uploads/2015/06/1991-Reflection-and-Reflexivity-in-Anthropology.pdf

https://www.semcoop.com/reflexive-ethnographya-guide-researching-selves-and-others

https://www.berghahnbooks.com/downloads/intros/SwancuttAnimism_intro.pdf

6

Proxemics

In this chapter, you will further hone your observational skills by designing and carrying out a small study on proxemics. Proxemics refers to the ways in which people use interpersonal space as well as the space between themselves and objects in their environments. These uses of space are largely shaped by culture, as are the meanings people associate with them. Understanding these meanings and uses is important to understanding important themes in social life as a whole, as well as how one's environment can impact one's behavior. For this exercise, you will observe how people use space and interpret the cultural norms involved in the ways people control and interact with the space around themselves.

Learning Goals

1. *Identify and document the cultural norms involved in the ways people control and interact with the space around themselves,*
2. *Differentiate how people use interpersonal space and the space between themselves and objects in the environment.*

Edward T. Hall coined the term "**proxemics**" in the 1960s, and elaborated on the concept in *The Hidden Dimension* (1966), one of several works he wrote on non-verbal communication among humans. "Proxemic" is made of the root /prox/ denoting the general space between things (proximity, approximate) and /emic/ denoting differences in actions that change the meaning of those actions within a culture, as opposed to differences that are noticeable but have no effect on meaning (see pp 6–8 for greater detail).

The emic/etic distinction is of considerable importance in anthropology in general and in fieldwork methodology in particular. It often, simplistically, gets translated into: ways of viewing data from an "insider" (emic) versus "outsider" (etic) perspective in anthropological discourse, but such a translation is rather misleading, although not entirely inaccurate. The nuances involved in applying the theory of emics and etics to ethnographic methods are too richly dense to be laid out in detail here. Your instructor may want to investigate this theory in more detail with you, and you may also consult https://www.researchgate.net/publication/246054591_Emics_and_Etics_The_InsiderOutsider_Debate if you want a broader analytical approach to the subject.

Doing Field Projects: Methods and Practice for Social and Anthropological Research, First Edition.
John Forrest.
© 2022 John Wiley & Sons, Inc. Published 2022 by John Wiley & Sons, Inc.

Proxemics, in general terms, is the study of how humans use space, whether it be interpersonal space, or the space between people and objects. Proxemics also provides insights into how and when differences in use of space mean different things to the participants. Hall divided horizontal space into four categories (each with subcategories):

1. **Intimate distance** for embracing, touching, or whispering
2. **Personal distance** for interactions among good friends or family
3. **Social distance** for interactions among acquaintances
4. **Public distance** used for public speaking

The precise distances vary considerably from culture to culture, and also within cultures depending on expectations and circumstances. A colleague of mine once pointed out a complicated "dance" being carried out at a faculty party between a professor from one culture who insisted on talking to a professor from another culture at a distance that was comfortable for the one and not the other. The first professor kept trying to get closer to the other professor, who kept backing away, which involved them weaving all around the room.

There are many other proxemic dimensions, including vertical distance, territorial space, and space between humans and objects. Vertical space between individuals can be used to assert dominance in a number of ways. When a teacher stands while all the students in the class are seated, the teacher is proxemically announcing control of the class. But this is a culturally determined rule. In some cultures, a person of high status sits, and subordinates are expected to stand. In other cultures, people of extremely high status sit, and their subordinates are expected to kneel or prostrate themselves below them. Likewise, people assert territorial claims to space in a number of ways. If you put your bag on a seat next to you on a bus, you are signaling that you own that space and you do not want someone sitting next to you. Leaning against a wall or sitting on a desk are also actions with social messages attached. Think of all the teachers you have had and think about all the possibilities they have exploited: standing with no furniture in the vicinity, standing at a podium, sitting *at* a desk, sitting *on* a desk, and any others you can think of. What signals are they sending out?

Now we can take the example one step further. Consider all the classrooms and lecture halls you have been in, perhaps beginning with the classroom where you study anthropology or fieldwork methods. Consider all of the variables you can think of: size of the room; number and placement of the students and furniture; number, size, and placement of windows; location of materials for the teacher to display information including whiteboards, projection screens, etc., etc. Then, consider how the individuals employ proxemic behavior in those spaces. How do students decide where to sit, for example? Do they always sit in the same seats? Do you? You probably have a set of rules you follow and are aware of the rules of others. For example, in a classroom where there are rows of desks facing the front, with the teacher at the front, there is a common habit for the more committed students to sit in the front rows and the least committed to sit toward the back. The proxemics of such choices is obvious. But other cultures have different rules. In nineteenth- and twentieth-century private secondary schools in England there was a common habit of assigning seats based on progress in class. The worst students sat in the front row, and academic progress was rewarded by giving students seats closer to the back, so that the most successful students occupied the back row.

Think about the arrangement of desks as well. For many years I taught fieldwork methods using standard rows, but one of my students suggested that we all sit in a circle. The quality of the classes changed instantly. By sitting in a circle, everyone could see everyone else, and discussion could flow much more easily. I sat in the circle also, which reduced my vertical dominance considerably, but also made it awkward for me to get up and write on the board. The formation also meant that students sitting with their backs to the board had to turn around when I wrote on it. I have also experimented with other arrangements, such as having the desks in facing rows, like the way members of Parliament in Britain sit. I was astounded at how quickly the class coalesced into opposition groups in those circumstances.

The proxemics activity in this chapter is not an experimental project, but an observational one. You should not be rearranging environments to see what happens, but simply observing what happens in spaces that are predetermined. Also, while you can think about the proxemics of classrooms and lecture halls you use, it is not a good idea to observe proxemic behavior in a class you are taking. You are in class to study. Observing proxemic behavior requires your undivided attention, so that if you are paying attention to proxemics, you are not being a good student in that class. Choose your location and your research question carefully. The project takes one hour to complete, and you will need to choose a location where you can sit undisturbed, observe a designated area without obstruction, and take notes without drawing attention to yourself or being interrupted.

For my first ever proxemics observation as a graduate student, I observed students heating items in a microwave at lunch time in one of the campus's snack bars. It was not a well-conceived project because it occurred to me on the spur of the moment. I happened to be eating a sandwich at a table opposite the microwave, and noticed how uncomfortable people were during the 60 seconds, or so, that their food was heating. They did various things for that time to occupy themselves (in the days before smartphones), such as staring at the oven, looking pointedly away, or fiddling with items. My research question, which evolved as I watched, was: "Why are people so uncomfortable for that short space of time?" There was something about the proxemics of the situation that contributed to their discomfort. There was nothing in the environment to hold their attention while the microwave was heating their food was my simplistic conclusion. Once I had formulated my question, I took detailed notes on their actions.

This example does bring up a vital point, however: *always pay attention*. As you become more proficient at ethnography you will probably become increasingly aware of the social dimensions of situations around you that you failed to take notice of previously. This is an element of the ethnographic mindset I referred to in my introductory remarks. Always be on the lookout for ethnographically interesting circumstances, and make a note of them when you can. Expand your awareness constantly. Being an ethnographer is a state of mind.

Instructions

1. Decide on a Topic
Once you have been assigned this project, you should immediately start paying attention to places you go to routinely, giving thought to possible research questions that

you could investigate in those places. Check out new places as well. Avoid the obvious. Do not, for example, hypothesize that people will sit on shady benches in preference to those in full sun on hot days in the park. If that were *not* the case it might be interesting, but if it is the case there is not much to investigate or conclude. Also, limit your research question to one or two of the possible proxemic variables. Do not imagine that you can document use of horizontal space, vertical space, territorial space, and relations to objects all at once. You could, for example, observe how much space strangers prefer to leave between themselves on those park benches, to see if you can determine the precise nature of social space and territoriality. That would limit your observation to horizontal proxemics.

2. Write Your Research Question
Your research question (and consequent hypothesis) should be narrowly focused. For example, how do people walk around blind street corners? Think for a minute about this question. If you are walking along a busy street and come to an intersection where you need to turn left, but you cannot see around the corner, what is your best strategy to avoid bumping into someone coming the other way? What happens when you encounter someone in your way? Do you attempt to pass on the right or left? You could observe such a street corner and hypothesize that people will put some distance between themselves and the wall when they turn the corner to minimize the possibility of bumping into someone. You can further hypothesize that when people come face to face at the corner they will normally pass to the side that they drive on – that is, in England they will pass on the left, and in the United States they will pass on the right. How often do they fail to pass automatically, but hesitate between right and left?

Obviously investigating how people turn corners or cross the street is not likely to reveal earth-shattering results, but do not let this discourage you. The early projects in this book are designed to be small and easily carried out, because their main purpose is to get you accustomed to looking at behavior as a fieldworker, meaning that you should be recording your observations in detail, and you should be targeting your observations to your research question, and not randomly recording whatever comes into your field of vision.

That said, I do want to put in a word about flexibility. Every anthropologist on the planet, at one time or another, has had the experience of writing up a careful and detailed research proposal, that has a sharply focused methodological plan with a cogent hypothesis (drawn up at home), and then gone into the field and discovered that the plan is unworkable, or the hypothesis is ridiculous, or for some unforeseen reason the research cannot be carried out as planned. It happens. At that point you have to be flexible and regroup. In the case of this project, it could be that the corner you picked does not have many people turning on it, but there are numerous people crossing the street at the corner, and they are encountering a problem. It is all right to shift your attention in this way, as long as the basic goal of the project is achieved. In this case, you note your original idea in part 1 of your data presentation, explaining why that idea did not work, and then explain why and how you switched topics. Failures are data too.

3. Plan Your Observations
Planning where to conduct your observations can get tricky and should be done with care, keeping in mind that you not only need to find a place where you can observe easily

without intruding, but you also need to find a situation that provokes interesting research questions. We can talk for a long time about what counts as an "interesting" research question, but the bottom line is to do something that interests you. If a project does not interest you, don't do it. If it does not interest you, it will not interest anyone else.

To give you some ideas for proxemics project types, here are some examples my students have chosen:

- Negotiating a complex turnstile in the subway
- Diners choosing their tables and seating arrangement in a restaurant
- People waiting at a bus stop with limited seating
- People choosing seats in a movie theater
- Finding the most frequented campus locations for a bulletin board

Perhaps the most difficult decision at the outset is choosing a location where you can sit with a notebook and take notes without being obviously out of place and noticeable. The project takes an hour to complete, which means that being in that one place for an hour should not cause problems. Sitting in a parked car can work in some situations, but usually you will be out in the open, and you will need to use a notebook that is larger than your pocket-sized one.

4. Be Mindful of Ethical Prohibitions

There are three hard-and-fast prohibitions when it comes to conducting proxemics projects. The observations must be carried out in a public space. In a public space there is a presumption that people might observe one another. Yet, even though you are not asking for informed consent, you are not exonerated from some ethical provisions. You must preserve the total anonymity of the people you observe and you must also consider your own personal safety. Therefore:

1. Do not observe children.
2. Do not observe illegal activity.
3. Do not observe groups that expressly prohibit it.

These are obvious prohibitions, although I can add some qualifications and comments. It is all right to observe one or two children if they are with adults, and your general observations concern adult behavior. It is not acceptable to observe children as your primary focus. Ethical considerations require you to obtain parental consent to observe children, even though the situation is anonymous.

Some behavior, such as jaywalking, is illegal, but is rarely prosecuted. Even so, you should not use jaywalking as your primary focus. If, however, in the course of watching people crossing a busy street, someone jaywalks, you can take note. Do not, under any circumstances, make as your focus activities that are illegal and are always prosecuted if uncovered by authorities, even if you have a vantage point that cannot be detected. Your failure to report a crime can, in many cases, also be considered a criminal offense. Furthermore, consent to observe cannot be granted, even if you were foolish enough to ask for it, because it is not legally possible to consent to an illegal activity.

Lastly, 12-step programs, secret societies, private religious practices, and the like quite explicitly tell participants that their activities are not to be divulged outside of their meetings. There are no exceptions to their prohibition.

5. Create a Shorthand

Before you begin your observations, draw a sketch map of the area that you are observing. Mark on the map all aspects of the area that you consider important. Mark the significant locations with convenient symbols, such as A, B, and C, so that you can refer to those locations without lengthy references in your notes. You don't want to have to write "a group of 3 sat at a table for 6 beside the window." If the table is shown on your sketch map as having 6 seats and the window is also shown, and you mark the table as B, then your notes need only say "3 at B." If you are concerned about exact seating decisions you can mark the chairs as 1, 2, 3 …, etc., so that each chair at table B is B1, B2, and so forth. The situation will dictate the symbols you choose, but keep it simple.

Also, decide on how you are going to designate the people in the study. Something simple, yet uniquely identifying, works best. It should be anonymous, but unmistakable. "Blue hair" (abbreviated to bh) or "steam locomotive belt buckle" (slbb) work, but "white shirt" does not. You probably will not get a lot of people entering your observation space with hair dyed blue, but you may get several with white shirts. Use your abbreviations in your notes but keep a reference key on a separate page. Also decide what variables about the people you are going to record. Does age matter? Or gender expression? Height? If they do, then you must record these variables in your reference key. Do not record variables that do not pertain to your research question. Also, do not record conversations that you overhear, or any other data not relevant to proxemics (except data needed to identify individuals in your notes).

Record the exact time when you begin your observations, and mark down the time every time that you make a new observation. It is technically possible to record your observations using a smartphone, and this practice has the added advantage of making you blend in with your surroundings. Someone tapping on a smartphone is nothing out of the ordinary. You can also keep a record of the times of events automatically. It is, however, cumbersome, and relies on you being proficient with your phone's notepad app. Notepad apps have many features that make them less than ideal for lengthy note taking. If you think that you are proficient enough with your phone to use it to take notes, experiment to be sure. Find a convenient spot and record proxemic data for 5 to 10 minutes. If you find that you can do it proficiently, then use this technique for the actual project. Otherwise, use an ordinary paper notebook, and have one with you anyway as a backup in case something goes wrong with your phone.

6. Make Your Observations

Make your observations for approximately one hour – not much longer, and not shorter. By the end of the hour you should have several pages of notes, with a left-hand column recording the times that events occurred beside which are your shorthand notations concerning those events. The timeline is important because it records the duration of events, even when they are passive. If you are recording seating patterns in a fast-food restaurant, for example, you automatically have notes concerning the duration of people's stay at tables via the timeline.

Before you do the actual project, practice your method for 5 to 10 minutes in a trial location to make sure that it is workable, and, also, to become proficient at it. Make any corrections necessary so that you are comfortable and confident when you do the actual project. This project is a lot harder than it sounds, because it requires you to pay careful attention to detail that you probably never even noticed before. Welcome to fieldwork.

7. Review Your Notes

After your hour of observation is over, immediately go to a private space and review your notes. Correct any obvious mistakes and elaborate on your notes where your shorthand is confusing. Immediate follow-up with your notes is also a good habit to get into in general, even though your preference might be to put your notebook away and go off and relax when the actual observation is over. Your memory is at its most acute immediately after an event, and drops off rapidly even within the first hour. You may know exactly what you meant when you wrote, "2 ghm to C5," but an hour later you are clueless because you forgot to write down what "ghm" means.

Once you are confident that your notes are as complete as can be, let them rest for a day or so. You would be surprised what having time to let things percolate can do. When you look again, decide whether your hypothesis was completely confirmed/disconfirmed, moderately confirmed/disconfirmed, or neither confirmed nor disconfirmed (or whatever scale suits you), and, most importantly, explain why you got the results that you did. You can then write up your results using the three-part guidelines laid out in chapter 4. Part 1 should be a description of your project at the outset, including a description of the location, an explanation of why you chose it, your research question, and an account of problems which you encountered. Part 2 is your data in readable form. Your field notes are shorthand. When written up for presentation they must be explicit, so that "f/lp from D3" becomes "woman in leather pants leaves seat D3." Replicate the timeline down the left side of your page, and include your sketch map and original notes along with these finished notes. Part 3 consists of your conclusions, noting any patterns or oddities that you observed, explaining how your hypothesis was confirmed or disconfirmed, and outlining any problems you found in conducting the research.

Further Reading

You can read Hall including (1963). System for the Notation of Proxemic behavior. *American Anthropologist* 65: 1003–1026, but there are a great many more recent explorations of proxemics for you to dip into to get a feeling for the method, such as:

Busbea, Larry D. (2020). Proxemics and the Architecture of Social Interaction. Columbia Books on Architecture and the City (Columbia UP) ISBN 9781941332672

Maiberger Institute. Proxemics and Nonverbal Communication in EMDR Therapy https://medium.com/@BarbMaiberger/proxemics-and-nonverbal-communication-in-emdr-therapyf0ee5b73353d

Maginnis, T. How's your personal distance – watch this space. http://www.friends-partners.org/oldfriends/spbweb/lifestyl/122/how.html

McArthur, J.A. (2016). Digital Proxemics: How technology shapes the ways we move. Peter Lang. ISBN 9781454199403

Mulvaney, B. Gender Differences in Communication: An Intercultural Experience. http://cpsr.org/issues/womenintech/mulvaney/

Olsen, C. J.. Proxemic Behavior of the Nonhandicapped Toward the Visually Impaired. University of Nebraska at Omaha. https://www.proquest.com/docview/1696286801

7

Mapping

As you explored in Chapter 6, the way that humans use and orient themselves in space is an important part of their cultural world. In this chapter, you will expand on your abilities to interpret the social dimensions of space by developing a map that is a visual representation of a specific and limited type of data. Mapping is a useful, albeit largely neglected, skill in fieldwork because it can help researchers appreciate the built environment of people's lives, how that space is used and the cultural meanings and values people associate with it. Importantly, it can also be a source of ethnographic data in itself.

Learning Goals

1. Collect data concerning the social dimensions of the use of space,
2. Plot the findings on a map that is either drawn from scratch or involves reworking an existing map.

Mapping is often neglected as a fieldwork skill, and there are many fieldwork situations where it is not necessary. Nonetheless, it is a useful ability to cultivate, for a variety of reasons. It can help organize fieldwork, appreciate the built environment of people's lives, and can also be a source of ethnographic data in itself. As we explored in Chapter 6, the way that humans orient ourselves in space and organize our surroundings is an important part of our cultural world. I draw sketch maps when I am doing fieldwork as a matter of habit, and find that the visual presentation of data on a map is also a good way, not only to see large amounts of data at a glance, but also to aid in interpreting data. When I did my doctoral fieldwork in Tidewater, North Carolina, I spent the first month mapping the village in sections, marking each dwelling, and noting who lived where. This was, among other things, a simple tool for finding my way around given that there was no official map. It was also an invaluable tool for locating people when I was told something like, "Margaret Smith would like to show you her grandmother's quilts," and I did not want to be asking all the time where people lived. Over time, I added details to the maps including kinship information, age of the properties, lines of inheritance, occupations of the occupants, and so forth, so that my maps were mines of information when it came to writing my dissertation. I also supplemented the large-scale maps with precisely measured drawings of individual

Doing Field Projects: Methods and Practice for Social and Anthropological Research, First Edition. John Forrest.
© 2022 John Wiley & Sons, Inc. Published 2022 by John Wiley & Sons, Inc.

houses and gardens. I used many of these drawings in subsequent publications to point out the social dimensions of interior and exterior spaces (see Forrest 1988a).

When I was doing fieldwork in Buenos Aires I had an entirely different purpose in drawing maps. I had any number of maps at my disposal, both on paper and online. Finding my way around was not the issue; I was much more concerned with how locals mentally mapped their environments, and how they navigated the city in their daily lives. What were their landmarks? What locations and routes were significant for them? How did they mentally map and traverse the city? These questions produced markedly different maps from standard ones.

Thus, think of mapping as a visual way of presenting data and not just a record of spaces. The maps you might consult when you are going about your everyday business have all kinds of purposes, and usually the most useful ones are targeted to *one* kind of information. So, for example, the London Underground map does not concern itself with distances between stations, curves in the tracks, or even where north is. All it is concerned with is how to get from one station to another, because that is the information that travelers most want to know. They may also want to know how long it will take to get from one place to another, but the map does not supply that information because that is not its purpose.

In the 1920s the London underground railway had blossomed into different lines, and there were also overground railways leading into various stations in the city. At that time, a map of the system looked like Figure 7.1.

Then in 1931 Harry Beck produced a new map that simplified things considerably. He used only vertical, horizontal, and diagonal lines to indicate the train routes, he did not worry about exact distances, and he eliminated all details except the train lines and stations. In this way he revolutionized mapping of train routes, and his system is used worldwide for both underground and overground rail systems from Tokyo to Buenos Aires.

In communications theory, the things you need to communicate are called the "signal" and the things that you do not need to communicate, and that obscure the signal, are called "noise." The job of the map maker is to determine what information for any given map is important (signal) and what information is not important (noise), and, thereby, to increase, as much as possible, what is called the "signal to noise ratio" (emphasize the signal and reduce the noise). On the London Underground map, distance between stations is considered "noise" for the purposes of the map. Distance between stations is not useless information in a general sense, but it is noise for the express purposes of this map. Some subway systems do include distance between stations in a single number on their maps, as it happens, because it is useful in gauging time between stations. But such information is rarely needed by passengers who use the maps.

In order to maximize the signal to noise ratio in your map-making endeavors, you must have a coherent research question first. Realize that I am using the term "map" in the broadest of senses, as a general term for a drawing that represents spatial relationships in a graphic way. Think about your local supermarket, for example. There are sections for fresh fruits and vegetables, meat and fish, refrigerated items, boxed foods, baking needs, canned foods, household cleaning supplies, toiletries, paper goods, and so forth. How the sections are categorized and where they are located is a decision the store manager has to make, and each manager's prime objective is to maximize sales. Therefore, a good starting research question would be, "How is this supermarket laid out to maximize sales?" A slightly more complex question would be, "What categories does this store break items into?" That question can partially be

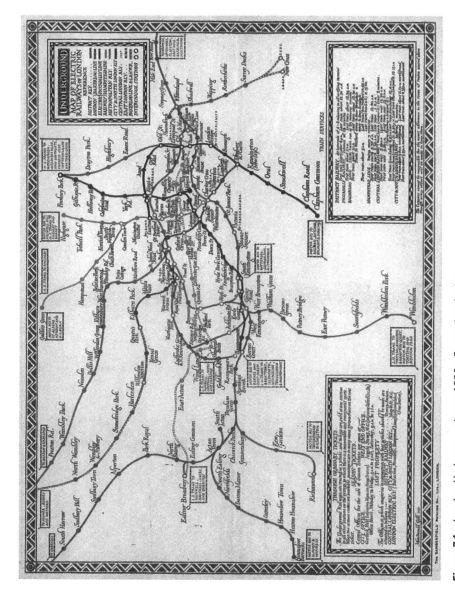

Figure 7.1 London Underground map 1920s. *Source:* Londonist.

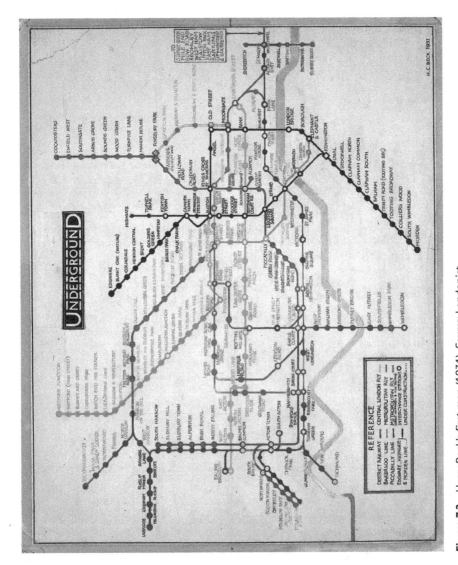

Figure 7.2 Harry Beck's first map (1931). *Source:* Londonist.

answered by the signs on aisles, but not completely, because some items, such as fruits and vegetables, typically do not have signs, and some aisles contain items that are not included in the signs.

A store manager might decide to place all the items needed for babies – food, diapers, toys, etc. – in one place, so that a shopper who has a baby can find all the baby supplies at the same time. But, an alternative would be to scatter those items throughout the store – baby food with canned goods, diapers with paper goods, etc., etc. – so that the shopper has to go hunting for them all, in the process spotting other things to buy on impulse.

The complication that you have to take into consideration is that maps are two-dimensional, but supermarkets are three-dimensional. Store managers are concerned with the floor plan when it comes to guiding shoppers around the aisles, but they are also concerned with the vertical arrangement of items on shelves. It is a common habit to place the most expensive items at eye level, and the cheaper items at ground level or well above eye level. A supermarket, therefore, needs at least two different kinds of map – plan and vertical – and the choice of which you want to draw will be determined by your research question.

In one section of Phnom Penh, in Cambodia where I used to live, I could go to one of three supermarkets depending on my needs. One was very close, and the two others were some distance away. The close one was useful for things I needed on short notice, such as butter and eggs, but the store was small with limited choices. Half of the store space was taken up with plates, cups, and glasses, cooking equipment, and storage containers which in a two-year period I never saw anyone buying. There was also a very large section devoted to bottled alcohol, including a huge array of wines and spirits, set apart from the rest of the store and across from the cash registers. The choice of fresh fruits and vegetables, meat, fish, and other perishables was extremely limited. Household cleaning supplies had their own section, away from the food items, but personal toiletries were scattered all over the store, in some cases in aisles that might have hair dyes on one side and canned fruit on the other. What was the store's logic? Were any cultural priorities exposed in its layout? Mapping could help answer such questions.

One of the larger supermarkets I went to less often had a layout whose logic confused me even more. It is situated in a popular mall, so you can enter it from a number of different directions. If you enter from the street, the first items you encounter are house plants, seeds, and gardening equipment. If you enter from the mall, you could enter through personal toiletries, organic packaged foods, or chocolate and sweet snacks, depending on the direction you approach it. Meats, fish, and fresh produce are at the back of the store. It would be an interesting project to map the plan of the store to figure out the logic.

Instructions

1. Select a location and define the research question

As with the proxemics project, you should begin by paying attention to the places you habitually frequent and consider what research questions you could ask about those locations. It is perfectly acceptable to use the same location as you used for the proxemics project, but now you will be presenting the data differently, and your research question may be altered somewhat. Chances are, however, that a new location will spark new questions. Here is a small sampling of potential projects that students have used to give you some ideas:

- A large cemetery, recording the ages of graves, and the location of graves in relation to features of the environment including trees and hills.
- Location of specific fruits and vegetables in an outdoor market.
- Use of space for different items in a closet.
- Alternatives for arranging furniture in a small dorm room.
- Layout of a professional kitchen.
- Places where sexual assaults have occurred on campus.
- Nighttime lighting in public spaces on campus.

Once you settle on a location and a research question, you have to decide on how you are going to draw your map. Mapping and design are complex technical skills, but do not be intimidated by that fact. This is not a project for professional publication. You are simply trying to express spatial information in a clear way. Squared paper can be very useful for this project. You may also be able to use a preexisting map which you subsequently modify.

2. Gather your data

Once you have decided on your research question, you must collect your data, and how you do this will be determined by the location and the question you are asking. First of all, you need to find out whether a map of the area already exists. For all geographical locations, there are various map options online. If you are studying, say, the number and types of vehicles owned by families in a neighborhood, you can download and print out the base map of the neighborhood to start you off, or, perhaps, you can buy a street map. In this case, you do not have to start from scratch in drawing the spatial dimensions of your map and, instead, you can concentrate on recording data concerning make and model of cars on your existing map. The existing map (plus data) is the equivalent of a sketch map. *It is not a finished map.*

Besides geographical locations, many places have preexisting drawings that are readily available. Public buildings usually have floor plans used for emergencies, for example. For many locations, however, you will have to start from the beginning. The basics of drawing a sketch map from scratch are straightforward. We can start first with the barebones, followed by a detailed example.

Squared paper is best when producing a sketch map. You can find paper with 4, 5, 6, or 10 squares to the inch, or other dimensions. You will have to decide what is best based on what is available, but 5 squares to the inch is fine for most sketch maps. Begin by drawing an outline of the space you are mapping, in pencil (so that you can erase easily). Next, mark the location of everything that is important to your research question on your sketch map, and exclude everything else. Indicate in writing what every object on the sketch map is, and include all necessary dimensions – overall size of the space, length and breadth of each object, and so forth. Your sketch map will not be perfectly to scale, so notation of all dimensions is essential. It does not matter for the sketch map whether things are out of proportion, as long as you have a notation of all of the dimensions. Your finished map is going to be a scale map (that is, without individual dimensions marked), and the objects on it will be symbols (identified with a key) which means that it will be interpretable without need of any lettering or numbering (compare Figures 7.1 and Figure 7.2). Now let us see, in detail, how to make a sketch map.

Imagine I want to map the furniture placement in the room where I am sitting right now, and ask, as I do once in a while, "Is the furniture placed in the most efficient manner for my own daily needs (writing, eating, watching movies, entertaining visitors, etc.)?" To begin a sketch map I need the dimensions of the entire room, but I do not have a tape measure or other measuring device. The floor is wooden tile, however, and that is sufficient to record dimensions. A map for these purposes does not have to be accurate to a micromillimeter; the number of tiles is enough because the tiles are small enough (10" by 10") to capture all the dimensions that I need. By good fortune, the room is exactly 13 × 13 tiles. I can lightly sketch the outline on a piece of squared paper, marking 13 tiles for each side of the room. I am going to add the furniture next, as well as any other features of the room (such as doors and windows) that affect the efficient placement of the different pieces of furniture.

The room has a door and two windows on one side, and the entrance to a hallway on the opposite wall. The door leads to my front balcony, and the rest of the wall where the door is, has a set of large windows. The placement of the front door, front window, and entrance to the hallway are all important features to include on the map because they influence the placement of furniture. The door and hallway entrance cannot be obstructed, so furniture must be kept clear of where people walk. Therefore, I have to put their location on the sketch map. The location of the front window is important also because it lets in light and has a good view, and so influences where I put my desk and chair.

Now I can draw the location of the various pieces of furniture on the map (see figure 7.3). The room has two easy chairs, a sofa, a coffee table, a desk and chair, a high-backed chair, a television center, and two sets of freestanding shelves. They can all be represented by squares or rectangles because their exact shape is not important. Their

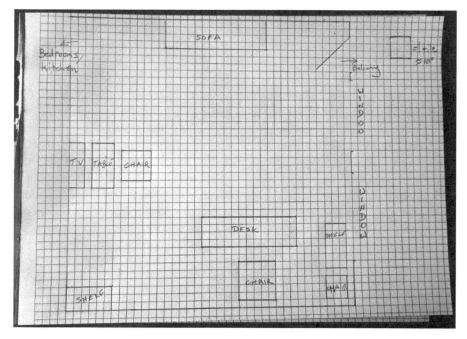

Figure 7.3 Sample Sketch Map.

size *is* important, so I need to count tiles to represent the piece of furniture, and also count tiles to mark the location. So, for example, my desk is 4 tiles long and 1.5 tiles wide and it sits 4 tiles from one wall and 3 tiles from another. So, I can roughly draw a rectangle inside my sketch map and mark both its dimensions and location. I also label it as "desk." I then repeat the process until I have marked the size and location of all the pieces of furniture. That results in something like this:

Last thing to consider is which pieces of furniture can be moved. All of the furniture is physically movable, but two pieces have to stay where they are because of their function. The television center is an absolute fixture because it is adjacent to the cable box on the wall. The freestanding shelves near the television are more mobile, but I use the top shelf for my electric kettle, and there is only one conveniently located electrical outlet for it. There are three other outlets in the room: one for the television, and two by walkways. So, the shelves have to stay where they are, or I would have to consider relocating the kettle to another room if I wanted to move the shelves. This point leads to consideration of the function of all the pieces of furniture.

I can tell you what pieces of furniture I use most often and what their functions are, but most of this information could be gathered by an observant outsider. Many horizontal surfaces, including one easy chair, a hard-backed chair and the sofa, have things piled on them which would have to be moved if you want to sit on them. Thus, it is easy to surmise that at the moment I rarely use them for seating. My desk is piled with books and papers and my laptop sits in the center. There is also a thermos plus mate and bombilla beside the laptop. Next to the desk is a service table with things I use occasionally when sitting at my desk including devices to plug into my laptop, a blood pressure cuff, spare reading glasses, earphones, my smartphone, tissues, toothpicks, and other assorted things that I need once in a while. The second easy chair sits facing the television with the coffee table in between. The coffee table has some incense and candles on it, plus the television remote, but is mostly clear. You might be able to guess, therefore, that I eat at the coffee table sometimes while watching television. Of course, if you did the necessary fieldwork (that is, watch me or ask me) you could confirm these surmises.

3. Identify your focus

At this stage you have to make a decision concerning signal versus noise, and this decision is influenced by the research question. Recall that in the example I gave, the research question was "Is furniture placed in the most efficient manner." In this case, the "signal" consists of the walls, doors and windows, and the size and placement of the furniture; the "noise" is everything else, including things on horizontal surfaces, the exact shape of the furniture, electrical outlets, light switches, and so forth. You will now identify which data are your "signal" and which are your "noise." Think carefully about the important data for your research question and which other data distracts from the focus of your map and your research question. Once you have identified the unnecessary information on your map then you are ready for the next step; finishing the map.

4. Finish the map

For this step you will eliminate the "noise" data and focus on your "signal" by redrawing your sketch map and creating a new polished finished map. How you go about producing a finished map depends on whether you are using a preexisting map for your sketch map, or working from scratch. Let us consider the case of a preexisting map first. If I had the architect's drawing of my apartment, which I do not, I could use it as the basis of my sketch map. This preexisting diagram might have on it such things as window and door placement, and possibly dimensions of my living room. But it might also have information that is not relevant to the map I need to draw, such as placement of wiring and light switches. I can mark the furniture placement on that diagram, but it is not a finished map; it is the equivalent of a sketch map. I have to make a copy of the map on a clean sheet of paper in order to produce a finished map that shows all, *and only*, the relevant information. You can use tracing paper to copy your map, or a light box that will allow you to trace on regular paper. There are also ways to project the map on to regular paper. You and your instructor will have to decide what is acceptable, as well as what equipment you have available and what you are comfortable using. Most college and university art departments have light boxes or tables, as well as ways of projecting images on to paper, which can be borrowed.

If you are using data from a sketch map that you created from scratch, producing a finished map is a much longer process than tracing a preexisting map. First you must create a base map. Going back to the example of the map of my living room, we know that it is 13 tiles by 13. So, the first job is to draw a square to start the base map, representing the room. Using squared paper, plus ruler and pencil, is the simplest option. The size of the room on the page is determined by the size of the squares on the squared paper. If the paper has 4 squares to the inch then a 2 × 2 square on the paper can represent one tile. That is the scale (4 squares: 1 tile). Your scale is the only dimension that will appear on the finished map. All the other dimensions can be calculated by counting squares on the map.

The next job is to mark all the necessary physical features of the room on the base map. In my example, these include the window, the outside door, and the entrance to the hallway. This is now an outline map. Next I need to mark the placement and size of all the furniture. At this point I have to decide how to add such data. This is the most challenging part. There are various templates you can buy to draw icons of everything under the sun, including chairs, lamps, desks, sofas, trees, bushes, etc., which may be useful for a map you are working on but are not necessary in my example. All I need to plot are the sizes of the pieces of furniture, amount of usage for each piece, and whether the piece can be moved. Indicating the amount of usage for each item of furniture is complicated. I could list each item on a scale of 1 to 5 from least to most used and just mark the number on each piece, but this is not the best way to convey this information. Color coding is much more easily comprehended visually (and quickly). I could choose dark blue for least used and bright red for most used and create a scale of dark blue, violet, yellow, orange, and red. Then shade each of the pieces of furniture in the appropriate color. Two of the items are not moveable, so I need to decide on a symbol for that. Maybe a really thick border. Instead of using colors to indicate usage I could decide on different borders for the items of furniture on a scale of least to most used (with immovable included) (see Figure 7.4).

You need to make these same kinds of decisions if you are modifying a preexisting map. Imagine you are plotting the location of graves in a cemetery based on their age, and in relation to physical features. If you have a cemetery plot map, you can use a light box to trace the positions of the graves and the extra features you want to map – maybe trees, or a pond, or driveways and walkways. Then you can color-code the graves based on age. If you just mark the year of the grave on the map, the data are not obvious, but if you use colors, the pattern of usage will likely emerge. You cannot use a different color for each year, obviously. That is no clearer than marking the dates on each grave. But you can use a different color for, say, each decade. When one of my students did this project, she discovered that certain features, a pond and an old shade tree, were focal points, so that when the graves were chosen, nearness to these features was important. This fact was shown clearly in the color-coding because the graves closest to these features were the oldest, and those farthest away were the newest, showing up as concentric rings of different colors.

To finish off the map you need to add the following:

- An indication of scale.
- A key explaining colors and symbols used.
- An indication of orientation, such as an arrow pointing north, when appropriate. Interiors with windows need this because of the position of the sun, but interiors without windows do not.
- A descriptive label.

As much as possible, your map should be self-explanatory: that is the point of maps. Look at my finished map (Figure 7.4). It is not a cartographer's dream, but it clearly shows the data I intend to convey.

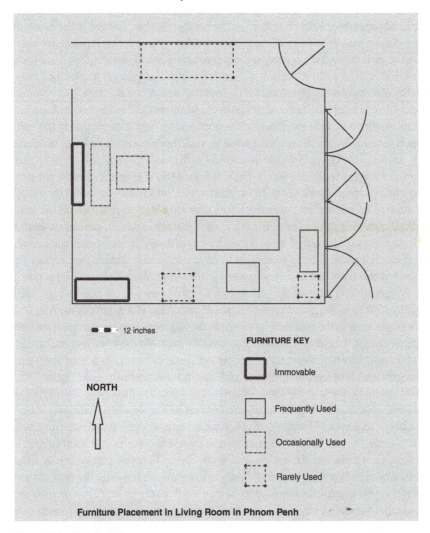

Figure 7.4 Finished Map.

It is possible to use computer-aided design (CAD) tools. CAD is certainly a helpful tool in producing high-quality maps, and there are numerous free apps available, such as:

- FreeCAD https://www.freecadweb.org/downloads.php
- Fusion 360 https://www.autodesk.com/products/fusion-360/students-teachers-educators
- Onshape https://www.onshape.com/products/free
- nanoCAD https://nanocad.com/products/nanoCAD
- OpenSCAD https://www.openscad.org/downloads.html

Just bear in mind that these are professional tools that have many features that will not be useful (such as 3D), and there is a steep learning curve involved. If you are already comfortable with a CAD package, then by all means use it, but I would not recommend trying to get yourself up to speed with one just for this exercise. Right now, the aim is to get a sense of the value of mapping in general, not ramp up computer skills that may not be valuable to you in the future.

Your presentation should have three parts. In part 1 you will explain how you chose your location and fixed on a research question. It should also explain how you collected your data, and should include your sketch map and other notes. Part 2 is simply the map itself (which can be presented in a computer file if you have used CAD – and can be projected if you are making a class presentation). In part 3 you will explain any problems that arose, and the conclusions you came to.

Additional Suggestions

This exercise is deliberately rudimentary (one map only), but there are a great many possibilities for more complex projects if mapping is useful for your overall research agenda. The most obvious extension is to take a comparative approach. Let's say you are interested in the layout of dorm rooms at your college. In many housing facilities on a campus, the rooms are more or less identical, and there is limited space. Therefore, on arrival the occupants have to make decisions about the placement of moveable items such as beds, desks, and chairs. Some students are not interested in how the furniture is placed, and may accept the layout as given when they arrive; others are much more creative and spend the first day or so moving things around until they find the optimal arrangement for their needs. By the time the students begin this mapping project, they will have already settled on their room design. Therefore (with permission), you can visit any number of different rooms and record the locations of moveable items in the various spaces and draw multiple maps for comparison.

Comparative mapping of this kind starts off with a base map (so that you do not have to keep redrawing the same space) and with fixed symbols for the common moveable items. The base map can be fixed and then you can use transparent overlays for the different rooms which can be placed over the base map, or can be compared side by side. Or, if you have the computer skills, your data can be built into an interactive map online. In the same vein, you can create a base map on your computer with tokens that you can move around to represent the moveable items. Then you can ask classmates to come up with designs of their own.

If you decide on a comparative approach you can then ask pertinent questions, such as, "Does gender play a part in room arrangement?" "Is age a factor?" "Are there commonalities from room to room?" "Does one arrangement strike you as particularly optimal or especially creative?"

You should not feel constrained by my instructions here; there are multiple possibilities that do not involve paper and pen or CAD. One year I had a blind student who created a tactile map of her room. Her map was an enclosed box with a hole to insert your hand. Inside were all the things that she had to navigate around her room, using her hands to guide her. Each item, dresser, desk, bed, chairs, etc. was made to scale, and placed in their correct positions within the map box, but each was constructed of materials with its own texture – wood, cork, corduroy, etc. To "read" the map you had to insert your hand and feel your way around the room in analogous fashion to the way she actually navigated her room in real life. This example might give you ideas for tactile mapping that can serve similar or unrelated purposes.

You can also work on this project in two distinct ways, either as an observational exercise or as an engaged one. That is, you can draw your map(s) without any input from the people who use the space(s), or you can ask pertinent questions of the people involved. In the case of dorm rooms, you can ask the occupants why they settled on the arrangement that they currently have. Did they experiment with other arrangements, and what decisions did they come to?

Another variation of this exercise is creating a sequence of maps. When I was mapping Tidewater houses for my doctoral fieldwork, I discovered that it had been common over the previous 100 years to start with a simple two-room house, and then for successive generations of owners to add rooms and floors as their needs changed and/or their finances improved. Figures 7.5–Figure 7.9 in *Lord I'm Coming Home* (Forrest 1988a: 70–74) show five evolutionary stages in the modifications of one house from two-room cabin to two-story, four-bedroom house. This is the relevant section:

> The house I consider in this exercise was built in 1868 by Cull Kinsey and added on to, up and out, by him and by later generations. Cull started by building two rooms side by side with a breezeway down the center. As you entered the house through the breezeway, you could turn left into the bedroom or right into the general-purpose room, used for cooking, eating, working, sitting, or whatever (Figure 7.5). As his family grew, Cull partitioned the bedroom into two bedrooms and then built a lean-to addition, for use as a bedroom, to the right of the general-purpose room. To complete the change he built a porch that ran the length of the building. *(Figure 7.6).*

Cull's son Paul built upward. He added a second story above the original portion of the house, making this floor into two large bedrooms, the size of the two old rooms downstairs. Downstairs he removed the partition wall between the two bedrooms and used the room as a sitting and work room, reserving the kitchen space for domestic tasks. Eventually he built a separate kitchen at the back of the house to keep the heat of summer cooking away from the main living space. Paul had only two children, and when the elder left home he began to take in boarders. To separate his family from the guests he built a dining room adjacent to the kitchen building and set aside the left-hand main room as a guest sitting room (Figures 7.7–Figure 7.8).

Paul's younger child Mary also had two children. Most of her life she had looked after the guests with her mother, so she simply continued existing practice when she inherited

Additional Suggestions | 71

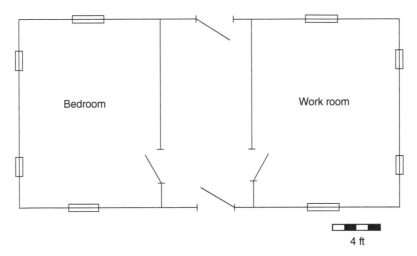

Figure 7.5 Original Kinsey house (1868).

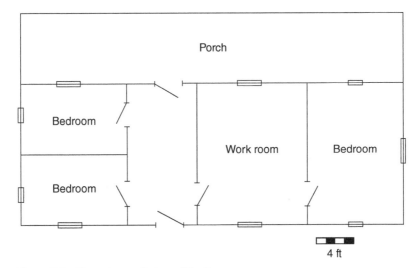

Figure 7.6 Kinsey house first modification.

the house. In the 1930s, when electricity and running water became available in the county, Mary could not take immediate advantage of the opportunity because it necessitated major structural changes. Before long, however, she had saved enough money to have the kitchen and dining room moved, forming a tee at the back of the house butted up against the old porch. She had the whole extension, including the porch, roofed continuously. The old porch, which was shortened somewhat, became a bathroom and washhouse, and the adjacent kitchen and dining room extension now had electricity and running water. The outbuildings had to be moved beside the house to limit plumbing and wiring for kitchen and bathroom facilities. To make up for the lost porch she had a new one built on the kitchen and dining room tee, forming a walkway into the main house (Figure 7.9).

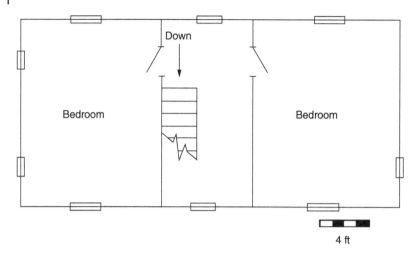

Figure 7.7 Kinsey house second modification (upstairs).

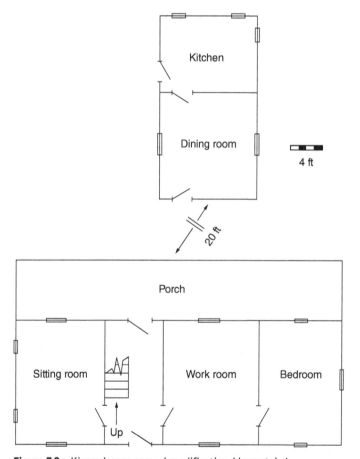

Figure 7.8 Kinsey house second modification (downstairs).

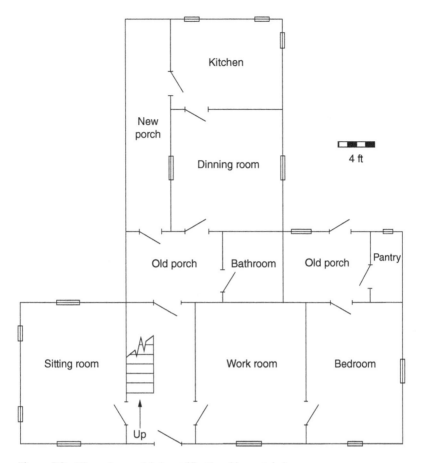

Figure 7.9 Kinsey house third modification (downstairs).

In the 1950s Mary grew tired of the arrangement of the downstairs and determined on a complete overhaul. She converted the lean-to bedroom into the kitchen and made guest bedrooms of the dining room and the old kitchen. She took out the right-hand breezeway wall to enlarge the center room, which served as a spacious congregating place for dining, bridge parties, dancing, and so on. Now people entering from the road walked directly into the main room instead of a narrow passage. She also screened in the new back porch (Figure 7.10). Since then the house has remained the same. Her husband died not long after the changes were made, and she has now lost interest in home alterations.

Sometimes comparing two (or more) different maps can be insightful in other ways. For example, I like to cook and I have lived in 7 different apartments in Argentina, Italy, China, and Cambodia over the last 12 years. When I select an apartment to live in, the

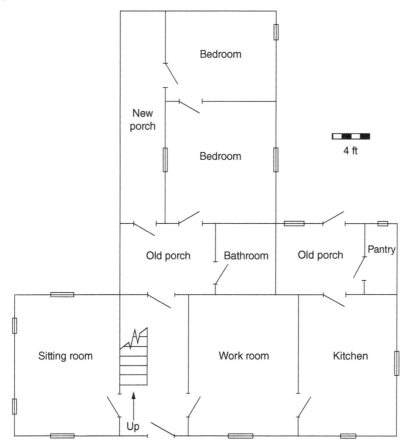

Figure 7.10 Kinsey house fourth modification (downstairs).

layout and equipment of the kitchen is one of my major concerns because I cook daily for myself and often for dinner parties. Comparing maps of these kitchens can reveal a great deal about the cultural variations in cooking in different countries.

These are just two sketch maps (on the same scale) giving an idea of how a comparison of maps gives the sense of how cultural values concerning cooking are reflected in kitchen layout and equipment; I could have drawn maps of all seven of my kitchens for a complete analysis, but two are sufficient for instruction. Comparing only these two I note that an Italian main meal usually consists of at least two cooked courses – a pasta dish (il primo) followed by meat and vegetables (il secondo) – whereas a Cambodian cooked meal can often be made in one pot, accompanied with rice from a second pot, or rice cooker. Therefore, an Italian kitchen ideally has a four-burner stove and an oven, whereas a Cambodian kitchen can make do with two burners (and no oven). There is also a great deal more preparation space (surfaces) in my Italian kitchen than in my Cambodian one because Italians do all their prep in the kitchen, whereas Cambodians do a great deal of their cleaning, peeling, slicing, chopping, and so forth in other parts of the house (or outside). Note also that my Italian kitchen is a separate

Additional Suggestions | 75

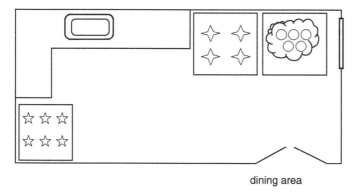

Figure 7.11 Kitchen #1 (Italy).

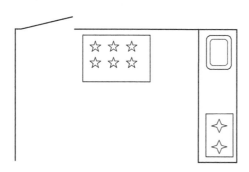

Figure 7.12 Kitchen #2 (Cambodia).

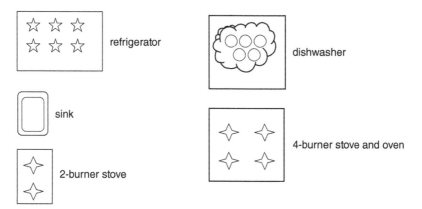

Figure 7.13 Map key.

room (with a door) so that it can be closed off completely, whereas my Cambodian kitchen is simply an open section of my general living space.

Finally, consider the possibility of analyzing imaginary maps and their usage, or online maps used in computer games. Dungeons and Dragons masters routinely design fantasy maps for the use of players, and these can be created on paper or online. Links such as https://www.solutionhow.com/en-us/dnd/dnd-map-maker-useful-links and http://pyromancers.com provide helpful resources. In this case you would certainly want to talk to a gamer to help understand issues in mapmaking and map usage.

Further Reading

Ethnographic mapping is not a common research method but you can find examples, such as this one concerning the availability of alcohol in Malaysia: file:///C:/Users/Acer/AppData/Local/Temp/Anethnographicmappingofalcoholaccessibilityindifferentethnic-communitiesresidinginurbanandsemiurbanareaswithinKlangValleyMalaysia.pdf or this exercise in mapping the layout of a library: https://blogs.lt.vt.edu/librarylc/category/mapping/ https://blogs.lt.vt.edu/librarylc/category/mapping

You can also consult such works as this classic, *The Image of the City*, by Kevin Lynch (1960) MIT Press, or the more recent *Image and Environment: Cognitive Mapping and Spatial Behavior*, edited by Roger M. Downs and David Stea (1975 and 2017) Transaction Press, which contains papers related to ethnography and uses of space that are mapped (both cognitively and physically).

This article also gives a good overview ("GIS, Ethnography, and Cultural Research: Putting Maps Back into Ethnographic Mapping"), https://www.tandfonline.com/doi/abs/10.1080/01972240903562712. The book *Mapping My Way: Map-making and Analysis in Participant Observation*, by Les Roberts, may also be helpful. https://link.springer.com/chapter/10.1057/9781137025050_12

8

Recorded Interviews

In this chapter you will practice one of the earliest established and most widely used ethnographic research techniques: gathering recorded interviews. Ethnographic interviews allow the anthropologist to get closer to an insider's perspective and to appreciate the ways that a person makes sense of and categorizes their world. By examining what people talk about as well as how they speak about such things, ethnographers gain valuable insight into the specific ways in which people understand their culture and communities. Learning to listen and ask questions as an ethnographer does is a valuable skill for nearly any profession or area of study.

Learning Goals

1. Practice person-to-person interview skills using both directed and undirected formats,
2. Articulate the advantages and disadvantages of various transcription methods.

Ethnographic interviews have a long and checkered history. At one time, interviews were the main, or sole, method of gathering data, but Malinowski's invention of "open air" fieldwork changed all of that. It was clear that Malinowski's method not only garnered a greater variety of data than simple interviewing could, but use of participant observation as a field strategy also pointed up the differences between what people say they do versus what they actually do. Nowadays, ethnographic interviews are more likely to be an adjunct to other field methods rather than the sole means of acquiring information, but they are still a fixture in the fieldworker's toolkit. Interviews can be formal or informal, voice-recorded or not, and directed or undirected.

You ought to familiarize yourself with the general styles of interview technique, even if you find short, simple interviews by themselves are of limited utility. Later projects in this volume, including Process Documentation (Chapter 11) and Life History (Chapter 15) involve interviewing as components of the process of data collecting, so it is useful to gain expertise in the method, and also develop disciplined habits of indexing and transcribing. This project is specific to using a voice recorder, although you could also use a video recorder or online applications just as well. There are notes on these methods at the end of the chapter. The point of this project is to familiarize you with interview technique as a tool in general. More than most other projects in this book, it can be treated as a dress rehearsal for methods to come.

Ethnographic Interviewing

Ethnographic interviews are quite different from the interviews you see on television talk shows or the news. Talk shows are entertainment, and are geared to that end. The interviewer has a set of questions prepared, the point of which is to amuse or inform the audience in some preordained format. News interviews add color to a breaking story, or add opinions to questions of the day. Some of the methods in an anthropological interview may look like these other kinds of interviews, but they are aimed substantially differently. Traditionally, an anthropological interview has an audience of one: you, the interviewer. Its purpose is to gather ethnographic data, and to record "authentic voice." You are not simply recording information; you are also recording the way people present that information in their own unique style. *How* people talk about a subject can be as important as *what* they are talking about, and can give you valuable insight into what the subject matter means to the interviewee.

What I call information here is a concept that needs to be teased apart. Data you collect using interviews are not necessarily empirical facts in any absolute sense. Some obviously are, for example, "I was 5 years old when I first went to school" or "I was 12 years old when JFK was shot." But such information is not the heart of fieldwork. You are trying to discover the ways people experience their lives and how their various mental abilities filter that experience. Their memories may be faulty, or they may deliberately lie about some events. Either way, your job is to try to see life through their eyes. This task is complicated enough but is made yet more complicated by the dynamic that exists between you and the person you are interviewing. There may be differences in age, class, ethnicity, etc. that influence how an interview proceeds, and you must be aware of that dynamic. Later exercises explore the workings of this dynamic more fully (see chapters 11 and 15), but for now it is sufficient to focus on some basics of interview technique.

There are two broad classes of interviews: undirected and directed. For an undirected interview you begin with only the most general of questions because your aim is simply to get your interviewee talking about the subject you are interested in, without leading the interview in any specific direction. If the interviewee goes off on a tangent that takes the interview completely off topic, it may be necessary to steer it back, but if the interviewee is on topic, all you have to do is sit and listen, showing attention, of course, but not interrupting nor contributing your own thoughts (engaged interviews where you actively add your own thoughts, and there is a clear dialog between interviewer and interviewee, are discussed in chapter 10). In a less formal context, undirected interviews can also be informal chit chats, spontaneous conversations, and brief exchanges of information. These can be as useful to anthropologists as more intentional interviews. Nevertheless, this represents a more advanced technique that you will not be exploring deeply in this book. What is important to keep in mind is that different kinds of interviews produce different kinds of data under different circumstances.

For a directed interview, you come prepared with a set of specific questions on a topic, and your goal is to get answers to those questions. In reality, the boundary between the two types of interview is not clear-cut, and they frequently merge into one another. You might, for example, have a very tightly organized set of questions prepared, and then find that your interviewee gets deeply involved with one particular question, and wants to range over the topic. In that case, the interview changes from directed to undirected. The reverse can happen also. You can ask the broadest of questions, and then find yourself narrowing your focus to one small detail. In short, good interview technique requires flexibility.

When you are interviewing you have to be thinking of several things at once. Obviously, of fundamental importance, you have to be paying attention. Think of the interview as a conversation, even though it is a bit one-sided. When you are talking to someone in daily life, you don't want that person's mind wandering while you are talking. You want them to be attentive and responsive. The same is true of interviewing. However, you do have to juggle several things at once. You need to have a notebook so that you can jot down a reminder of questions that you want to follow up with, while not disturbing the flow of conversation, for example. You can do this by writing down a single word as a reminder. You also need to keep an eye on the recorder to be sure it is still working, the battery is not running out, and so forth. This means, incidentally, you need to buy a recorder that allows you to check periodically, and unobtrusively, that it is operating correctly (see chapter 2). You need to have your research question foremost in your mind also, so that you can keep things on track. Interviewing is hard work.

Anthropologists debate constantly about the "purity" of interview material, and there is one school of thought that thinks that too much talking on the part of the interviewer taints that "purity." Another school of thought believes that there is no such thing as "purity" of information, and the interview situation itself inevitably taints the process. They argue, instead, that the interviewer should be part of the conversation, not necessarily as an equal contributor, but certainly as an established and active presence. So much depends on the nature of the subject matter, the relationship between interviewee and interviewer, and a host of other circumstances. You should tailor your discussion to particular interview projects. The instructions here for this project are deliberately simple to start you out. After the main instructions there are some suggestions and comments on variations on technique including video and online interviewing. Engaged interviewing is a completely separate technique with its own project (chapter 10).

Before you conduct an actual ethnographic interview it is a good idea to test out, and hone, your skills with the method. Read the instructions through and then do a dry run with a willing participant. One option is to pair up with a classmate and to take turns interviewing each other. That way you get a sense of what it feels like to be interviewed as well as learning good habits as an interviewer. Once you have a partner, discuss with each other what topics each of you would like to be interviewed about. Even though this is only a trial interview, the subject matter should, nonetheless, still be engaging to you.

Instructions

Pick an appropriate person to interview, set up a time and place for the interview, conduct an interview of around 30 minutes, and then transcribe about 10 minutes of the interview. These time frames are simply a convenient guideline and are not written in stone. At this point, you are simply developing the skill of interviewing, not getting deeply involved.

The steps can be broken down as follows:

1. **Choose an Interviewee**

Who you want to interview and what information you want are a single piece. If you want to know about coal mining in Kentucky, you interview a Kentucky coal miner. The person you interview should be an active and current specialist in the topic. Whether the topic comes first or the person comes first is determined by circumstances. It could be that you already know a person who was involved in something you are interested in, or you may have an interest in an event, but do not know anyone who was involved. Your choices are determined by practical considerations.

The events of 9/11 in 2001 in the United States are seared into the memories of many people above a certain age, and the fallout in terms of political activity, national security, public surveillance, and overall changes in social attitudes towards terrorism and violence in the United States have been long-lasting. I was not far from the trade towers when they were hit, and I was following the sequence of events at my university from the time the first plane hit until the towers fell. I have my own memories (including the fact that the second plane hit the Twin Towers while I was teaching Fieldwork Methods), but if I wanted to record the memories of others it would not be too difficult to find interviewees. I know people who were in the buildings at the time and got out alive, people who were part of rescue operations, people who were involved in the cleanup, and people who lost friends and relatives. I could pick any one of them to interview about their experiences on that day, or in the aftermath. Which one(s) I should pick to interview depends on my research question.

2. **Write a Research Question**

If I wanted to conduct interviews concerning 9/11, or the 2021 US Capitol insurrection, or the COVID-19 pandemic, my two questions to pose to myself initially would be (1) What do I want to know? (2) Why do I want to know it? Question #1 guides the interview primarily, and question #2 guides the analysis. You might think that the events of 9/11, and the insurrection, are intrinsically interesting, and maybe they are. But interest alone cannot drive question #2 if you are conducting an ethnographic interview. You must have a research question. The process of developing a research question is not necessarily straightforward, however. Recall that you should start with more than general interest, and instead focus on the question, "Why ... ?" "Why did this person race to help the victims of 9/11?" "Why did this particular individual storm the Capitol?" etc. But remember to also always entertain a degree of flexibility. It is completely normal to start with one research question, and then modify it as the interview progresses. You may find that the original research question is not as important as you thought, or cannot be answered for some reason. Or maybe a new question, that you find more engaging, occurs as the interview progresses. Those things happen. Even so, there must always be a research question in there somewhere.

3. **Choose a Time and Place**

The most important factor in choosing a time and place for an interview is that you need to be somewhere that is comfortable and private, and where you will not be interrupted or distracted in any way. It is possible to conduct interviews in quiet sections of coffee houses or parks, but they are less than ideal locations because they are potentially stimulating environments. A person's home is, more often than not, the ideal location, as long as there are not scores of people running around all the time. You want your interviewee to be focused on the interview itself, and at home that is much easier to accomplish than elsewhere – usually (dogs, children, spouses, etc. have a habit of interrupting). Nonetheless, always be mindful of your own safety (see chapter 3). For every interview, consider the risks involved in being isolated, alone, in someone's private home. When setting up the time for the interview, ask your interviewee where they would be the most comfortable and where you will not be distracted.

Set a time for the interview that also guarantees that you will not be interrupted (and during the interview itself turn your phone off). Likewise, be on time for the interview. When you arrange the time with your interviewee explain how long the actual interview is likely to take (in this case, about 30 minutes), but explain that it will take a little while to set up, and that the interview may run a little longer than planned. Budget for yourself approximately an hour, which allows for getting settled and setting up your equipment, running longer than expected, and packing up. Do not make plans to do anything else immediately after the interview. You should not in any way make your interviewee feel rushed. For the duration of the interview, your interviewee must have your complete and undivided attention.

4. Conduct the Interview

When you arrive for the interview you will, of course, exchange pleasantries and whatnot, but do not get into the meat of your topic without having your voice recorder on. Valuable information can get lost that way. Certainly, you can ask for your interviewee to repeat something that got mentioned before the recorder was on, but there can be a loss of spontaneity the second time around. At most, explain how the interview is going to happen in a few words, and what your purpose is, and then switch your recorder on. You may need to explain why you are using a voice recorder rather than taking notes, but usually not. Explain that you want the interview to be about 30 minutes long, but that you do not have a stopwatch. It is quite possible that you may want to return later for more interview material for other projects. Overstaying on the first interview is a bad idea. If the first interview goes on for 2 hours, you may both have a good time, and you may gather some wonderful data, but your interviewee may balk at having you come back. Thirty minutes is a long time for someone to talk who is not used to interviewing, but it is short enough that it is not overly taxing.

Physical situations dictate exactly how you sit with your interviewee and where you place your recorder. Sitting facing one another, with the recorder between you, works well enough. Your recorder should have a timer or some other readout that indicates it is on and working. You should place the recorder in such a way that you can check it periodically to make sure it is recording, without drawing undue attention to it. People vary in their habits when they know they are being recorded, but some will be wooden or tongue-tied at the outset if they have never been recorded before. Over time they will get into their subject matter and forget the recorder is there, moving into a casual way of speaking. But if you are constantly checking the recorder in a marked manner, you will break the mood of naturalness.

When recording an interview, you should get into the habit of recording informed consent first thing. This does tend to make the very beginning of the interview a tad formal and off-putting, but it is a necessary ingredient (see Ethics chapter). Over time you will develop a stock introduction something like: "I am (name) talking to (name) about (topic) on (date). Before we start I want to explain that I am recording this interview for a paper I am writing for a class, and I want to ask you if you agree to allow me to use the interview for that purpose. I will not use the interview for any other purpose without asking you. Is that all right with you?" Make sure that the affirmative answer is clearly audible. In many cases, informed consent may seem a bit ridiculous. After all, when discussing why granny always knitted socks as birthday presents, you are unlikely to uncover earth-shattering secrets. But you must get into the habit of recording informed consent because it is a fundamental ethical requirement of all fieldwork, and there is no telling what information will emerge. At some point an interviewee may say something like, "I am going to tell you this, but I don't want you repeating it." You have to respect those wishes even though you have a generalized informed consent on record.

You have to decide ahead of time whether you will be conducting a directed or an undirected interview. For an undirected interview, all you need is a mental idea of the most general sort of questions or prompts you will use to get things started: "What is your favorite memory of growing up in Brooklyn in the 1950s?" "Describe a typical day working in a coal mine," etc. Do not be too general; otherwise, the interviewee will not know where to start. If, for example, you ask, "What was Brooklyn like in the 1950s?" the interviewee will likely not know how to begin nor what to talk about, and may well ask in return, "Well, what do you want me to talk about?" But, if you ask for a favorite memory, or a typical day, you have a starting point. Sometimes the topic itself presents a natural starting point. If you interview me about 9/11 it would be reasonable to start by asking, "What were you doing when you first heard the news?" If I were your interviewee I would then start by saying, "I had just come into work and the department secretary had her television on, showing an image of one of the Trade Towers with smoke pouring from the side." I would then go on to talk about the events of the day without much need for prompting. Because I have been a teacher all of my life, I know how to talk. Some interviewees will need very little help from you, some will need a great deal. There are no strict rules. Your job in an undirected interview is to keep things moving along in whatever manner seems best. You may have to do no more than say "Uh-huh" or "Then what?" occasionally, or you may have to take a more active role, and be thinking constantly about questions that will help someone who has a difficult time giving information. Try your best, however, not to complete your interviewee's sentences or offer suggestions to an indecisive line of thinking.

For a directed interview you will to have a set of questions written down that you can refer to, and which guide the proceedings. They should not be questions with yes/no answers, because there is a strong chance that those are the answers you will get given back to you and nothing else. Your questions should be such that the interviewee needs to elaborate on them, but not so open-ended or general that they could go in any number of directions. Here is a simple example of how a directed interview can flow:

> What was your favorite dish as a child? (answer)
> Who cooked it? (answer)

> Was it from a recipe? If so, whose was it? (answer)
> When did you eat it? How often? (answer)
> Who ate with you? (answer)
> What was so special about it? (answer)
> Etc.

If you have all the questions you want to ask written down, you can check them off when they are answered. Sometimes the answer to one question will answer another of your questions in the process. Sometimes a second question will be only partially answered in the course of answering another, so you have to return to it to get the full answer. Just keep a running tally of answers as you move along, and don't get fixated on your list of questions. Just glance at your notes from time to time to make sure you are covering all the topics you want covered. However, do not be rigid about the order and content of the questions. If a question occurs to you in the middle of an interview, jot it down, or ask it as it occurs to you.

I will confess that I, like many of my colleagues, do not like directed interviews, and I have conducted only a small number of them over the course of my career. But if your research question is narrowly defined, a directed interview may be your best tool. The only time I have used directed interviews successfully was when I was conducting extensive fieldwork projects of a year, or more, and there were very specific things I wanted to know about, such as, documenting a kinship chart, or detailing the steps in a technically skilled process. I deal with such interviews in later chapters.

5. **Transcription**

For your presentation, pick around 10 minutes of the interview to transcribe. This is just a little sampling exercise to get you familiar with transcribing. The transcription needs to be done by hand, not by using some kind of voice-to-text software, because hand transcribing entails *really listening*, which is a fundamental part of the interview process. You probably think that having been present at the interview you are on top of all the information, and you do not need to do more than summarize the main points, perhaps pull out a salient quote or two, to write an essay on the topic. If you think that, you are dead wrong. In every interview there is much more information available than what you absorbed the first time through. During the interview itself, even if you paid attention most of the time, you were thinking about other things, such as whether the recorder was functioning, what the next question was, and so forth, and, of course, once in a while, your mind wandered. You need to familiarize yourself and re-familiarize yourself with the interview.

It is good practice to make multiple copies of interviews and store them in different places, such as on your laptop, in a cloud, and/or on a thumb drive. There is a long history of anthropologists misplacing their field data, and you do not want to join their ranks. Make copies as soon as possible. Mark each interview file with the name of the person interviewed and the date, time, and place of the interview, plus a header indicating subject matter. Then listen to the interview at least twice. First time through, simply listen and make a note of the points that are important to you. Second time through, make an index of the subjects on the recording as a simple list with a running tally of the relevant times in the recording down the left column and then a brief description of the topic in the right column. That way you can go immediately to a point on the recording you want to listen to again, or transcribe.

Transcription is the best way to get to know the content of an interview inside out, because you are going to have to write out the transcription verbatim, and that is a slow, tedious process until you develop competence in it. Even if you were to use voice-to-text software, you still have to go through the text word-for-word, because voice-to-text can make mistakes and you need to correct them all. By the time you have been through a voice-to-text transcription and checked it with the recording, you will have spent almost as much time checking and correcting as doing the transcription by hand, so you might as well just do it by hand in the first place. More importantly, hand transcription forces you to listen closely to the interview in ways that you have probably never listened to anyone before – every word, pause, change of tone, repetition, stumble, and nuance. This method is irreplaceable.

I go into greater detail about the transcription process in later chapters where the interviews are more targeted and transcription methods are more specialized. For now, I will give you the fundamentals. The project requires the transcription of 10 minutes of the interview that you believe captures something essential. If possible, it should be a segment that is complete in itself. How you go about the transcription process is something to discuss with your instructor. I present some possibilities here, but there are others. Here is a brief extract from an interview conducted by one of my students with a woman who was put in prison for trying to escape East Germany in communist times. I will walk you through four transcription methods.

It is best if you upload the interview audio file to your computer and play it using an audio player. I recommend you have the player in some convenient place on your monitor so that you can access it easily, and then practice playing a very short segment and then repeating the same segment so that you know how to stop and start with ease. Pick the segment you want to transcribe and then start the recording at that spot. Stop as soon as you have played enough to remember, write it down verbatim, go back to the beginning, play the segment again to check the accuracy of your writing, then repeat with the next segment. Do this until you have finished the passage you want to transcribe, and then play the whole passage again, checking your transcription for accuracy.

The raw transcript should be verbatim, with no punctuation, capitalization, or other conventions of written prose. You should simply note pauses in speech, which may be caused by having to take a breath or stopping to think. I usually record pauses with an em dash. Remember that punctuation marks in writing are primarily indications of pauses as well as other indications of intonation. They do not exist in oral language, but pauses do. You can also decide whether you want to record phatic remarks (er – um – eh) or not. They too are pauses.

Spelling of the speaker's words is a thorny issue you should discuss with your instructor. You do want to convey the authentic voice of the speaker but you should not be condescending. I tend to err on the side of conventional spelling to avoid condescension, even though, by so doing, I lose some of the flavor of the speaker's voice. You will see in the transcriptions throughout this book that I, and my students, make adjustments when appropriate. For example, I usually write "dunno" rather than "don't know" if that is what I hear, but I am inclined to write "I be from Somerset" (for an interviewee from England) rather than "Oi be from Zomerzet" even though the latter captures the West

Country accent better. Take a look at Zora Neale Hurston's *Barraccoon* (Hurston 2018) for some ideas concerning how spelling can evoke a speaker's voice. The purpose for your transcription, and its audience, will influence your choices.

a. pauses with dashes

My first transcription example here is the basic raw transcription that I and my students routinely produce first time around. This transcription was made by a student of mine conducting an interview with a woman who was imprisoned in East Germany before the fall of the Berlin Wall because she made repeated illegal attempts to cross the border. Every time the speaker pauses to take a breath or think, the transcriber puts two hyphens (or an em dash). Otherwise there is no punctuation of any kind. Everything is transcribed including repeats, phatic remarks, stammers, and the like. Only proper nouns are capitalized. Following this raw transcription are three other methods for transcribing the same sample.

> everybody had a number– I was number 79– and my cell number was 89– and– at one point they put me again in a single cell– which was 69– they put me in a single cell– because at one point– ahm– I was underage– and there was a problem what to do with me– and– they decided that they would have to– release me– and– ahm– so right before I got out– a week or five days before I got out– they put me into this single cell– because they didn't want me– it was also before they told me that I am going to– go– because– ah– they didn't want me to carry any information or anything somehow out– so they put me– without me knowing about it– one day they just came in– said like: O.K. five minutes to pack all your stuff– come with us – so– and– then I just took all my belongings– said goodbye– and they put me into a single cell– and then soon after– I heard that– ahm– they release me from prison– which was at my point– in my situation– I was not happy about it at all– because in a way I felt comfort in there– because I knew that everybody else in there– was in the same boat– everybody was thinking the same way– it is probably kind of silly– but sometimes like at night– we would just scream– things like– I hate this country – which of course you couldn't do outside– there is no way– I mean people were thrown into prison for saying things like that.

b. numbered lines with breaks

Academics sometimes use a similar transcription process but use a line break to mark pauses in the original in place of the dashes or hyphens. The result, quite deliberately, has a poetic look to it. Certain speakers' verbal styles when transcribed this way show a reasonably regular pattern of rhythm and meter that can even be broken into stanzas (see Forrest 1988a: 175–180, 247–250, and below in Chapter 15). Numbering the lines makes it easier to refer to sections of the narrative. Despite the changes in presentation format, this is still a totally verbatim transcription without punctuation, omissions, or editing of any kind:

1. everybody had a number
2. I was number 79
3. and my cell number was 89

4. and
5. at one point they put me again in a single cell
6. which was 69
7. they put me in a single cell
8. because at one point
9. ahm
10. I was underage
11. and there was a problem what to do with me
12. and
13. they decided that they would have to
14. release me
15. and
16. ahm
17. so right before I got out
18. a week or five days before I got out
19. they put me into this single cell
20. because they didn't want me
21. it was also before they told me that I am going to
22. go
23. because
24. ah
25. they didn't want me to carry any information or anything somehow out
26. so they put me
27. without me knowing about it
28. one day they just came in
29. said like O.K. five minutes to pack all your stuff
30. come with us
31. so
32. and
33. then I just took all my belongings
34. said goodbye
35. and they put me into a single cell
36. and then soon after
37. I heard that
38. ahm
39. they release me from prison
40. which was at my point
41. in my situation
42. I was not happy about it at all
43. because in a way I felt comfort in there
44. because I knew that everybody else in there
45. was in the same boat
46. everybody was thinking the same way
47. it is probably kind of silly
48. but sometimes like at night
49. we would just scream

50. things like
51. I hate this country
52. which of course you couldn't do outside
53. there is no way
54. I mean people were thrown into prison for saying things like that

c. simple edit – basic punctuation and tidying

Both of the first two methods of transcription can be burdensome to read, especially if the speaker stumbles and backtracks to the point where the written version is not at all smooth and readily comprehensible. The next level of transcription is, therefore, meant to preserve the verbatim text as much as is possible, but to clean up the text in several ways. First, the pause dashes or line breaks become regular prose punctuation, with a comma marking a short pause and a period marking a longer pause or the end of an idea. Some pauses are left unmarked if a speaker would not normally pause at that spot in the narrative. Even with punctuation, the prose produced may still be awkward in places. Second, some er's and um's are edited out, as are repeated words and false starts. The text becomes a little easier to read, but this ease comes at the expense of strict accuracy of transcription as well as a loss of information concerning the verbal style and quirks of the speaker:

> Everybody had a number. I was number 79, and my cell number was 89. And at one point they put me again in a single cell, which was 69. They put me in a single cell because at one point I was underage, and there was a problem what to do with me. And they decided that they would have to release me, and so right before I got out – a week or five days before I got out – they put me into this single cell because they didn't want me … It was also before they told me that I am going to go because they didn't want me to carry any information or anything somehow out. So, they put me without me knowing about it. One day they just came in, said like, "O.K. five minutes to pack all your stuff. Come with us." Then I just took all my belongings, said goodbye, and they put me into a single cell. And then soon after I heard that they release me from prison, which was at my point, in my situation … I was not happy about it at all, because in a way I felt comfort in there, because I knew that everybody else in there was in the same boat. Everybody was thinking the same way. It is probably kind of silly, but sometimes, like at night, we would just scream things like "I hate this country," which of course you couldn't do outside. There is no way. I mean people were thrown into prison for saying things like that.

d. complex edit with omissions and full punctuation

At the farthest end of the spectrum is a transcription that seeks to present the interview in language that is as close to grammatical prose as possible while still maintaining as much of the verbatim narrative as is consistent with producing readable text. Words, including phatic er's or stumbles, are omitted if by so doing the narrative is smoother. Likewise, words may be inserted in square brackets to indicate that the speaker did not say them, but with them added the speech becomes clearer. In the process the text is closer to a literary form, and therefore some of the authentic voice is lost:

Everybody had a number. I was number 79, and my cell number was 89. And at one point they put me again in a single cell, which was 69. They put me in a single cell because at one point I was underage, and there was a problem what to do with me. They decided that they would have to release me, and so right before I got out – a week or five days before I got out – they put me into this single cell. It was also before they told me that I am going to go because they didn't want me to carry any information or anything out. So they put me without me knowing about it. One day they just came in, said, "O.K. Five minutes to pack all your stuff. Come with us." Then I just took all my belongings, said goodbye, and they put me into a single cell. Soon after I heard that they [would] release me from prison. I was not happy about it at all, because in a way I felt comfort in there; I knew that everybody else in there was in the same boat. Everybody was thinking the same way. It is probably kind of silly, but sometimes at night we would just scream things like "I hate this country," which of course you couldn't do outside. There is no way. I mean people were thrown into prison for saying things like that.

I guarantee that after you have painstakingly transcribed a segment of an interview, you will know that "text" better than any other you have ever read, and you will see things you did not realize were there. Keep all your transcriptions from now on. You never know what use you will put them to. I have copies of transcriptions of every interview I have ever conducted in the field going back over 40 years. I have mined them repeatedly for publication over the years, and can still imagine uses for them in the future.

6. Compose Your Written Presentation

As always, section 1 of your written presentation should include information about why you chose this person to interview, what your topic was, and what problems arose in the process. You also need to lay out your research question. Section 2 is the transcription. Section 3 is a larger discussion of the whole interview and an assessment of your research question. Was it confirmed or not? Did you have to modify it? You can also select quotes from the interview as a whole that support your conclusions.

Additional Options

Video Interviewing

In the early stages of learning interview technique, video interviewing adds unnecessary complications to the learning process. In fact, there are not many advantages to using video recording equipment for most interviews. The main disadvantage to recording an interview using video is that the video equipment itself is much more intrusive than a simple voice recorder. You are best off using a tripod so that you can set up the video camera, turn it on, and let it record without having to pay undue attention to it during the interview. It would be even more intrusive if you had a person operating the camera because that person could be moving the camera from you to the interviewee, which is distracting in itself. It is equally distracting if you are operating the camera, and, more importantly, your attention is unnecessarily drawn to the operation of the camera and not to the interview itself. A tripod becomes almost indispensable because you can set the camera going and forget about it.

It is best not to spend a great deal of time setting up the framing of a tripod-mounted video camera. Have the interviewee sit down for the interview and, while you are setting up the camera, keep up a steady conversation. That way, you can make sure that the shot is not too tight, and you can also ensure that if the person being interviewed shifts around a great deal or makes wide hand gestures, they are all captured within the frame. Generally, you should choose a frame that errs on the side of being too wide. Remember that you are not making a movie; the video is for documentation, so that the aesthetics of videography are not at issue.

Make sure that your control of audio is adequate. Microphones are always invasive to one degree or another, so you need to minimize this effect as much as possible. Having a powerful omnidirectional microphone attached to the camera or tripod is a good choice because you can essentially set it and forget it. Lavalier microphones can also be an option. They have to be attached to the interviewee (and you need one too), but once they are in place it is possible to ignore them once the interview starts – particularly if they are cordless.

Set up the camera and tripod beside you, with the monitor set in such a way that you can keep an eye on it, but the interviewee cannot see it. Start the camera and then look at it as little as possible. You want the interviewee focusing on you, not on the camera. Once the camera is rolling and you are happy with the framing and the operations of the camera in general, turn your attention exclusively to the interview (with maybe an occasional glance at the camera to be sure it is still recording, and the framing is holding up).

If you are intent on using videography for any of your projects, it is a good idea to work with a second option here as your first port of call, to check and refine your interview skills. Pick a classmate to work with, and conduct a dummy interview following the general guidelines given above.

Online Interviewing

Ever since the COVID-19 pandemic forced many businesses and employees to find ways to work at home in countries worldwide, there has been an explosion of interest in using internet services for a variety of functions, and the necessary apps have proliferated. Therapy sessions between counselor and client, for example, are now commonplace, and even certain diagnoses by physicians can be made remotely (particularly if the main requirement is gathering patient history). In the same way, ethnographic interviewing online is eminently feasible and a reasonable substitute for conducting interviews in-person provided certain conditions are met. In particular, your interviewee must be comfortable with online technology and have the necessary app (or apps) at hand. This provision does limit your possibilities slightly, but only slightly. There is a handful of older people who will be excluded from your circle of potential interviewees, but not many. I know a great many people, all over the world, who are in their 70s and who are completely at home with video conferencing by laptop, tablet, or smartphone. The main limitation of using a smartphone or tablet over a laptop with a webcam is the narrow field of vision. If placed correctly, a laptop's webcam can have a wide enough range that it will capture gestures and other bodily movements along with facial expressions. A laptop is also less likely to run into battery or memory problems than the other options. A lengthy recorded interview online has a hefty overhead.

If possible, you should use an app that does not require an additional charge over and above the standard broadband fee you are paying to be online, and the app should not have a time limit. For this exercise you need only 30 minutes, and most apps will be able to accommodate that time period. But you should not feel pressured by an arbitrary cutoff. The interview may be only 30 minutes, but you also need time at the beginning and end for opening and concluding pleasantries, and these should not feel rushed because of technical time constraints. Free ZOOM apps limit contacts to 40 minutes, which is tight for a 30-minute interview. If you spend too much time setting up the interview, you will be cut off before the end. In this case, adjust the length of the interview accordingly – or break it into two sessions.

The app you use should have a record function. Not all of them do, so check to be sure, and then make sure that you are comfortable with using it. If it does not, you can still use a voice recorder in the same way that you do with in-person interviews. As with in-person interviewing, it is a good idea to conduct a trial run with a friend or classmate before doing a real interview. Review the instructions given above, making the necessary modifications for online usage. That is, set up a date and time, get connected at that time, run through your protocols, and at the conclusion of the rehearsal, assess your performance. Decide if your location was appropriate, for example. Was your background cluttered and distracting, or reasonably neutral? Were your sound levels adequate? Check all of the relevant technical issues, and also be sure that you are comfortable and relaxed as an interviewer when online. Then proceed to an actual interview.

Bilingual Interviews

Historically, it was built into ethnographic inquiry that researchers had to conduct fieldwork in a language other than English (or whatever their first language was), which meant either employing a translator or learning the language beforehand. There is a whole branch of linguistic anthropology that deals specifically with the complexities of language usage, but standard ethnographies in the twentieth century rarely paid much attention to the language that the fieldwork was conducted in, except to note local terms when they were especially culturally significant. If you happen to be bilingual (and perhaps bicultural as well), you will know that social dynamics are different when you are using different languages. To carry out this project you need to be fully bilingual, not simply fluent in a language other than your first language. The task is to use a language other than English for your interview, but then translate information you have gathered in another language into English.

Translation is a skill in its own right, and the task is always more complex than simply making an "accurate" translation. What counts as accurate is more than simply making sure that the meanings of words and phrases are conveyed correctly in English. In Italian, for example, to wish someone luck you might say, "In bocca al lupo," which is simply translated as "Into the wolf's mouth." But to translate in this way misses the point. The expression was perhaps first used by operatic and theatric performers who believed that wishing someone good luck at a performance would result in bad luck. The English equivalent would be "Break a leg," which would be a more culturally accurate translation than the word-for-word literal one.

If you are bilingual, you can take notes and make recordings in a language other than English, but you have to translate your findings into English for an academic readership. How you do this will hinge on how much of the flavor of the original language you wish to convey, and how sensitive you are to cultural nuances. The following is a short excerpt from a long life history conducted by Janette Yarwood when she was a student of mine. The interviewee was intent on producing a complete – written – life history for her children, but lacked the ability to do it on her own. Yarwood, who has since earned a PhD in anthropology and now works as a professional, recorded the life history for many hours in Spanish, and also transcribed it in Spanish. The language used here is idiomatic such that transcribing in Spanish alone is not a straightforward task. More is at stake than simply smoothing out punctuation, pauses, stumbles, and repetitions. There is the question of whether or not to keep the original idiomatic Spanish, or to translate it into standard Castilian.

> J: yo quiero saber de tu vida entera no solamente de lo malo que te paso yo quiero saber lo que usted cree que es lo más importante – de tu familia del viaje de Puerto Rico – donde naciste cuando naciste
>
> S: Me paso lo que me paso a los diez años entonces tuve que ir de mi casa yo seguí andando hasta que tuve a la hija mía a los quince años entonces seguí mi vida – pa aquí pa allá – hasta que mi dio con irme a club y esa cosa – usted sabe – después de allí tuve a mi otro hijo como a los 23 años en ponce donde yo caí presa después yo fui a buscar lo pero no me lo dieron nunca – yo lo tuve presa después salí y me ajunte con el papá de Gabriel – entonces como sufrí mucho con el y eso decidí a venir a este país salí en cinta con Francis me vino a este país y el se vine detrás hasta que tuve los otros hijos de el …
>
> J: ¿usted vino a quedarse con alguien?
>
> S: cuando yo vino – vine en case de mi mam porque no tenia mas sitio entonces de allí coji un furnished room – entonces di a lu a Francis y eso fue en Dekalb Avenue y tuve a Milagro y después a Gabriel y me quede aquí viviendo – tu sabe la vida esa …
>
> J: me puede decir más de cuando usted era joven de donde naciste donde vivía que hacía
>
> S: yo nací en Puerto Rico en Yauco en un sitio que se dicen los guandules entonces desde que yo nací mi vida era yendo al río lavando ropa estaba en escuela de chiquita pero no llegué ir más de a séptimo de allí no fui más porque usted sabe mi mama nunca mi dijo vaya ni ve ni na después a los diez años me paso lo que le dije …

Yarwood translated parts of the interview into English using dashes for breath pauses and an asterisk to mark her questions.

* I want to know about your entire life not only the bad things – I want to know about what you think is most important – about your family – about the trip from Puerto Rico – when you were born – where you were born

what happened to me happened to me at ten years old then I had to leave my house then I kept on going until I had my daughter at 15 years old – then I kept on with my life here and there – until I started going to clubs and things like that – – you know – then I had my other child at 23 years old in Ponce – where I went to jail – – then I went to get him when I got out but they didn't give him to me never – – I had him in jail – – that where I got together with Angel's father – then since I suffered a lot with him and things I decided to come to this country I was pregnant with Michelle – I came to this country and he came right behind me and then I had my other kids from him –

* you came to stay with someone?

when I came here I came to my mother's house because I didn't have nowhere else to go then from there I got a furnished room – then I had Michelle that was at Dekalb Avenue and I had Jessica and then Angel – and I stayed living here – living you know that kind of life –

* can you tell me a little more about when you were younger where were you born –

where did you live – what kinds of things did you do? I was born in Puerto Rico in Yauco in a place that's called Los Gandules – and from the time I was born my life was going to the river to wash clothes – and going to the hills to get coffee – over there people had to go pick their coffee – I had to be getting different fruits and things like that – I was in school from little but I didn't get to go past the 7th grade I didn't go after that because my mother never told me to go or I should go or nothing like that.

Obviously, if you cannot speak Spanish you will not be able to get into the technical problems of translating dialect in this particular example, but my overall point is much more general. You have to be genuinely bilingual to carry out this project, and not simply conversant with a language other than your native tongue. You have to be aware of the specific feelings engendered by statements made in the second language and work on conveying those feelings in English. There is a cultural element also. As an ethnographer, you have to translate the cultural essence embodied in the dialect you are using. Sometimes this may involve the use of footnotes in your translation.

Take this simple example. In the Rioplatense dialect of Buenos Aires there are numerous differences from standard Castilian Spanish in grammar and vocabulary. In particular an argot, Lunfardo, which evolved among criminals in the nineteenth century, is used to some degree or other by all speakers of Rioplatense, but how much is used, and which words are used, varies according to the social status of the speaker: the higher the status, the fewer Lunfardo words. The greeting "che" (hi) is very common, but is considered a little too informal for polite society. If someone says to you, "No tengo mango," you have many decisions when it comes to conveying the meaning in English. It literally means "I have no mangoes" but in this case "mango" means "money." In 1960s slang you might translate the phrase as "I don't have the bread," but that is old-fashioned (even older would be "I don't have the dough"). In so doing you might convey the level of informality as well as the status of the speaker, but a footnote might also be necessary.

Further Reading

James Spradley's *The Ethnographic Interview* (http://faculty.washington.edu/stevehar/Spradley.pdf) is a classic resource for beginners. It is a self-teaching text that moves step by step through interview technique from developing a research idea to the actual process of asking questions in an interview. It is a good tool for getting started. You can also look at:

http://www.aogaku-daku.org/wp-content/uploads/2012/04/Ethnogaphic-Interview-Questions.pdf
https://course.ccs.neu.edu/is4800sp12/resources/EthInterview.pdf
http://www.worshiplife.net/Interview%20Worshiplife%20Frame.htm

9

Participant Observation

Like ethnographic interviewing, participant observation is a quintessential ethnographic technique. Compared to other qualitative research approaches, participant observation allows the ethnographer to understand the cultural content and context of behaviors and their motivations more intimately by virtue of being actively engaged in the same sorts of activities as their research participants. Bodily perceptions, feelings, and experiences all become part of the data collection process. In this chapter you will engage in an introductory participant observation exercise and document the data you gather as well as the challenges and possibilities inherent in this technique.

Learning Goals

1. *Articulate the complexity and difficulty of participant observation fieldwork.*
2. *Practice a variety of data gathering techniques, and also develop ways of balancing them in intensive sessions.*

Extended participant observation is one of the pillars of social and cultural anthropology as described in the Introduction. This kind of fieldwork can take a year or more to complete and has a whole slew of difficulties associated with it that you do not have to face. Even so, you should have some hands-on familiarity with the method, and doing fieldwork in your own backyard is quite legitimate. There was a time when locals doing fieldwork in the United Kingdom or the United States was frowned upon as inauthentic. This stance had to do with the history of the discipline in which travel to an exotic destination was considered mandatory, and is no longer applicable. Nowadays, fieldwork within one's own culture is normal.

Despite major changes in outlook within anthropology, there is still a prevailing, though weakening, sense that the fieldworker must maintain some distance from the people under study in order to observe them as an outsider (as well as participating as a (quasi-)insider). Other projects problematize this classic stance considerably (e.g. chapters 10 and 13), but for the moment the goal is to replicate the classic method. Whether you conceive of yourself as an insider or an outsider when conducting fieldwork, certain procedures are normative. Even as an insider, you are still an observer and you are still bringing anthropological theory to bear on your observations. This last point gets us into some choppy philosophical waters that I am going to sidestep for now. Read DeWalt et al. (1998) and Emerson et al. (2001) for more consideration of these issues. The current exercise, for pedagogic purposes, does expect a degree of distance from you and the event you are focusing on – and the parameters are outlined in the instructions. The idea is to get the flavor of the method, which you can continue to employ in other research projects, or modify later as you see fit.

Instructions

1. Choose Your Event

For your participant observation project, choose an event that is open to the public and lasts for around an hour. It can be longer, but should not be significantly shorter. Plan your schedule in order to arrive at the event somewhat in advance so that you can take note of how people assemble, and give yourself a little time afterwards so that you can see how they depart, and maybe talk with them if you do not have the opportunity during the event. Because the event is public, you do not need to seek permission to attend, but, if asked, you should be honest about why you are there. You can take photographs if other people are, but be sparing about it. You may also keep written notes as long as it does not interfere with participating. Do not, under any circumstances, choose an event, such as an open 12-step meeting, that is open to the public but does not allow outside reportage. Do not use a voice recorder, or any other device, that is essentially secretive. Everything you do should be open to inspection, and obvious.

The event you choose should be something you have never participated in before. The degree to which the activities are alien to you will be the degree to which you are prompted to observe closely. If you were raised going to a Baptist church, it is not a great idea to choose a Methodist church service for this project. Yes, it will be unusual to you, but not especially so. The layout of the church will be quite familiar, and much of the service will look like what you are used to. Going to a Buddhist or Hindu temple will definitely be different. There are twin traps here. The more the event is like something you know, the more you will be lulled into thinking that you know what is going on; the more the event is unlike something you know, the more you will be lost. Being lost is not necessarily a bad thing, especially if it prompts you to ask about what is going on, but it will limit your ability to participate in any meaningful way.

It goes without saying that the event should interest you, but the interest does not necessarily mean that you like the event. You could, for example, go to a football pep rally even though you hate football and cheer leaders, but are interested in understanding why people attend them. For one of my training participant observation projects as a graduate student I attended a political rally in a tobacco barn in Durham, North Carolina, where George Wallace gave a speech as a presidential candidate. I was not remotely attracted to Wallace as a candidate or as a person, but I was interested in the nature of the event and the people in attendance. I learned a great deal about Wallace's rallies and his followers, but it was not something I wanted to repeat. Better, all things considered, to choose an event that both interests you and will be a positive experience for you. Also, avoid events where there is the potential for physical danger. Political protests, for example, could be peaceful, but could turn ugly.

There are always numerous public events advertised weekly in local publications and on the internet. Decide what kind of event you would like to attend and then choose from what is on offer, bearing in mind that you need time after the event to write up your experiences. Timing is often an issue, because public events do not shift to accommodate your schedule. However, do not make too many compromises. Better to be a little late turning in a project than doing one that does not interest you, yet can be completed quickly. Always choose engagement over expediency. Remember that the people you are investigating are not lab rats. They need to be treated with respect at all times.

My students have often chosen religious events because they are usually well defined, frequently offered, and limited in scope. Be careful, though. You must avoid events that are too close to ones you are familiar with. I have had students familiar with Protestant church services attend Quaker meetings and Russian Orthodox services. These were fine choices because they were well outside their normal experiences, yet had points of contact with services they understood. Buddhist and Hindu services were much more challenging, because they involved a worldview that most of my students were largely unfamiliar with. In many ways, secular events proved to be more successful, because my students did not have to engage with belief systems that were foreign to them. One student went to a police auction of confiscated vehicles. He immersed himself in the technicalities of the event but vowed that he would not bid on any of the cars on offer. Then toward the end, when the highest-value cars were put on the block, he could not resist bidding on a Mercedes Benz convertible. It went for more than he could afford, as you might expect, but he did end up being a true participant. Other students have attended Friday night bingo in a church hall, polo matches, and Rocky Horror showings.

Avoid the temptation to attend the event with a friend, especially if that friend is a member of the group holding the event. It is often awkward to show up alone to an event full of strangers, especially if they all know one another and you are a complete outsider, but do it anyway. Going with a friend will make it easy to talk to that friend instead of the participants, nullifying the whole purpose of attending. You may find the people at the event to be completely welcoming, or they may ignore you. Both are common experiences. Here is where you might want to revisit your self-study. What do you usually do in awkward situations or new situations? Be yourself. There is no need to say up front that you are doing fieldwork and will be writing a report. You can quite genuinely say that you are there because you are interested. But if you get into conversations that are more than superficial, be clear about your intentions.

You must always be prepared for disappointments and missteps. Events get cancelled or postponed at the last minute. People at the event may tell you that they are uncomfortable with your project. There are many reasons for the project to fall through. In that case, move on to plan B. For this, and all of the following projects that involve engagement with people, you should have some idea of an alternate project just in case plan A cannot be accomplished. There is no need to get too involved in planning alternatives but keep the notion in mind – just in case.

2. Plan Your Arrival and Note-taking
Give yourself plenty of time to get to the event sufficiently in advance so that you can see how people assemble. Do they all come at the last minute? Slowly over time? Well

in advance? How do they arrive? Car? Bus? Walk? You can jot notes on these things in a pocket-sized notebook if you like. You can also take a photo of the situation if it does not interfere with events. Do not take photos of people unless this is a normal part of the proceedings. Draw a sketch map of the location if you have time. It does not have to be to scale, nor overly detailed. In many ways, a map is better than photos because it indicates the entire physical location, whereas photos give only one angle.

Settle into a place where you can see as much as possible (if the event is sedentary, or you need not move from one location). Continue to observe how people gather, and make special note of what marks the beginning of the event. From this point on, taking notes may be impossible or inadvisable. If you must be an active participant all of the time, such as at a bingo game, you will not have the time to take detailed notes, except during pauses. Even then, people may wish to talk to you, and you should give them priority over note taking. Whatever happens, you will need to remember much of what occurs. Any aids to memory should be considered. If the event has a leaflet, a bulletin, or a printed order of events, take one and use it to jog your memory. Take anything that is being distributed, or is available to take.

As a student you should be used to taking notes whilst listening to a class, but you will also realize that paying attention and taking notes at the same time work against each other. While you are writing notes, you are not giving complete attention to what is happening around you. Unless you can write without looking at what you are writing, you will miss seeing what is going on. During an event where movement of participants plays a key role, not seeing what is happening is a problem. Given that this will likely be your first experience at participant observation, it is better to concentrate on participating and observing rather than taking notes – especially detailed ones. After all, you are getting the feel for the method, and not publishing groundbreaking research findings.

3. Write a Preliminary Research Question

Your research question can be your guide, although your focus must not be too rigid. The most obvious general research question is, "Why do people do this?" but you should not limit your observations to trying to answer this question. There is no telling what may be central, and what peripheral. You should pay attention to seemingly minor points, such as what people are wearing, how and when they speak, and modes of interaction, along with more specific information pertinent to the event itself. At the outset, assume that nothing is intrinsically irrelevant.

I went to a Chinese wedding in Yunnan province a few years ago at the invitation of the groom, who was a work colleague, and I had never been to a Chinese wedding before. It turned out to be the Chinese equivalent of the reception in the United States, in that it was mostly a massive banquet with the official state marriage having taken place the day before. The event opened with a video of the previous day's ceremony on a large screen, followed by a series of formal ceremonies, beginning with the bridal party entering in pairs, followed by a complexly staged ritual in which the bride and groom exchanged vows. Then their parents were introduced, and they and the couple performed a sequence of rehearsed activities, such as dancing together (on a stage), proposing toasts, singing, and drinking together, all directed by a professional master of ceremonies. Meanwhile the guests – about 300 – ate a long and elaborate series of dishes, presented in a well-established sequence. I wore a suit and tie, as I would have done to a wedding in the United States, and was surprised to see that the other guests were dressed in various ways. Some were as formally dressed as I was, and others were in T-shirt and jeans. This was one of my first clues as to how people treated the event. Formality of clothing was directly correlated with the age of the participant. People of the couple's age were dressed casually, and people of the parents' generation, and older, which, thankfully, included me, were dressed much more formally.

Dress turned out to be a very precise indicator of function and meaning for the event. The bridal party all wore Western wedding clothes – white chiffon for the bride, matching green dresses for her bridesmaids, black tie for groom and groomsmen, and formal evening wear for the parents. The video from the legal wedding the day before showed that the bridal party all wore traditional Chinese dress to that event. The younger guests all treated the wedding as party time, drank more than usual, and were generally boisterous, while the older guests treated the wedding like a big, formal dinner party, and were much more reserved than the younger people present. The room was set out in tables that sat ten people, with an informal, but carefully calculated, seating arrangement. Overall, the formally dressed sat together, and the casually dressed sat together – separate from the formally dressed. In my case, all the guests who were work colleagues of the groom sat together even though our style of dress varied.

The invitations indicated a time to arrive, but some guests were well ahead of time (including me, because I had no idea what to expect, and the event was far from where I lived, in a part of town I was completely unfamiliar with). In fact, I had time to scout out both the neighborhood and the facility where the wedding was held. It was a combination luxury hotel and several banquet halls (on different floors of the building, with different weddings happening simultaneously – so that guests had to figure out which wedding they were going to, and for a time there was a mass of people milling outside in the street). Guests arrived in dribs and drabs for well over an hour past the time indicated on the invitation, and were still arriving while the video of the previous day's events was showing. Some – all younger, casually dressed guests – even arrived after the formalities had started.

As I arrived, the bride and groom plus their bridal parties were standing in a line in the hall immediately outside the banquet hall, with the couple in the middle and the groomsmen and bridesmaids flanking them on either side. They greeted guests at a distance and quite formally as they arrived and entered the hall, and continued to do so until near the end of the video when the bridal party began assembling at the entrance in preparation for their formal parade into the hall (on a raised, decorated platform).

It was fortunate that I was able to document the entire event with multiple photographs because a great many guests were taking photos all the time: hall, decorations, wedding rituals, food courses, etc., etc. When the last of the wedding rituals was performed, the guests left immediately, and the hall was stripped and cleaned in less than 30 minutes, even though it was only around 8 p.m. Younger guests made arrangements to continue the party at their favorite bars – with the groom going along with men I knew from work – and the older guests (including myself) going home.

Note that my attention to dress, plus arrival and departure protocols, was as important to me in understanding the nature of the event, as to the actual actions during the event. This should be a lesson for you to pay attention to *everything*. You will not necessarily know what is useful information for your research question, and what is not, when you are taking notes. As with other projects, be prepared to be flexible about your research question as events proceed. Indeed, you might look back at the data you have collected and realize that a different research question opens up as you review what happened.

4. Write Up Your Field Notes
Absolutely as soon as you can when you are away from the event, write down everything you can remember about the event – everything. Do not wait. Think of the first 60 minutes after the event as the "golden hour." During that time your memory is at its sharpest. The longer you wait, the more you will forget. You can return to these notes later and add pieces that you have forgotten, but they will be the main foundation. Chances are that you will remember details for several days afterwards, so keep adding to your notes. Mark your notes with the time you arrived, the time the event began and ended, and the time you departed. Also make note of the date and location. I will say this over and over and over again. TIME DATE LOCATION. Drill them into your memory.

4. Prepare Your Presentation
As you did for the exercises in previous chapters, prepare your notes for your presentation. In the first part, you should recount your research question, picking the location, problems encountered, and missteps. The second part will be a finished description of the event including all supplementary materials such as a sketch map, photos, and handouts. The third part contains your conclusions, including an evaluation of your research question.

Further Reading

There are numerous analyses and critiques of participant-observer fieldwork, dating all the way back to the early part of the twentieth century when the method was in its infancy. The following short bibliography provides a fair sampling of recent concerns with participant-observation as a fieldwork method.

DeWalt, K.M., DeWalt, B.R., and Wayland, C.B. (1998). Participant observation. In: *Handbook of Methods in Cultural Anthropology* (ed. H.R. Bernard), 259–99. Walnut Creek, Calif.: AltaMira Press.

DeWalt, K.M. and DeWalt, B.R. (2011). *Participant Observation*. Walnut Creek, CA: AltaMira Press.

Emerson, R.M., Fretz, R.I, and Shaw, L.L. (2001). Participant observation and fieldnotes. In: *Handbook of Ethnography* (eds. P. Atkinson, A. Coffey, S. Delamont, J. Lofland, and L. Lofland), 356–357. Thousand Oaks, CA: Sage Publications.

Ambert, A., Adler, P.A., Adler, P., and Detzner, D.F. (1995). Understanding and evaluating qualitative research. *Journal of Marriage and the Family* (57): 879–893.

Richardson, L. (2000). Writing: A method of inquiry. In: *Handbook of Qualitative Research*, 2e (eds. N. Denzin and Y. Lincoln). Thousand Oaks, CA: Sage Publications.

10

Engaged Anthropology

Engaged ethnography is an emerging research approach within anthropology. While traditionally, interviews and participant observation involved an unbalanced power relationship between the researcher and participant, engaged research techniques are designed to better level out these differences and even produce new knowledge or uncover different perspectives. In this chapter you will use your ethnographic skills to document an event in which you are a cultural insider. You will explore what can be gained from moving away from outsider observation, as well as some of the drawbacks of such an approach.

Learning Goals

1. Re-examine old ways of understanding the relationship between the fieldworker and the people/community investigated in research.
2. Understand how engaged interviews differ from classic ones.
3. Experiment with engaged participant-observation.

The recorded interviewing and participant observation projects are classic approaches and techniques that are important to both practice and master. As has been well discussed in anthropological circles for many years, they have many drawbacks. The classic interview separates the interviewee from the topic under discussion, and also separates the interviewee from the interviewer in significant, sometimes critical, ways. I have already discussed (p 78) the first shortcoming in relation to anthropological theorizing in the past. Malinowski's development of participant observation methods was a giant leap forward from the days of using interviews alone to gather data, not only because it added layers of richness to the information being gathered, but also because interviews are subject to bad memory, prevarication, and other avenues into misinformation. And, there are many other techniques besides participant observation, outlined in this book, that uncover details that interviews alone cannot provide. Classic participant observation has two, somewhat intertwined, objectives. One is to observe activities from the outside; the other is to become immersed in them from the inside (as much as such a goal is achievable). It is one thing to be told that planting rice involves wading in flooded paddies for 10 or more hours per day, stooping and

Doing Field Projects: Methods and Practice for Social and Anthropological Research, First Edition.
John Forrest.
© 2022 John Wiley & Sons, Inc. Published 2022 by John Wiley & Sons, Inc.

thrusting seedlings into mud repetitively. It is quite another thing to go out in the paddies with the farmers and work with them all day. The latter draws you into the farmers' world much more directly. It also helps build a rapport with them that sitting and chatting usually does not – at least not the same kind of rapport. Interviewing in the classic sense, as articulated in chapter 8, captures the observing side of participant observation, but not the participating, meaning that the information that you are gathering is (deliberately) one-sided. Sometimes this method is necessary, sometimes not.

The classic interview is not an exchange. The interviewer asks for something and the interviewee gives it, without the interviewer necessarily giving anything in return. There was a time when ethnographers paid interviewees, which solves the exchange problem, but creates several new ones. If being paid for information – that is, being an "informant" in a traditional sense – is lucrative, then all manner of dubious practices may surface. If informants are paid by the hour, they have an incentive to elaborate on information, perhaps even invent stories and customs in order to talk longer and, thus, earn more. Even if they are not paid directly, they may still see the fieldworker as a potential source of desirable things. In whatever manner it is conceived there is always an asymmetry in the interviewer–interviewee relationship with a complex power dynamic in play.

Typically, the fieldworker is the one who holds the power and controls the dynamic, although the reverse can also be true depending on circumstances. Historically, fieldworkers came from colonial nations who held power over local populations, so that when an individual fieldworker sought to establish relations in a local village, he/she stood as a representative of that colonial power to the locals. This power dynamic cannot help but skew the relationship between fieldworker and locals. In modern times we are sensitive to this dynamic, and, to some extent, especially with the decolonizing of large swathes of the globe and the increased impact of globalization, the stresses within that dynamic have softened when it comes to international fieldwork – but not completely eradicated.

When you start to do fieldwork, you are immediately assessed for who you are and what your intentions are, no matter where the fieldwork takes place. This fact is one of the underlying driving forces of the self-study. How will people evaluate you based on your appearance and your behavior? These are always critical factors to consider when embarking on fieldwork. Imagine you were to sit down with an 80-year-old, former share-cropper, descendant of slaves, with a fourth-grade education, who had lived in coastal North Carolina all of his life as had his parents and grandparents (whose graves are located in the fields he used to work), how do you think that the power dynamic would evolve between the two of you? I do not know you, so let us imagine you are a 22-year-old daughter of Puerto Rican immigrants living in New York, and you are a first-generation college student in your senior year at a state university, barely getting by on financial aid and student loans. In the overall urban landscape in New York, you are likely to have many social pressures on you because of your age, ethnicity, gender, and financial status, and you may feel oppressed. As such you may also feel an affinity with other oppressed people, including the North Carolinian sharecropper. He, on the other hand, may see you as a representative of a power elite because you are from a prosperous city, you look white (in his eyes), you are in college, aspiring to be a professional, and you have control over resources that he does not. There are multiple asymmetries in the relationship, all of which are going to affect the field data that comes out of it.

One way to ameliorate the effects of the asymmetries in field relationships is to be open about them from the outset, and another is to seek a different kind of relationship from one of giver and receiver. You could, for example, conceive of the relationship as a partnership involving some kind of (quasi-)exchange. What gets exchanged affects the relationship, of course. Exchanging information that has value to both parties can be rewarding, and can open up a different kind of relationship involving the production of new types of knowledge and involving different insights and perspectives. This discussion leads to thinking in terms of *engaged* fieldwork.

Contemporary anthropology is deeply aware of, and concerned about, its own colonialist inclinations in the past. In the early twentieth century, anthropologists came from financially and politically dominant cultures to study deeply subordinate cultures: subordinate to the anthropologists' cultures, and also often subordinate within the nations where they lived. It is not surprising, therefore, that these anthropologists were treated with suspicion by local peoples, and, in return, the anthropologists' views of the local populations were inevitably colored by their social backgrounds within dominant cultures. When you read Malinowski's diary from the Trobriands, you can immediately see his ambivalence and his self-awareness that he belongs to the "other":

> Then I went to the village; the moonlit night was bright. I felt not too exhausted, and I enjoyed the walk. In the village I gave Kavaka a bit of tobacco. Then, since there was no dance or assembly, I walked to Oroobo by way of the beach. Marvelous. It was the first time I had seen this vegetation in the moonlight. Too strange and exotic. The exoticism breaks through lightly, through the veil of familiar things. Mood drawn from everydayness. An exoticism strong enough to spoil normal apperception, but too weak to create a new category of mood. Went into the bush. For a moment I was frightened. Had to compose myself. Tried to look into my own heart. "What is my inner life?" No reason to be satisfied with myself. The work I am doing is a kind of opiate rather than a creative expression. I am not trying to link it to deeper sources. To organize it.
> (Malinowski 1961 [1922]: 30–31)

Malinowski's stance is quite obviously one of the interested outsider peering in for "scientific" purposes, such that local populations are reduced to the status of abstract objects to be studied in much the same way as biologists or chemists go about their experiments. Nowadays, anthropologists are quite aware of the problems inherent in this stance, although we still have a way to go to rectify the sins of the past. Engaged anthropology is one way to redress the balance, by treating the people we are working with as partners who work with us on an equal footing rather than as subjects to be examined and analyzed. That is an essential element of engaged anthropology. In life history projects I have conducted or directed I have called a version of this stance "reciprocal empowerment" (see Chapter 15).

A significant percentage of my students chose to do life histories on people who shared similar (typically undervalued) backgrounds. A gay man interviewed a much older gay man concerning New York City before the AIDS crisis, an African-American woman from a poor neighborhood interviewed a man from the same neighborhood who had been incarcerated for a petty crime (to survive financially) and was a survivor of the Attica rebellion, a woman raised by two mothers interviewed a man raised by two fathers, a woman with a physical disability interviewed a man who had lost his right arm in childhood, and so on. In each case there was a deep reciprocity of feelings as well as of action. This was not just a case of exchanging empathy, but of being able to help one another in active ways. The interviewees had a valuable story to tell which inspired and provoked the fieldworkers (and got them class credit), and the fieldworkers in turn had the resources to be able to turn their interviewees' stories into tangible products that could potentially be disseminated to a wider audience. In one case, the interviewee, a longtime drug user, wanted to craft a book to give to her children as a way for her to reconcile with them by having them understand her background (among other things, she had been repeatedly raped and sexually abused as a child). This is one species of engaged fieldwork.

On a more general level, engaged anthropology is the intellectual opposite of supposedly "objective" fieldwork. There are advantages and disadvantages to both approaches; both have their values and their failings. You can get a good introduction to the issues involved with engaged anthropology through the summary article "Engaged Anthropology: Diversity and Dilemmas" by Setha M. Low and Sally Engle Merry (2010). They list six ways in which fieldworkers can be engaged: (1) sharing and support, (2) teaching and public education, (3) social critique, (4) collaboration, (5) advocacy, and (6) activism. This list echoes the work of Shepard Forman's *Diagnosing America: Anthropology and Public Engagement* (1993), in which he issued an "outspoken call for a committed and engaged anthropology" (1993:3). In his "Statement to the Profession" he argues for "an anthropology that includes prominently among its missions empirically grounded social criticism on the one hand and theoretically guided participation in public policy processes on the other" (Forman 1993:298). He identifies five aspects of engagement: (1) anthropology as a source of social criticism, (2) community engagement, (3) policy voices, (4) classroom engagement, and (5) reengaging anthropology defined as continuous self-criticism from within the discipline.

Engaged anthropology runs up against the once normative cultural relativism that was vaunted by classic anthropology, and the abrasion points between the two have been evident for some time. Cultural relativism was at one time an intellectual stance within the discipline that seemed almost axiomatic. Boas noted as early as 1887 that "civilization is not something absolute, but ... is relative, and ... our ideas and conceptions are true only so far as our civilization goes" (Boas 1887:589). This stance was the mere beginning of his conversion to the notion that cultures were not units on an absolute evolutionary scale but were individually distinct and needed to be treated in their own terms. The older evolutionary models were misleadingly ethnocentric, so that adopting a stance of cultural relativism was a move in the direction of counteracting this ethnocentrism. To a great extent it did, but there were dangers lurking in misinterpreting the intent of cultural relativism.

It is easy to confuse cultural relativism with moral relativism, and very early on in American anthropology there were clear danger signs that needed to be confronted. To see a cultural practice through the lens of the culture as a whole is a far cry from saying that we cannot make any judgments on that practice. Certainly, we must reserve judgment until we understand the practice in its cultural context, and such understanding may take time and effort, and may never be complete. Nonetheless, we are ethically obligated to intervene where human rights are clearly being abrogated. How we intervene is a complex issue, however.

The example of female genital cutting (FGC), which exists in numerous cultures, underscores the problems that anthropologists face when dealing with the potential clash between human rights and cultural relativism. Shell-Duncan and Hernlund note:

> The work of scholars who stress the fundamental importance of offering perspectives on cultural factors that promote the practice of female genital cutting has brought the debate surrounding cultural relativism into sharp focus. Greunbaum (1996) notes that analyses that do offer emic interpretations and cultural contextualizations are often criticized as bordering on advocacy for the practice.
>
> (Shell-Duncan and Hernlund 2000:25)

It is possible to explain *why* FGC is a culturally valued practice in certain cultures without condoning it, but even while condemning it, intervention may be complex. Take the seemingly more benign feminist objective of equal pay for equal work as an analogy. Suppose you find a situation where women are routinely paid less for the same work as men and you decide to intervene on moral grounds. Objections from the boss and male workers are to be expected, but you may also find women objecting. Then what? You are going to have to engage in a program of education in social values and processes for both men and women, and you are likely to continue to meet opposition. You are going to have to explore the reasons for their opposition (both men and women). In all situations that involve morals and human rights, you cannot begin from the stance that your moral values are self-evidently the best ones. You have to re-examine yourself as strenuously as you examine the practices you are challenging.

This project can be carried out in a number of different ways and before you do it you should have a detailed discussion with your instructor, because there are numerous methodological pitfalls and ethical traps to avoid.

Engaged Interviews

Classic interview technique stresses the need to hear the point of view of the interviewee (including his/her authentic voice) and the interviewer's role is to stay in the background as much as possible. This practice is not so much in the service of objectivity, given that, as discussed (pp 11–15), objectivity is a nonexistent ideal, but in order to obtain a certain kind of one-sided information. There are many times when this sort of information is precisely what you are seeking. But interviews can be multi-vocal in different ways, and one of these ways is for the interviewer to become engaged with the interviewee and treat the interview more as a conversation than as a data gathering exercise. The following interview took place between three people: an African-American professor (Prof), a former undergraduate student, who is also African-American, who at the time of the interview was enrolled in a PhD program in Sociology

(Liz), and her mother (Mom). The interview concerned institutional racism in university departments, and the ways in which African-American students actually accept the strictures of racism without complaint, and sometimes even without awareness.

PROF: So, what I want to know is how are we going to overcome hundreds of years of racism and oppression when that's all that we've got. Your professors at [X University] are fitting right into that mold. They're saying "if you don't write and speak in a certain way [academic standard English] we can't accept your work." And it's the four Black women in the class that get told that. What they're doing is using language as a weapon against people. They're using it as a way of subjugating people because of the way they speak.

MOM: What you're saying, professor is so true. I was reading a study that said that eighty five percent of young blacks do not feel that racism is a problem. It's what you said. You become so comfortable with being rejected or living in the negative that you don't even realize what is happening to you.

PROF: And also like [your interviewee] was saying, you end up with these internal racial categories – how dark is your skin?

MOM: How straight is your hair?

LIZ: I was telling her [mother] that as children you don't see the larger picture, so you start blaming the people right in your household – in your community for the situation that we're having. So instead of saying we were enslaved for four hundred years, and this is what perpetuated the problem... The teenagers are not seeing the larger problem they're seeing the surface.

PROF: Right, and blaming each other.

LIZ: And that's exactly what Willie Lynch said – you start playing them up against each other.

PROF: That's what I'm saying – the people who want to subjugate you don't even have to bother because it's already working for them.

MOM: The Communist Manifesto

PROF: And what the White world does not understand is that Whites benefit from the subjugation of African-American people without being directly involved or even directly racist themselves.

LIZ: Yeah, but I can understand young White children who have never been taught the full picture. You have a lot of Whites who say, "I don't think we should apologize for slavery – I had nothing to do with it." But you forget that you benefit from it. You have the outcome; you're living the outcome of it. So, there is a responsibility there.

MOM: But it goes beyond childhood. That CEO – he knows very well that if there is a Black or Hispanic who qualifies for that job – his own self-esteem his own brotherhood to his brothers will not let him go beyond ...

LIZ: ... a certain point. Exactly. You know what's scary about what she's saying. If the White males – the White CEO's who run companies – eighty percent of the people in upper management are White – this is scary to any of the educated Black people who are trying to get something out here because they're going to look at the brotherhood of it. We don't have any people who own anything, that have anything. So, you're always sending your resume out to some White man or some White woman somewhere and hoping that they give you a chance. Give you a chance – not that you've earned it because you have a Master's degree or a PhD or because you're really skilled in computers or because you know how to work with DNA. You think they should be giving you a chance? A chance? I earned it to try to apply what I've done. I'm not trying to steal anything from anybody. I'm trying to make an honest living the honest way – the hard way. Isn't that part of the American dream? And for us to feel that we have to get to that point – "could you give me a chance? [My informant] said it, he felt uncomfortable working for crackers because he just felt that as a man not having any power – it diminishes you – it breaks down your self-esteem. He knew he could make glasses but he said he would run through seven, eight jobs because he was just a token. It was OK to produce the glasses but never getting past that point. Never feeling in control. Someone's telling you what to do with your skill.

You might best think of an engaged interview as a conversation as opposed to a one-sided request for information. Because the three participants in this interview share an ethnic/cultural background, the information gathered is not strictly instructional, as it might be with a classic interview. Rather, the conversation is mutually supportive, underlining those areas of culture that all participants agree are continually problematic even as the world changes. You will also note that at one point Mom starts a thought and then Liz finishes it seamlessly – indicating that their perspectives on this topic are congruent.

The following project is only one kind of engaged interview. Another version of engaged interviewing is to conduct a classic (one-sided) interview, but when you have prepared a version for presentation, return to the interviewee and ask for comment and other input, so that the shaping of the final product is a truly joint effort. This engaged project can also be combined with activism in multiple ways. A person who has a story to tell that can affect public policy or other social organs might be encouraged to speak out in suitable venues, for example.

Instructions

In this project you are encouraged to engage with the person you are interviewing, and not simply record information.

1. Identify your interviewee and topic

Your first task is to find a person to interview who shares critical values, interests, or personal history with you. Similar to the recorded interview activity, you should choose a topic that interests you and one you would like to discuss in detail. Identify an interviewee who also shares your opinions on this topic and finds the topic interesting. Your goal is to record an interview in which you are both roughly equal voices and both contribute to and further the discussion. Topics might include:

- Ethnicity
- Gender
- Sexual orientation
- Family history
- Poverty
- Schoolwork
- Politics

Follow the general instructions for interviewing outlined in Chapter 8, including setting up your equipment, finding a suitable time and place for the interview, and indexing and transcribing your materials, but, instead of using the guidelines for directed and undirected interviews, treat the situation as a partnership or as a conversation between equals.

2. Prepare and plan

Developing a research question is also fundamentally different. Instead of asking what you can learn as the sole objective, your agenda concerns how each of you can mutually benefit from the exchange. Nevertheless, you can prepare by writing down a series of topics or open-ended questions that you wish to discuss. You might consider sharing this with your interview partner ahead of time.

Be aware that there are some ethical traps you need to avoid. For example, if you have been a victim of domestic violence and you interview another victim, there are all manner of potentially harmful triggers that could emerge during the interview. Otherwise, follow the general guidelines for a classic interview.

3. Interview and wrap-up

Record an interview for about one hour, index the whole interview, and then transcribe salient sections for presentation. As you transcribe, pay attention to the ways in which your voice and your interviewee's voice work together. For instance, does something you say generate a new idea for your interviewee? Does something your interviewee said lead the conversation to topics you did not expect? Are the ways you agree or disagree important to the conversation? Did one of you speak more than the other? How did this impact the conversation?

When you present your transcription, highlight the ways in which engaged fieldwork differs from classical norms, and point out the specific kinds of information that are elicited using this format.

Engaged Participant Observation

As ethnographers, we must maintain a level of detachment, however illusory, from our data in order to analyze what we see. Instead of seeing insider/outsider as a simple binary dichotomy, however, we can plot "insider" and "outsider" on a multidimensional spectrum, and place ourselves at different times in different locations on that scale. When eating Thanksgiving dinner with your family (assuming you are from the United States), you are close to the insider end of the scale, whereas when you are shopping in Bangkok on vacation (and do not speak Thai), you are much closer to the outsider end.

When you are involved in observation of a culture as a clear outsider, the "external" nature of your observations is self-evident. Can you turn that "external" gaze inward to reveal and analyze aspects of the cultural world that you inhabit and are intimately familiar with from the inside and can you become directly engaged with that world while still observing? The process is fraught with difficulties because as an insider you are prone to overlook details in situations that you take for granted, or think of as "obvious" and not worth noting or commenting on. But, if you have been methodical with previous projects, you will have become more sensitized to critical detail, and can scan your own cultural environment more like an ethnographer.

Choose the Event

For this engaged participant-observer project you will participate in an activity as a clear insider, but document it ethnographically as you would any other participant-observer exercise. In your first participant-observer project, you were required to choose an event that was patently outside of your experience. Now you are expected to do the opposite. Pick an event with which you are intimately familiar as an active and regular participant. For example:

- Special family dinner, such as, Passover seder, Thanksgiving, or breaking fast during Ramadan (or other special family activity).
- Religious services
- College (or any other) sporting event
- Club activity where you are a member

Research Question

Review the instructions for the classic participant-observer project (Chapter 9) and make the necessary changes for this activity. The most general research question that must always be present is, "Why do we do things this way?" Realize, though, that the question can be answered in many different ways – personal, historic, psychological – but your quest is to seek anthropological (that is, cultural) answers.

Data Gathering

You have a little more flexibility with your research methods with a familiar situation than with one you are approaching as an outsider. You do still have the same ethical considerations, so that you must make participants aware of what you are doing and get informed consent before proceeding. But subsequently you can use methods, such as audio and video recording, that would be intrusive when approaching the project as a distinct outsider. Even so, care must be taken not to be too intrusive, even as an insider. That is, at a Thanksgiving dinner it may be typical to take a few photos, so you can take some also. But continuing to take photos throughout the meal, or setting up a video camera on a tripod to record the event is going to change the nature of the event. On the other hand, at an event, such as a class reunion, the participants might welcome a video as a memento. You have to be the judge, and decide to what extent your methods of data collection are changing the event. You should, however, ask whatever pertinent questions come to mind to you as an insider: "Why do we always do this in this way?" "Were things different in the past?" etc.

Presentation

Your presentation of data should emulate the practice described for the classic participant-observer exercise, but for the presentation of an engaged project you must also pay attention to the ways in which engaged fieldwork highlights certain kinds of information but obscures other kinds, and you should point out the things that you learned that surprised you, or that you were unaware of.

Additional Projects

In many projects that follow in this book, you have the flexibility of choosing to use classic or engaged techniques. Discuss this decision with your instructor before you begin them. Be aware that the method you choose (classic vs engaged) crafts the data produced. It is not fair to say that one method is "purer" or more "authentic" than another, or more useful. The data they produce are *different*, and have different uses (and flaws). You must be completely open about your methods from the start of your project until you present your data.

Further Reading

Engaged ethnography has been the subject of heated debates for decades, with its implications alternately applauded and vilified depending on the circumstances. You can look at these for ideas:

Beck, S. and Maida, C.A. (eds). (2013). *Toward Engaged Anthropology*. Berghahn.
Babül, E.M. (2017). *Bureaucratic Intimacies: Translating Human Rights in Turkey*. Stanford U.P.
Bringa, T. and Bendixsen, S. (eds). (2016). *Engaged Anthropology: Views from Scandinavia*. (Approaches to Social Inequality and Difference). Palgrave.
Cox, A.M. (2015). *Shapeshifters: Black Girls and the Choreography of Citizenship*. Duke U.P.
De León, J. (2015). *The Land of Open Graves: Living and Dying on the Migrant Trail*. University of California Press.
Edwards, D.B. (2017). *Caravan of Martyrs: Sacrifice and Suicide Bombing in Afghanistan*. University of California Press.

Hodžić, S. (2016). *The Twilight of Cutting: African Activism and Life After NGO's.* University of California Press.

Howard, P.M. (2017). *Environment, Labour, and Capitalism at Sea: "Working the Ground" in Scotland.* Manchester U. P.

Kirsch, S. (2018). *Engaged Anthropology: Politics beyond the Text.* University of California Press.

Robben, Antonius C.G.M. (2007). *Political Violence and Trauma in Argentina.* University of Pennsylvania Press.

Rojas-Perez, I. (2017). *Mourning Remains: State Atrocity, Exhumations, and Governing the Disappeared in Peru's Postwar Andes.* Stanford U.P.

Skidmore, M. and Wilson, T. (eds.) (2008). *Dictatorship, Disorder and Decline in Myanmar.* ANU press.

Tsing, A.L. (2015). *The Mushroom at the End of the World: On the Possibility of Life in Capitalist Ruins.* Princeton U. P.

Verdery, K. (2018). *My Life as a Spy: Investigations in a Secret Police File.* Duke U. P.

11

Process Documentation

In this chapter, you will locate a participant who has a particular skill or ability to produce something tangible. You will then document the process by which they use their skill using photographs, notes, and audio recording in order to produce a step-by-step description of the process. Finally, you will interview your participant about their skill to uncover how they learned it and what it means to them. Documenting such processes in ethnography can be useful for a variety of reasons not limited to research on particular processes or skills. Understanding why people do what they do, how they do it, how and why they learned it, and why it is important can reveal valuable cultural themes that other research techniques cannot replicate.

Learning Goals

1. *Document a person at work on a skilled project*
2. *Integrate interview technique, voice recording, photo documentation, and possibly videography.*

This project requires you to locate someone who is skilled at a process, and to document the process in action. In this case "skilled" does not necessarily mean a professional, but it can be. Someone who is a good cook or who makes one dish well is perfectly adequate. The absolutely hard-and-fast rule is that the finished product must be something physical, such as a bowl of soup or a picture frame. Do not consider an actor rehearsing a part for a play, or a musician writing a song (Chapter 14 can deal with these).

Many of my students chose a cherished family member, such as a grandmother, to demonstrate cooking a dish that they had heard about or tasted, but did not know how to prepare. Therein lies another important factor. You should not be documenting a skilled process that you are familiar with. Grandma's gefilte fish is fine as long as you have eaten it once or twice and never seen it made, but not if you sit with her and make it every year. You could learn about crafting picture frames, laying bricks, welding joints, or crocheting. Be imaginative; you would be surprised what skills people around you have.

The amount of time that it takes to document the process is going to be determined by the process itself. It could be an hour or a day. The central purpose of the project is

Doing Field Projects: Methods and Practice for Social and Anthropological Research, First Edition. John Forrest.
© 2022 John Wiley & Sons, Inc. Published 2022 by John Wiley & Sons, Inc.

to document the process in enough detail that you can produce a "recipe" – that is, a list of equipment and materials needed, plus a step-by-step description of the process. You are not simply creating a "recipe," however. There should be a research question driving the inquiry, and you are documenting the meaning of the process to the person involved and not simply the mechanics of the process.

This project has two halves that may be completed on the same day or on different days. One half is observing a person actually engaged in the process. The second half is conducting an interview concerning the process, but also getting into allied questions driven by your research question, and also taking up issues raised during the first half of your documentation. If possible, the process should be one you can document from beginning to end. If the process takes more time than you have, but you are intrigued by it, you can select a component that you can observe in a short time. For example, building a house takes months, but plastering a wall or framing a window can be done in an afternoon. You will need to know ahead of time how much time the process takes to complete so that you can budget your time accordingly.

This project requires use of a voice recorder and a camera. You will need the voice recorder for both halves of the project, and the camera for the first half. If you did not carry out the interview project in this book (Chapter 8), read the chapter now to familiarize yourself with using a voice recorder and setting up your equipment for interviews. The section in the chapter on transcription is only minimally pertinent, but you should familiarize yourself with the rest of the method. A dedicated camera is better than a smartphone camera, although a phone is adequate for this project. You do need to keep voice recording and photography separate, though, and this means having at least two pieces of equipment. Juggling voice recording and taking photos with a smartphone is not absolutely impossible, but is difficult, and can lead to numerous technical problems including running out of memory or battery power – and the complication of voice recording and taking photos at the same time (which your phone may not be equipped to handle). One important component of this exercise is learning to develop photographic skills beyond basic pointing and shooting, so you need to give this aspect careful attention. Consider this project to be your introduction to the basics of ethnographic photo documentation.

Instructions

Make an appointment for a time and place for your observation of the process, and let the person know that the project involves both observing the process and conducting an interview. It may be possible to do both on the same day, or you may have to schedule two separate visits. Acquaint yourself fully with all that this project entails before setting up appointments. Get a sense ahead of time concerning how long the process takes to complete. Chances are that you will have to devote a whole day, or a significant portion of a day, to your observations, so be prepared.

1. Write your research question
At the outset, your research question is likely to involve some version of, "What made you learn this skill?" and the answer to that question may come up during the process

itself or in the follow-up interview. The answer to that question will also, almost certainly, raise new questions, and will lead down multiple paths of inquiry. For example, I used to make cock-a-leekie soup in a practicum for my students in my field methods class. This is a traditional Scottish soup that involves poaching a whole chicken in broth with chopped up leeks, boning the cooked chicken, and serving the broth, chicken, and leeks together. It is not the most complex dish to make by any means, but it has very deep meaning for me.

I learned to make the soup by watching my father make it. He was from Scotland, and it was one of several traditional Scottish dishes that reminded him of his homeland. My mother was the family cook, but my father always made Saturday dinner, and he had a stock of recipes he liked to cook. I first began learning baking skills with my mother, but my father taught me about main course dishes. That is because he was a great cook, and my mother, except for baking, was an average one and hated cooking. When my sisters were married and living away from home, but I was still a teenager living at home, my father always made a big pot of cock-a-leekie soup for Christmas Eve, because my sisters and their husbands came over on Christmas Eve, and stayed the night so that they could spend all of Christmas Day with us ... but it was always uncertain when they would arrive. Cock-a-leekie soup was a good choice for a Christmas Eve meal (along with other things), because it could be kept warm on the stove, and served when hungry people arrived – without waiting. In consequence, cock-a-leekie soup is one of the tastes of Christmas for me, and I always make it on Christmas Eve if I can, even if I am living alone. I make it all year though, because it is one of my comfort foods. The dish has also spawned a rabid interest in using leeks whenever I can in a host of dishes – in place of onions in recipes, as a side dish, and as a base layer on serving platters.

When making the soup for the practicum I usually mentioned all these facts as I was preparing the dish. Think about what follow-up questions could be prompted by that initial set of statements:

> Why do you say your mother was an average cook?
> Where did your father learn to cook?
> How did your father teach you how to cook?
> What is the importance of Christmas for you?
> Why is cooking important to you?
> What is your favorite dish to cook now? Why?

I am sure you can think of many others. Each one will lead you down a different path which you can then explore. Watching the process in motion and talking about it with your informant will tell you about the process *and* the person. Learning about the process by itself is not your purpose; you are exploring the person through a skilled process, and from there expanding into wider horizons.

2. Document the Meeting

For the first part of the project you will need to use your voice recorder and a camera, plus your notebook. Before the person begins telling you about the process and showing how it is done, set your recorder going. Make a point of asking at the beginning if it is all right to record, and explain your purpose. Make sure the consent from your interviewee is audible. You can say something like, "Is it all right if I record what is happening? The recording will help me remember all the steps in the process when I am writing my paper." Informed consent is always necessary, and should become second nature to you. You can use your notebook to keep general notes so that you are not relying completely on the voice recorder. You can also jot down questions you want to ask if there is no time to ask them when you think of them.

Take some photos of the workspace and equipment at the outset. Having a general sense of the environment is important, and will also clue your interviewee in to the fact that you will be taking photos – but make sure, also, that you ask if it is all right to use your camera. Usually interviewees are helpful if you want to take photos, although they may be reluctant to have their faces in the images. Follow their lead. Your interviewee may tell you what parts of the process it is important to have a photo of and will give you direct instructions, but you can range farther as you wish. As a rule, having a camera shows you are serious about documenting the process. Just be careful not to let the camera become too much of a distraction for you or your interviewee.

Once you have your recorder working, just follow the process, being guided by your interviewee. Take note in your notebook of any questions that you have that there is no time to ask during the process, and also start thinking about how you are going to define the steps in the process. Take note at the outset of equipment, workspace, and supplies needed. After you have taken photos of the workspace, narrow your attention to key parts of the process. Let your interviewee and the process direct you. Let that be the flow of events, and do not interrupt them. If your interviewee is silent because the work is demanding at particular points, use the time for photography or note taking. If your interviewee gives you the opportunity to practice the skill, then do it. If you can be helpful in other ways, that is fine, as long as you are not intruding or interfering with your ability to document the process.

3. Subsequent interview

After the process is completed, if there is time, or on another day, if there is not, sit down with your interviewee for a formal interview. One component of this project is to write a "recipe" for the process. What I mean is that you will be producing a document that includes a list of equipment, a list of "ingredients," and a list of steps to be carried out in the process. So, a good way to start the interview is to check to see if your preliminary understanding of the "recipe" is correct. Do you have all the steps understood correctly? What are the most important steps? Which are the most difficult?

If you have not done the interview project in this book (Chapter 8), review the section on setting up your recording equipment and making the interview situation comfortable. This will be a directed interview, so you can ignore the sections on undirected interviews. If this interview takes place on a day separate from the observation of the process, listen to the recording you made during the process and write down all the questions that you have based on what occurred. Otherwise, rely on the notes you took during the process. At minimum you need answers to such questions as:

> Why did you learn this process?
> Who taught you?
> Why is the process important to you?
> When did you learn, and are you still learning?
> How long have you been doing it?

These are very general questions, but they are fundamental, and there is no telling where they will lead. Obviously, your own project will engender more specific questions. Nonetheless, remember that the project is about process *and* person. Go where the person takes you, but do not get so caught up in the process that you short-change the personal component. You are training to be an anthropologist, not a chef, or a wood carver.

When you have finished both parts of the project, listen to both recordings you have made. As always, label them with NAME, DATE, PLACE, TIME, and make copies. Store the copies on a thumb drive, in a cloud, and/or on your hard drive. As you are listening to the recordings, make note of two things. First, if your interviewee says anything especially memorable that you might want to quote verbatim, make a note of the time on the recording so that you can return to it easily. Second, index the recordings. When a new topic comes up, note the time on the recording and what the new topic is. Make a file with times in the left column and topics in the right column. That way you can find everything you need effortlessly. Such indexing may also be one way to organize the steps in the process, depending on the nature of your fieldwork (that is, if the steps were manifest as the project progressed).

4. Write up your findings

Next, organize all of your photos. Get into the same habit of organizing photos as you do with sound recordings. Create a file that you label with your interviewee's name, and the date, place, and time that you took the photos. You may also label each photo with specifics to help recall details. This can be time-consuming, however, so you will need to decide whether to label each photo, or only key ones. By this time you should have a good mental idea of the steps in the process, so, at minimum, you should have one photo selected as representative of each step and labeled as such.

At this point you are ready to write up your findings. The steps in the process can be the backbone of the write-up. How you integrate person and process is up to you, but the simplest method is to give units like this sequentially:

> Step #
> Describe the step
> Give personal details
> Photo

It is paramount to learn to give each of your photos a number and a short descriptive title, and to refer to the photo (by its number) in the body of your text. This is a cardinal rule for presenting images in a paper (or book). Do not leave your reader guessing what an image is or where it belongs. An image that is not specifically keyed to descriptive text is mere decoration. You want your images to be integrated into your text, and to add to it, not distract from it. Furthermore, the image should be very close to the text that refers to it, not in a separate file or on a different page. Do not make your reader hunt for images.

The presentation of your data will have many components and the final method of presenting it is up to you. In some fashion you must give a complete account of all the personal details you have learned as well as of all the technical details. All of this material goes into the middle section of your final paper (or oral presentation). The first section should describe how you chose your interviewee and why, and what research question(s) you had going into the project. The last section of your paper contains a summary of what occurred: the things that went well and badly, adjustments you made to your research question, and a careful summary of your conclusions.

For this project you may feel that standard paper/file format to present your findings does not capture the flavor of your data, or is in some other way too limiting. Discuss the various possibilities of presentation with your teacher. There are a great many software packages (some quite expensive), available for the visual presentation of data, but they tend to focus on making statistical charts and graphs, and, for the most part, are much more than you need for this project. Your school probably has some in-house tools such as Moodle, Infogram, and PowerPoint. See what is available and what is useful – and what you can learn easily. Maybe one such package is used in your class as courseware.

I recommend PowerPoint for presenting this project either for the private critique of your instructor or for public presentation. Each step of the process that you are documenting, including one or more photos plus verbal description, can be contained on a single slide, so that as you (or your instructor) page through the slides, the process unfolds in a natural manner. From now onward, you will have numerous opportunities to present your findings in different formats other than in conventional papers.

Further Reading

At this point it would be a good idea to acquaint yourself with discussions of ethnographic photography as a research tool because its use will be invaluable to you both in this project and going forward. The following readings provide a starting point:

Banks, M. and Zeitlyn, D. (2015). *Visual Methods in Social Research*, 2e. Sage: London
Collier, J. and Collier, M. (1986). *Visual Anthropology: Photography As a Research Method*, 2e. University of New Mexico Press.
Edwards, E. (1994). *Anthropology and Photography 1860–1920*. Nachdruck.
Grimshaw, A. (2001). *The Ethnographer's Eye: Ways of Seeing in Modern Anthropology*. Cambridge: Cambridge University Press.
Morton, C. and Edwards, E. (eds.) (2009). *Photography, Anthropology and History: Expanding the Frame*. Farnham: Ashgate Publishing
Pink, S. (2013). *Doing Visual Ethnography: Images, Media and Representation in Research*, 3e. London: Sage.
Pinney, C. (2011). *Photography and Anthropology*. London: Reaktion Books.

12

Visual Anthropology

Visual anthropology is a specialization within cultural anthropology that has a long and storied history. Visual anthropology remains an active area of research and practice and contributes to anthropological knowledge and methodology in numerous ways. The project in this chapter builds on a number of fieldwork skills you have developed in past projects. Here you will focus on the visual nature of the subject or topic you are documenting using either still photography or videography. The goal of this project is to tell a story in pictures: either crafting a portfolio of still images or producing a sequence of raw video footage.

Learning Goals

1. *Improve observational acuity to enhance visual ethnographic documentation.*
2. *Use either a still or a video camera, or both, as ethnographic tools.*

The anthropological study of the visual arts and the use of visual documentation of ethnographic data in general– film and still photography plus drawing and painting – have been around since the nineteenth century, but until the latter part of the twentieth century they were not seen as particularly central to the discipline. Nowadays visual anthropology is a recognized branch of cultural anthropology, and this project sensitizes you to the many possibilities of visual ethnography. Before getting into the specifics of the project, it is useful to begin with a brief history of the early use of still photography and film in ethnographic documentation so that you are aware of the pitfalls as well as the benefits of cameras in the field.

The use of photography and film had a slow start in representing ethnographic data because the technology was difficult to master at first, and because there was an unfortunate bias against the myriad details they captured. Edward Sheriff Curtis (1868–1952) is a celebrated pioneer of the use of still photography and motion pictures in the documentation of indigenous peoples of North America whose work is well known, although subject to considerable criticism for its ethnographic accuracy in recent times. Curtis was not trained in ethnography, but from the age of 17 (in 1885) he had developed a passion for photography, and in 1887 he set up a professional photographic studio with a partner in Seattle, Washington. By 1895 he had embarked on documenting Native American culture, first in portraiture, and then in a series of ethnographic photographs in collaboration with professional anthropologists.

In 1906, J.P. Morgan provided Curtis with $75000 to produce a series on Native Americans that was to be published in 20 volumes with 1500 photographs. In the introduction to his first volume in 1907 he wrote, "The information that is to be gathered ... respecting the mode of life of one of the great races of mankind, must be collected at once or the opportunity will be lost." Thus, his photography comes under the rubric of "salvage ethnography." Curtis took more than 40000 photographic images from over 80 distinct groups, and made over 10000 wax cylinder recordings of Native American language and music. He recorded indigenous lore and history, and he described traditional foods, housing, clothing, recreation, ceremonies, and rituals. While his data are invaluable, they are not without problems.

Critical appraisal of Curtis's work is mixed. He staged and posed many of the shots, which are well known for their inaccuracies – such as in the misuse of "authentic" clothing. At the time of shooting, Native American peoples had largely moved away from their former ways of life, so Curtis was attempting to re-create them, rather than document them with his camera as they actually were at the time. He frequently doctored images to remove modern objects, and staged events, such as war parties, that were obsolete activities in his day. On the other hand, his portraits, while obviously posed, are deeply evocative of a people and their time. They are also reliable documents of numerous famous people, such as Geronimo.

At the end of 1912, Curtis decided to create a feature film depicting Native American life, partly as a way of making money because his still photography was not producing a living wage, and partly because film technology had improved to the point where it was conceivable to create and screen films more than a few minutes long. Curtis chose the Kwakiutl (Kwakwaka'wakw) of the Queen Charlotte Strait region of British Columbia, because they had been the subject of intense ethnographic documentation by anthropologists, including Franz Boas, since the late nineteenth century, and because their traditional way of life was forcibly dying out through relocation, army massacres, deliberate starvation, and other forms of federal intervention. This film, entitled *In the Land of the Head Hunters*, was the first feature-length film whose cast was composed entirely of indigenous North Americans. You can view it here: https://www.youtube.com/watch?v=73u7eugbbu8 (original) or here https://www.youtube.com/watch?v=QB93E0Ct3W8#action=share (restored). *In the Land of the Head-Hunters* premiered simultaneously at the Casino Theatre in New York and the Moore Theatre in Seattle on December 7, 1914. It was a silent film but was accompanied by a score (to be played in the theater) composed by John J. Braham, a musical theater composer who had also worked with Gilbert and Sullivan. The film was praised by critics but was not a commercial success.

Fortunes for ethnographic documentary film changed when Robert Flaherty (1884–1951) produced *Nanook of the North* in 1922: https://www.youtube.com/watch?v=3IAcRjBq93Y In 1913, Flaherty began filming the Inuit of Belcher Islands under the direction of his employer, the Canadian railroad magnate Sir William Mackenzie, and produced over 30000 feet of stock film. However, he described it as "utterly inept, simply a scene of this or that, no relation, no thread of story or continuity whatever, and it must have bored the audience to distraction. Certainly it bored me" (Griffith 1953). To excite more interest, Flaherty set out in 1920 to produce a more commercially viable film depicting the Inuit, and ended up creating 1953 *Nanook of the North* which we might now call "ethnographic fiction." The main character's actual name was Allakariallak ("Nanook" was an invention) and the woman who played his wife was, in reality, Flaherty's mistress (by whom she bore a son – whom he never acknowledged). The story of the film – night is approaching and Nanook must hastily build an igloo for his family or they will freeze to death – was scripted by Flaherty, and a set with a half-built igloo had to be designed because there was not enough light inside a completed igloo. Flaherty also made Allakariallak hunt with a spear for the film even though he customarily used a rifle, and asked him to bite on a phonograph record as if he did not know what is was (Flaherty apparently told him that this part of the film was meant to be comedy).

Nanook, unlike Curtis's film, was a huge commercial success leading Flaherty to make *Moana: A Romance of the Golden Age* (1926), set in Samoa, and *Man of Aran* (1934), set in the Aran Islands of Ireland. All these films have the same basic theme – the struggle of marginal communities to eke out a living in a difficult environment – and each of them is carefully scripted using locals as actors in fake family situations. The stage was set for genuine anthropologists to do a better job of ethnographic reportage.

Margaret Mead and Gregory Bateson produced the film *Trance and Dance in Bali* in 1937, although it was not released until 1952. https://www.youtube.com/watch?v=Z8YC0dnj4Jw Bateson shot the film using a silent (clockwork) camera that held a short reel of film (several minutes long only), so that the final product is a series of snippets pieced together, and narrated by Mead. Modern critics note that the performance was staged and paid for by Mead (on her birthday) and is really a patchwork of two different dance/dramas: the Rangda or Witch play (Tjalonarang) combined with the Barong and kris-dance play, both of which had been developed as show pieces for tourists. Nonetheless, the vital aspect of the film is that it documents movement styles, in dance and ritual, that are difficult to record accurately in other media. Over the next few years, Mead and Bateson produced a number of shorts from Bali and New Guinea, all of which record the subtleties and complexities of movement: *Learning to Dance in Bali* (1978), *Bathing Babies in Three Cultures* (1954), *Childhood Rivalry in Bali and New Guinea* (1954), *First Days in the Life of a New Guinea Baby* (1952), *Karba's First Years* (1952), *A Balinese Family* (1951).

The technology of still photography and film has made enormous strides in recent times, such that the technical strictures of the past no longer hamper documentation. Now the challenge is to understand the pros and cons of photodocumentation. This topic has already been addressed briefly in the Process Project (Chapter 11). Now is the opportunity to dig deeper into visual anthropology in general. There are also plenty of helpful anthologies listed at the end of this project. Visual anthropology is not just about making ethnographic film, but is as much about analyzing visual aspects of culture, aesthetic and otherwise.

If you undertake a video project there are some basic issues to consider. Most importantly, realize that you will not be making a finished, edited film. You will simply be shooting and presenting raw footage. By all means, screen samplings of the well-known offerings of Jean Rouch, John Marshall, Robert Gardner, Tim Asch, David and Judith MacDougall, Noémia Delgado, John Melville Bishop, Flora Gomes, Ruth Behar, Véréna Paravel and Lucien Castaing-Taylor, Robert Lemelson, et al. But bear in mind that these finished products have all the advantages *and disadvantages* of published ethnographies. For example, in the vast majority of films, the camera crew and equipment are invisible as if they are not present at all. Yet, obviously they are influencing the action – not in the same ways as Curtis and Flaherty did, but they are a major factor. In some cases, for example *Dead Birds* (Robert Gardner 1964) or *The Ax Fight* (Tim Asch 1975), the film creates a self-contained story with built-in drama that more closely mimics the storytelling drama of a movie than plain ethnographic reportage.

Here again the thorny question of what counts as "unbiased" ethnographic reportage comes to the fore, and you should discuss this issue in the context of visual documentation with your teacher. To some extent, your project is going to sidestep the complexities of this debate because you will not be editing video into a completed film. You are going to allow the raw footage to speak for itself. Nonetheless the camera always has a point of view. This discussion continues in the instructions, but should always be in the forefront when you are using a camera.

Instructions

This project builds on a number of fieldwork skills you have developed in past projects, although which you use will depend on your subject. Your focus must be on the specifically *visual* nature of what you are documenting, and, as such, you have two options: still photography or videography. Either way, the common goal of this project is to tell a story in pictures: either crafting a portfolio of still images akin to a storyboard or producing a sequence of raw video footage.

You can make your choice based partly on what you are interested in documenting, but also on your comfort level with, and availability of, different technologies. Do not, however, be limited simply because of lack of knowledge or experience of a certain technology. One of the purposes of the projects in this book is to gain familiarity with new techniques and to learn from your mistakes. Digital photography and videography are much easier to work with than old-fashioned chemical-based film that had to be developed and printed. What is more, the results of digital media are available for immediate scrutiny and selection. You should use this project as an opportunity to expand your abilities operating such equipment. Using editing software and other advanced skills is not required because you will be producing raw data only. You will also be writing a narrative to explain your visual productions.

Option 1: Still Photography
To a degree, this option overlaps the Process Project (Chapter 11), and, as such, may be redundant for you if you do not have interests in this direction. This version of the project is, however, much more directly focused on the visual aspects of the process under study, and is much more wide ranging in its execution. The task is to select a person who works in the visual arts or in the display or presentation of items visually (either for practical or for aesthetic purposes), and your goal is to document some aspect of their process – which could be creating some kind of visual art, setting up a museum exhibit, or organizing some kind of practical display for advertising a product, announcing an event, or the like – using still photography as your primary method. The guidelines are deliberately open here to give you the widest opportunity to

investigate people who are either visual artists specifically, or those who make visual presentations, whether these are primarily aesthetic or not.

1. Select the Person of Interest and Research Methods

The first objective is to choose the person you wish to work with and then you can decide which fieldwork methods, apart from photo documentation you will need to use to carry out your investigation. Choice of methods will also be influenced by your research question. Make sure to keep your target of attention narrow and precise. Do not approach a museum curator wanting to know about curating exhibits in general, or go to a store owner and ask about fashioning displays of merchandise in general (even though such general questions will be somewhere in the background). Find someone who is engaged in a specific project, and investigate what is involved in the preparation for, and execution of, that particular project.

My students have chosen:

- A billboard designer.
- A curator putting together an archeological exhibit of local artifacts
- A wedding photographer.
- A sculptor
- A shop window designer.

There are similarities between this project and the Process Project, but there is a major difference in that the entire focus is on the visual aspects of the process so that your portfolio of photographs is your prime source of data. You can, and should, take a voice recorder with you and set it to record as you conduct your fieldwork because your interviewee will have a great deal to say about the process of designing an exhibit or working on a sculpture. One of your main questions will, of necessity, be asking how the form and function of the product work together, and you will also want to know what your interviewee is trying to achieve – *visually*. Your photo documentation must illustrate the answers.

It is certainly possible to record a performance using still photography, and you may choose to do so. Just remember that bodily movements are vital components of these events so that videography can capture more detail. Even so, still photos have their own advantages. A single shot can record a striking pose or an especially noteworthy line. To do so, however, you will need some skill and experience in photographing movement, and a high-quality camera.

2. Write your research question

Your research question is likely to be similar to the research question for the process project, but it need not be. For example, I am particularly interested in the curating of ethnographic and archeological exhibits because I routinely dislike museums. Many (not all) displays strip artifacts of their contexts. I once went to the opening of an exhibit of traditional quilts in a local art museum and got the opportunity to interview the curator. My research question: "Why did you display all the quilts stretched out flat on white walls under stark white lighting when they were designed to be placed on beds?" This was something of a leading question, I admit, but my underlying question was: "Why treat quilts in the same way that works of art are treated?" The immediate answer to my question is not difficult: curators of exhibits of quilts usually see it as their purpose to "elevate" them to the status of art by displaying them in the same way that they display paintings which are meant to be displayed on walls. I find such an attitude condescending. The veiled assumption is that these women could have been "real" artists if they had been able to work with oil and canvas instead of being relegated to colored cloth and thread.

Thus, my more general question, which applies as much to displays of cultural and archeological artefacts in museums as to similar displays in art galleries, "How much does cultural context matter in the display of these objects?" followed by "Why or why not?" In other words, does it make sense to display a dance costume or a drinking cup as something simply to look at, or should the viewer have some sense of how these objects are used? Shouldn't quilts be displayed on beds under appropriate lighting (as opposed to harsh gallery lights)?

3. Conduct your observations

Choose a time and place where you can observe your chosen subject at work designing a store display, carving an image, setting up an exhibit, or whatever, and make sure that person knows that you will be photographing the process. As with the Process Project, having a voice recorder will be helpful, but is not your main focus. Your job is to tell the story of the process visually. Creating a rapport with someone while you are snapping photos repeatedly can be awkward, and you will have to use your best judgment. You do not want to interrupt the process unnecessarily with incessant questioning, nor do you want to be so distant from the person you are documenting that all you are doing is taking photos and not talking at all. There must be a balance. Let the process flow naturally, and ask questions when it seems appropriate and will not disturb the action too greatly.

You may also consider the relationship between your interviewee and that person's intended audience (where "audience" can be construed in the broadest terms to include people passing by and looking at a shop window display or visitors to an art gallery). You can, for example, ask what response to the art or display is expected or desired. You can also address questions to viewers if you are able to attend the opening of a display or exhibit. Questioning viewers does create an issue of fieldwork ethics. You must be careful to inform people you talk to (at some point), that you are doing research. This can be done at the end of the conversation to avoid making it too formal at the outset, but it needs to be done somewhere along the way so that you have informed consent to use data collected in this way in your presentation.

4. Prepare your presentation

It is certainly best if you have a finished product to document for this project, such as a completed work or a finished display, but time constraints may not make this outcome possible. In an ideal world, being able to talk to your informant in the stage of preparing for an event, attending the event, and assessing the event with that person afterward will give you a complete picture. But there are many factors that can hinder the ideal. You will likely have to limit your objectives because of either your own time constraints or your informant's. A curator setting up an exhibit may be rushing to meet a deadline, and not have much time to sit and talk about it. You have to be flexible.

One solution might be to contact the person you are interested in, explain that you are going to attend, say, the opening of an art exhibit where you will be taking photographs, and then set up an interview afterwards to talk about the event, including questions about how that person prepared for the event. Questions either before or after an event can include:

> What are/were your goals for this event?
> How do/will you judge success or failure?
> Is success important to you?
> What are the most important aspects of preparation for this event?

Whereas with the Process Project the voice recording was central to the documentation, here it is secondary. Having a voice recorder set up while you are taking photographs is simply a supplement to your visual documentation.

Presentation of your project should be in-person if possible. Prepare a sequence of your photos as slides using an app such as PowerPoint so that you can click through them in order. You will provide the narrative (at most put a very simple caption for every image on the screen). Begin by explaining how you picked your topic, what difficulties arose (if any), and how you carried out the project. Explain your initial research question, what adjustments had to be made and so forth. Then present your data. Click through each image in turn explaining each step in the process as you go. Conclude with a summary of your findings as well as an assessment of the difficulties you encountered.

Option 2: Videography

Before commencing a video project you must meet a number of criteria. First, you will need a video-recorder that has certain minimum specifications. It must be able to record continuously without interruption. Many devices, including smartphones and DSLR cameras, have video capacity, but they are typically time-restricted. You need to be able to record without time constraints. Second, you must check the sound quality of your device. All video cameras have built-in microphones, but they are normally not of particularly high quality, so you will need to investigate external microphones. Third, you need to be completely comfortable with using the equipment. You should be fully conversant with framing, zoom, focus, etc. so that you can record what you want when in the field without fumbling. If need be, do a number of test runs before doing your actual fieldwork.

The task here is to document a performance of some sort, or an activity in which bodily motion is a major element. This could be a dance, circus act, street performer, or mime; or it could be a ritual activity in which the actions of the participants are primary. Your goal is to document the human body in action. As such, there is a degree of overlap between this project and the Performance project, but the goals of the two are markedly different, and the types of event documented may also differ.

1. Pick an event

First, pick an event. Outdoor activities are convenient because lighting is usually not a problem and camera location may also be relatively straightforward, depending on the size and placement of audience members. Major cities in the United States such as New York and Los Angeles have famous spots where street performers appear all through the day. Tourist spots in Buenos Aires commonly have areas where tango is displayed. London has its street buskers, especially in the theater district. You need to seek permission to record such events, even though you may see others in the crowd with cameras, because you are under professional ethical guidelines. You may not be able to secure permission until after the event, but it must be done before you display your findings.

Certain technical considerations, such as camera placement and location, are paramount. Margaret Mead and Gregory Bateson had an extensive, published, debate concerning the pros and cons of using a tripod versus hand holding a camera for filming ("Margaret Mead and Gregory Bateson on the Use of the Camera in Anthropology" in *Studies in Visual Communication* 4/2 1977 – https://repository.upenn.edu/cgi/viewcontent.cgi?article=1052&context=svc). Though dated, the points in the article continue to resonate. Mead advocated putting the camera on a tripod with as wide a view as possible, setting it going, and letting it record everything in range. Bateson preferred holding the camera and turning it to focus on specific events as they happened. Which method you decide upon may be dictated by your research goals or by the situation you are dealing with.

Back in the days when video cameras were big and cumbersome, I used to carry one on my shoulder, but did not pay attention to the monitor. I simply pointed the lens in the direction in which I was facing so that the camera roughly mimicked what my eyes were seeing at any one moment. Such a method was particularly useful when I was filming parades and other activities that involved constant motion. In such cases, a tripod is not possible. Talk over the various possibilities, as well as your chosen site, with your instructor.

2. Record the performance

The ideal for this project is to record a complete performance. This does not mean that you need to record every part of a 2-hour recital made up of individual pieces. Rather, it means that you should record a whole piece from start to finish. For pedagogic purposes, a 30-minute presentation is more than adequate. You should make contact with the performer ahead of time, not only to secure permission to film, but also to begin the process of documentation. Ask the performer questions about their skill, such as:

- Why did you learn this activity?
- Who taught you? Where?
- Why is this kind of performance important to you?
- When did you start learning, and are you still learning?
- How long have you been doing it?
- What are your expectations for this performance?
- How have you been preparing?

After you have made your video recording, if at all possible, play the recording back to the performer(s) with a voice recorder going – with permission – and note any and all responses.

3. Present your recordings

Presentation of your data as analogous to Option 1. Begin with an explanation of how you picked your topic and how you carried it out. Talk about preliminaries (tripod vs handheld), including if you conducted an initial interview, and lay out your beginning research question. Next show your raw, unedited, footage accompanied by a scripted narrative. You can even pause the video at key points, if need be, to point out specific actions. Your narrative should contain information about the performance and the performers as well as your research question(s), and any other pertinent information. After showing the video, give a final assessment of the project including any conclusions you came to, and any ways you would consider adjusting your methods.

Additional Possibilities

One common tactic, that has been used with mixed results, is to hand your camera over to the people you are investigating and ask them to take photos of what they deem to be important. This approach is likely to be more fruitful with still photography than with videography because these days people are in the habit of taking photos with their smartphones during special events, but may not know much about videography. Analyzing how other people use their phones for photography is covered in Chapter 17, but this exercise is rather different. In this case you are isolating actions that you want to document, and which the people you are engaged with may not see as particularly worthy of photography in the normal course of their lives.

When I went deer hunting with a group of men in Tidewater, North Carolina, it was not common for the group to kill a deer. In fact, in the course of 10 day-long hunts that I participated in, only one man shot one deer the entire time, and there were many days when we did not even sight a deer, let alone have a clear shot. On the day that the deer was shot there was intense excitement back at our base. When the hunter arrived with the deer, all the men in the hunting party helped to string it up by the hind legs from a tree and then the hunter posed for photographs with it. Subsequently they commenced to gut and butcher the animal which was a long, skilled procedure. I photo-documented this process completely, and at one point the hunter looked at me and asked, "Why are you still taking pictures?" Butchering was simply not of visual interest to him.

Once I attended a traditional day's pig slaughter in the village where I lived in the Catskills in New York, at the invitation of the pig farmer who wanted to have the day recorded because it was a tradition that was rapidly dying out. When I started my documentation, the farmer, and several of the helpers, specifically told me things like, "This part is important, get close and take pictures." Some of these admonitions were a test – "Would a college boy flinch at seeing a pig's throat slashed?" But most of them were genuine points of interest, particularly where a rare, and much admired, skill was involved.

The methodological problem with handing your camera over to a participant, or having that person take photos with their own equipment, is that you are necessarily injecting your needs on them, and in that respect you are interfering with the spontaneous flow of events. One solution I have used to great effect is to attend an event, such as the Chinese wedding I described (pp 97–98), where almost everyone was taking photos at some point or another, and ask some of the participants to share their albums with you. What do they focus on and why?

Another possibility for photodocumentation is to take a photograph from the same location at the same time of day, every day for some determined period. There are many published examples of this kind of photography that cover a whole year, and that is obviously out of the question for a smaller class project. But there are compromises that could work. For example, you could take a photo from the same location multiple times a day for a week. That would capture some of the same feeling as a more extended project.

This is the kind of project that art photographers get involved in (https://www.diyphotography.net/photos-show-exact-location-changes-different-times-year) and you need to be careful to keep your aims clear. Art photographers tend to be concerned with changes in lighting, environmental effects, and the like, that affect the aesthetics of their finished product. They also have a tendency to photograph the natural world: a single tree, a specific horizon, or a show garden. Typically – not always – they are interested in depicting changes in the weather, lighting, and plant growth, not in the social world or changes in person-to-person interaction.

This project, conducted on a street corner, gets at more of what could be a useful fieldwork exercise in anthropology, although it still needs serious modification (https://www.digitalphotomentor.com/street-corner-exercise-new-monthly-photography-challenge). The instructions and ideals described on this site are still about aesthetics, but they could be altered to meet the needs of ethnographic fieldwork. The first task would be to find a location where it would be possible to set up a camera without being obtrusive or in the way. The aesthetics of the situation are not the issue. As long as the lighting is adequate for clear photos, there is no need to pay additional attention to composition. The main concern is finding a clear view of some situation that holds some social interest. It could be a street corner or a park bench. Then you have to decide how often to take a photograph – and when. To a large extent this decision is going to depend on your own schedule.

Be aware that there is a danger with this kind of project that the methods can end up driving the results. It does not take much effort to find a convenient spot to set up a camera and begin taking photos. If you are not careful, however, the task can become a species of data collection without direction. It is always useful to be on the lookout for situations that have the potential to reveal deeper social realities than appear on the surface, but to go into a project with no more orienting idea than "let's do this and see what happens" is never a good plan. On the other hand, you might prepare for this project by doing a few test runs in different locations and scanning the results to see if any promising patterns emerge which you might then subsequently work into a hypothesis as you design your research plan. Fieldwork always entails a synergy of this nature.

Time lapse photography is also a possibility in some situations if you have the right equipment and the necessary skills. For example, you could document how people fill up seats in an outdoor arena where they have free choice or how people set up their positions at the beach. Time lapse is perfect for such occasions because it allows you to string individual still images into a continuous video that is much faster than a conventional video, and, because of that difference, patterns that are obscure in real time can more easily emerge.

Further Reading

The following list includes a great range of topics in anthropological discussions of art and aesthetics, and of visual anthropology. Only some will be useful for your particular project:

Bakke, G. and Peterson, M. (2016). *Anthropology of the Arts: A Reader*. Bloomsbury.
Morphy, H. (1999). *Rethinking Visual Anthropology*. New Haven: Yale University Press.
Banks, M. and Zeitlyn, D. (2015). *Visual Methods in Social Research*, 2e. London: Sage.
Barbash, I. and Taylor, L. (1997). *Cross-cultural Filmmaking: A Handbook for Making Documentary and Ethnographic Films and Videos*. Berkeley: University of California Press.
Collier, M. et al. (1986). *Visual Anthropology. Photography As a Research Method*. University of Mexico.
Daniels, I. (2010). *The Japanese House: Material Culture in the Modern Home*. Oxford: Berg Publishers.
Coote, J. and Shelton, A. (eds). (1994). *Anthropology, Art and Aesthetics*. Clarendon Press. 1994.
Edwards, E. (1994). *Anthropology and Photography 1860–1920*. New Haven & London: Nachdruck.
Engelbrecht, B. (ed.) (2007). *Memories of the Origins of Ethnographic Film*. Frankfurt am Main: Peter Lang Verlag.
Grimshaw, A. (2001). *The Ethnographer's Eye: Ways of Seeing in Modern Anthropology*. Cambridge: Cambridge University Press.
Harris, C. (2012). *The Museum on the Roof of the World: Art, Politics and the Representation of Tibet*. University of Chicago Press.
Harris, C. and O'Hanlon, M. (2013). The Future of the Ethnographic Museum. *Anthropology Today* 29 (1): 8–12.
Heider, K.G. (2006). *Ethnographic Film* (Revised Edition). Austin: University of Texas Press.
Paul Hockings, P. (ed.) (2003). *Principles of Visual Anthropology*. 3e. Berlin: Mouton de Gruyter.
Layton, R. (ed.) (1991). *The Anthropology of Art*. Cambridge U.P.
MacDougall, D. (1998). *Transcultural Cinema*. Princeton: Princeton University Press.
Martinez, W. (1992). Who Constructs Anthropological Knowledge? Toward a Theory of Ethnographic Film Spectatorship. In: *Film as Ethnography*, (eds. D. Turton and P. Crawford), Manchester: Manchester University Press. 130–161.
Mead, M. (1963). Anthropology and the Camera. In: *Encyclopedia of Photography*, (W.D. Morgan). New York.
Morton, C. and Edwards, E. (eds.) (2009). *Photography, Anthropology and History: Expanding the Frame*. Farnham: Ashgate Publishing.
Morphy, H. and Perkins, M. (2006). *The Anthropology of Art: A Reader*. Blackwell.
Charlotte, M.O. (1971). *Anthropology and Art: Readings in Cross-Cultural Aesthetics*. Natural History Press.
Peers, L. (2003). *Museums and Source Communities: A Routledge Reader*, Routledge.
Pink, S. (2006). *Doing Visual Ethnography: Images, Media and Representation in Research*. London: Sage Publications.

Pinney, C. (2011). *Photography and Anthropology*. London: Reaktion Books.

Prins, Harald E. L. (2004). Visual Anthropology. In: *A Companion to the Anthropology of American Indians*, (ed. T. Biolsi), Oxford: Blackwell. 506–525.

Prins, Harald E. L. and Ruby, J. The Origins of Visual Anthropology. *Visual Anthropology Review*. 17 (2): 2001–2002.

Ruby, J. (2000). *Picturing Culture: Essays on Film and Anthropology*. Chicago: University of Chicago Press.

Svašek, M. (2007). *Anthropology, Art, and Cultural Production*. London: Pluto Press.

13

Sensory Observation

Research that focuses on sensory observations is not common in anthropology, in part because we lack a common vocabulary for such descriptions. Nevertheless, documenting one's detailed sensory observations can prove to be valuable ethnographic data. In this chapter you will identify an event in which you will document your sensory observations (other than sight). You will produce your own specialized vocabulary, test it out, and then use it to document your event. You will reflect on the ways these sorts of observations can aid the ethnographer as well as on the challenges in gathering such data.

Learning Goals

1. *Establish a baseline methodology for documenting the senses other than sight in an ethnographically informed manner.*
2. *Critique your methods.*

You will not find an overabundance of readings on sensory anthropology, although the field has been expanding of late. Paul Stoller's *The Taste of Ethnographic Things: The Senses in Anthropology* (1989) was a step in the direction of rectifying the problem, followed up with his *Sensuous Scholarship* (1997). Meanwhile, *The Varieties of Sensory Experience*, edited by David Howes (1991), showcased numerous efforts to advance research in the area. You will find additional resources listed at the end of this chapter, and you can consult them when casting about for ideas.

Sensory anthropology is still not fully incorporated into mainstream ethnography for two reasons. First, language to describe sensory experience is rudimentary at best. As anthropologists have known for decades, not having a vocabulary for smell that is comparable to color terms is critically debilitating, and, other than using formal chemical analysis, there is no really useful alternative to employing vague linguistic terms for describing the smell of a field location. Taste and touch are similarly encumbered. In addition, recording sensory information outside of the visual and auditory is limited to verbal descriptions. Cameras and sound equipment are now indispensable field tools, and they can capture a wealth of data easily. The rest of the sensorium is relegated to the written word, and such descriptions are profoundly impoverished when it comes to the interpersonal exchange of data.

Second, the sensorium, the totality of the human sensory experience, cannot be reduced to five basic senses as commonly taught. Contemporary Western scholarly analysis recognizes up to 21 different senses depending on how you count them. There are senses for temperature (thermoception), kinesthetics (proprioception), pain (nociception), balance (equilibrioception), vibration (mechanoreception), as well as for various internal stimuli (e.g. the different chemoreceptors for detecting salt and carbon dioxide concentrations in the blood, or a sense of hunger and of thirst). Move outside of Western cultures and things get more difficult. The Javanese include talking as one of the senses, and there are a number of Native American cultures in which the use of hallucinatory drugs stimulates its own sense.

When planning this project, bear in mind that there are multiple dimensions of sensory research that you will not be able to cover in a first effort because the senses are fiendishly difficult to document. Fields such as the arts, aesthetics, and the sensorium were shoved on the back burner in fieldwork for many decades in the twentieth century, partly because ethnographers did not have the necessary expertise to carry out focused research in some arenas, and partly because finding an acceptable vocabulary to be able to communicate effectively about the sensory has been an ongoing problem. Over and above these thorny issues is the fact that aesthetics and the sensory are deeply personal, subjective experiences. Finding some kind of intersubjective agreement within a community under study concerning the sensorium is, more often than not, maddeningly elusive.

In light of the above, this project has narrowly defined, and limited, objectives. The purpose here is primarily to hone your observational skills in a difficult area, and to provide you with the necessary tools to delve deeper into the sensorium in a structured way. The German terms from ethology, *Umwelt*, *Umgebung*, and *Innenwelt*, are helpful in this regard. Biologists use the term Umwelt to describe the overall sensorial abilities of a particular species, and philosophers have long been concerned with how one's personal Umwelt (one's Innenwelt) affects one's construction of reality. If you had compound eyes like a fly, eight eyes like a spider, the exceptionally complex color vision of the Mantis shrimp, or eyes that can rotate independently like a chameleon's, how would you conceive of the world around you? In what ways would your construction of reality be different if you had the olfactory capabilities of a bloodhound or the echolocation sensibilities of a bat or a dolphin? These are imponderables because of our inability to enter into the consciousness of these animals. That is, our Umgebung, our ability to appreciate their Umwelt, is extremely limited because we share neither their sensory organs nor their cognitive abilities.

When studying the human Umwelt, we have a better chance at Umgebung in relation to others, but there is always going to be a degree of uncertainty which becomes more and more acute the more unlike us those "others" are. Do you, for example, eat rice with almost every meal? Probably not. Yet, there is a preponderance of people in various parts of Asia who eat rice in one form or another with most meals. If you eat rice only a few times per year, when you go to an Indian, Thai, or Chinese restaurant, you are going to think about its smell and taste in a wholly different way from someone who eats rice two or three times per day – *every day of the year*. Learning how to appreciate that person's Umwelt is going to take considerable practice and effort.

The first step towards understanding the Umwelt of others is to come to terms with one's own, that is, your Innenwelt (the way that you map yourself on to the world you perceive). This task is the focus of the sensory project. The effort involved in charting a small portion of one's own sensorium is difficult enough – so as to be all-consuming – so, this project does not entail the additional complications related to charting the deeply personal experience of sensory input. When my sister smells lilacs she is instantly transported back to her teenage years taking state exams because there were numerous lilac bushes outside the hall where she sat her exams (and it was a stressful time). When I smell acetone, I conjure up memories of building model ships as a boy – acetone being a major ingredient in the glue I used (and making models was my great joy). Some people relish the taste of cilantro, others find it repulsive. The senses can trigger deep responses, emotional and otherwise, instantly, and such responses may or may not be linked to cultural norms. Another of my sisters was a professional baker for many years, and she exploited the power of aroma in multiple ways. When doing a demonstration in a mall she would set a pot of chocolate simmering at her stall so that shoppers would catch the smell and be attracted to seek out her show. She would also be sure to allow the scents of her baking to waft into the street around her shop so that passersby were drawn in.

Affective states associated with the senses, because they are internal and because our vocabulary for them is so impoverished, are difficult to articulate, let alone study ethnographically. The so-called affective turn in the humanities and humanistic wings of the social sciences began to take hold in the late 1990s but there were major pre-echoes of this approach going all the way back to Durkheim:

> The very act of congregating is a powerful stimulant. Once the individuals are gathered together, a sort of electricity is generated from their closeness and quickly launches them to an extraordinary height of exaltation. Every emotion expressed resonates without interference in consciousness that are wide open to external impressions, each one echoing the others. The initial impulse is thereby amplified each time it is echoed, like an avalanche that grows as it goes along. And since passions so heated and so free from all control cannot help but spill over, from every side there are nothing but wild movements, shouts, downright howls, and deafening noises of all kinds that further intensify the state they are expressing.
>
> (Durkheim 1915 [1912]: 217–218)

Later, in the *Affecting Presence* (Armstrong 1971), Robert Plant Armstrong sought to find a cultural foundation for affect in relation to aesthetics and the senses that bypassed language and symbolism completely, and argued that there was a direct communication between the sensorium and human emotional responses, and, as important, that this communication was guided by distinct cultural conventions. There are numerous readings on the role of affect in ethnographic analysis at the end of this chapter that you can consult if you wish to extend your explorations into the senses at a later date.

To a great extent, you are on your own in this project. You will be mapping new territory in many ways, so you should work closely with your instructor in the beginning phases. The basic exercise here is to do a second participant observation project, except this time you will focus on one of the classic five senses only, and you may not use sight. If you use hearing, you cannot focus on speech per se because the exercise requires you to document sounds, not linguistic meaning. That is, you can document the tone, pitch, duration, and other aural qualities of speech, but not the words themselves. In other words, you can treat speech around you as "music" but not as verbal communication.

Two problems arise immediately. First, we have to navigate the sensorium carefully. As mentioned earlier, modern science recognizes 21 senses (more or less). However, taste, smell, and hearing can still stand as areas of investigation without undue modification. Some of the "newer" senses are really the old ones broken into components. For example, touch is now divided into sensations related to pressure, temperature, vibration, and pain. You must decide how you are going to document such sensations individually or collectively. Other senses, such as awareness of acceleration or hunger, are probably too limited in scope to be useful in this exercise, but you can discuss this issue with your instructor.

It is possible to conduct your study using one of the old-fashioned five senses without doing grave injustice to contemporary science, but, if you decide that a focus on temperature reception or hunger by themselves are worthy projects for investigation, then by all means proceed. The instructions here can accommodate this decision. Check with your instructor first, and be sure that you understand the limitations of such a project. If you want to document thermoception, for example, there will be long periods when nothing changes, and then brief periods of rapid change (as when you enter or leave a building). In order to get anything close to a usable file of data, you will need to be taking notes for some time – days, perhaps. You will also need a carefully defined research question that targets that specific sense, which could be difficult. With this project you may also edge into ethically suspect territory if you are not careful. Pain reception is an obvious example of dangerous ground.

Second, talking about things that you sense can be exceedingly difficult because of a general lack of precise vocabulary. Outside of sight and sound we have little in the way of technology to make permanent recordings of the senses. Video can do an adequate job with sight and sound, but we do not have a smellograph or a tasteograph for recording those sensations. Developing a usable vocabulary is a major component of this project.

Classic ethnography is almost completely devoid of information about tastes and smells, because they cannot be described accurately, and because they have not been considered significant in the past. Given that our senses of taste and smell can be remarkably acute, this state of affairs is rather puzzling. Walking around the food stalls in the markets in Phnom Penh is always an assault on my nose – some good, some not so good. I can identify all of the smells and I can tell you what they come from, but I cannot *describe* them in a way you will understand either physically or mentally. If I tell you that something smells like lemon, maybe you will grasp my meaning. But, what if I say it smells of fermented galangal? That does not help unless you have directly experienced it yourself. I cannot possibly describe the complex taste of a broth that has been simmering for hours with seven or more different spices, most of which you have likely never tasted, along with a mix of vegetables that are unique to SE Asia.

Not only are smell and taste potentially really acute, they are also capable of triggering memories from long ago that have been stuck in the dungeons of our minds. Conveying a sense of those smells and tastes requires creative work on your part – hence, the methods outlined here. If I tell you to conjure up a mental image of a lilac-colored equilateral triangle, you can picture something fairly close to what I am describing. What about a chimpanzee with bright purple hair wearing a black suit with white pinstripes? You should still be able to visualize something not too far from my original thought, even though it is totally imaginary. I am completely at a loss when it comes to describing the smells emanating from a street vendor near my apartment in Phnom Penh who serves noodles and vegetables in broth.

There are, in fact, professionals in the fields of taste and smell who have extremely well-educated senses, and they also have a professional vocabulary for communicating to other professionals. This information is, unfortunately, of little use to you because you do not have the time to take the necessary training, and because professionals in these fields typically focus on a limited inventory of products, such as wines or perfumes. You can research their vocabularies if you like, but without the requisite training, they will be meaningless. Wine tasters, for example, use words such as angular, cigar box, bright, cassis, and flabby, and other wine tasters will understand when a wine is described in those terms. They are not helpful to me or you. What you have to do instead is to start thinking about how to convey information about things that you sense in a way that you can understand (and recall), and that others can also understand.

Instructions

1. Select your event and sense

First, pick the event you want to experience and the sense you want to document. My students have chosen the following in the past (as a small sample):

- Getting a tattoo – touch.
- A wine tasting – taste (and smell).
- A classical music concert – hearing.
- A cheese tasting – taste.
- Visiting a food market – smell.
- Buying cologne – smell.

This project is meant to be a kind of participant-observation exercise, but the rules can be somewhat looser, because you are not documenting an event from start to finish, necessarily, but documenting senses at an event for which you can set your own time frame. Some of the projects in the above list have built in beginnings and endings, but not all of them. Walking around a food market, for example, has no time constraints.

2. Create your vocabulary

Once you have settled on your project, begin creating your vocabulary. You will need to do some experimenting here as well as using your imagination. Start with the words that come to mind immediately and then broaden from there. Keep in mind that there are more dimensions to documenting a sense than you might conjure up at first blush. Take taste as an example. Without too much trouble you can come up with bitter, sour, sweet, and salty. They are four of your taste buds. But you have a fifth taste bud, the one for umami. You may not even know you have this one, but you do. It is the taste sensation engendered by certain seaweeds and mushrooms, and is concentrated in monosodium glutamate (MSG). However, that is just the beginning. Much of your taste perception is triggered by smell. That is why you frequently cannot taste well when you have a cold: your sense of smell is blocked by your stuffy nose, limiting how you taste things. This means that the complexities of taste involve defining the nuances of smell as well. Here you must rely on comparisons: like lavender, like orange, like mothballs, etc., etc. I will call these sensations "types" of tastes. They are only one dimension of taste, however.

Continuing with the example of taste, I am going to exclude what gourmets, and chefs, call "mouth feel" because, as the name implies, this is the sense of touch, not of taste. The difference between al dente pasta and overcooked pasta is mostly a matter of touch (in the mouth), not taste – although there is a slight difference in taste as well. Likewise, the "hot" sensation of red peppers is more a matter of touch than taste. You will know this if you have ever touched your eyes after cutting hot peppers (DO NOT DO THIS !!). Even so, hot peppers have a genuine taste as well, and the different varieties are all different. You may have to trust me on this matter if you have trouble with any variety beyond the mildest. Your taste vocabulary, therefore, should not include touch words, such as, "hot," "crunchy," "soft" and the like.

You do, however, need to consider questions of where you feel the sensation of taste in the mouth, how strong it is, and how long it lasts. You need to educate yourself on the whole spectrum of qualities of the sensation of taste. A good way to do this is to draw up a table like this one (which I have merely started for you):

Table 13.1 Table of Tastes.

TYPE	DURATION	INTENSITY	LOCATION
Bitter	Lingering	Faint	Tip of the tongue
Sweet	Brief	Overpowering	Throat
Salty			
Sour			
Floral			
Fishy			

Fill in the blanks, of course, and pick your own vocabulary. Also, decide if you want to quantify some of the values. Duration, for example, can be measured in seconds, and strength can be measured on a scale of 1 to 5 or 1 to 10, or whatever you decide. You do not need to replace words with numbers; merely give them better definitions by quantifying them. Fill in the whole table as you see fit (you can add rows and columns as you wish). With suitable adjustments, the same kind of table can be used to create a vocabulary for any of the senses.

3. Test your vocabulary

Next step is to test out your vocabulary. You should not have to put a great deal of effort into finding a location for the test, and you need not spend an immense amount of time on it. But you do need to have some assurance that your vocabulary is adequate to the task. If you have chosen sound, for example, sit in a noisy street for a while. Have your table of words handy, and make your observations. Do you need to add words? Are your location, duration, and intensity words adequate? As important: how easily can you document your chosen sense as it floods into you? You can "cheat" somewhat if you have chosen sound because you can use a recorder. For smell, taste, and touch, you are on your own.

4. Gather your data

When you are as satisfied as you can be with your vocabulary table, participate in the activity you have chosen. Your descriptions at the time are going to be much more crucial than for your first participant-observation project because there is much less opportunity with sense perception to fill in the blanks after the event. You cannot go back to your car when the event is over and round out your description of the taste of a fruit in the way that you can fill in the details of a conversation that you had. Before anesthesia, some surgeons used to comfort patients before surgery with the aphorism, "Pain has no memory." While not strictly true, it is legitimate to say that describing a pain while it is happening is closer to the experience, than the memory of being in pain.

As always, mark down the place, date, and time of your project when you start. Have your notebook drawn up into three columns: a thin one on the left, and two roughly equally spaced ones in the middle and on the right (see Table 13.2). Use the left column to note down the time as often as you can, use the middle column to describe the sense you are documenting using your vocabulary, and use the right column to make a note of what was happening. Again, this is merely a beginning using a hypothetical smell vocabulary:

Of critical importance to remember in this project is that your task is to document what you observe, not your likes and dislikes. Although I have already dismissed the distinction between so-called objective and subjective experience, it is also true that some subjective observations are not particularly useful anthropologically. The fact that you crave rare steak or detest the taste of cilantro, is not of any great social importance (although a general survey of the likes and dislikes of a community is useful). Your goal in this project is to make an effort to map the nature of a human sense in general, not its effect on you in particular. There is a place for "reflexive anthropology," but this project does not directly involve likes

Table 13.2 Activity Log.

TIME	SENSE	ACTIVITY
10 : 22 am	Floral, rose, sweet, brief, faint, watery	Walking by a flower stall
10 : 28 am	Spicy, meaty, long, strong, oily	Passing a food stall
10 : 35 am		

and dislikes (nor sensory memories). Of course, it is reasonable to record all manner of personal reactions to sensations, but your personal preferences are not the focus of this study, and should not be in the forefront. Your goal is a certain type of objectification of the senses for the purposes of communication. Other projects in this volume deal more directly with autoethnography and active engagement (Chapters 5 and 10).

You will note that I have, more or less deliberately, avoided talking about possible research questions driving this project. That is because the most directly relevant research question is, "What can research into the sensorium contribute to anthropological data?" That is a particular hobby-horse of mine, but it is, nonetheless, a salient question that should hover over this project, along with, "How can I incorporate sensory data into my general fieldwork in the future?" Think back, for example, to your original Participant Observation exercise. How much sensory data did you include, and what might you have included? Churches and temples have distinctive smells. How would you describe them? If you attended a church service, did they use organ music? How would you describe that sound (and the sounds of people singing)? Adding sensory information of this kind adds an extra dimension to your data. Otherwise, the same kinds of research questions that are pertinent to participant-observation studies are also pertinent here, with suitable adjustments made for the fact that your dataset is highly focused.

5. Prepare your report
In the first part of your report, apart from the usual discussion of your choice of field site and research question, explain why you chose your single sense for this site. Then lay out your work on developing a sensory vocabulary, along with your table of words and explanation of what they mean and how you arrived at them. In the data section of your report, reproduce your field notes in the same fashion as you recorded them, that is, in three columns. In the third section, explain all the problems you had in documenting sense, and give any conclusions that you reached. "This project is impossible" may be the most salient conclusion you come to, but it is not especially original or enlightening. You might, however, explain how documenting the senses will be useful or not useful to you in the future.

Sensing and Mapping

Take a look at this paper: https://culanth.org/fieldsights/what-does-anthropology-sound-like-activism. It offers an example of combining sensory data with mapping, and could be another approach to the topic. I could easily imagine drawing a rough map of a market or street in Phnom Penh (or using a commercial one), and then documenting the smells (and the feelings they engender) as I walk around. Street sounds, as in the paper, would be equally instructive. How about what the surface of the road feels like on your feet and the rest of your body? Be creative.

Further Reading

For a general overview of the sensorium and anthropology take a look at this website: http://www.sensorystudies.org/sensorial-investigations/doing-sensory-anthropology/ by David Howes and Constance Classen. David Howes edited a useful volume: *The*

Varieties of Sensory Experience: A Sourcebook in the Anthropology of the Senses. 1991. Anthropological Horizons. There is also the anthology, *Ritual, Performance and the Senses,* 2015, edited by Michael Bull and Jon P. Mitchell.

Constance Classen is more involved in cultural historical studies than in contemporary ethnography, but she has produced a number of volumes on the senses and their cultural meanings that can provide insights for fieldwork projects:

The Deepest Sense: A Cultural History of Touch (Studies in Sensory History). 2012. U. Illinois Press.
(2005). *The Book of Touch* (Sensory Formations). Berg.
(1993). *Worlds of Sense: Exploring the Senses in History and Across Cultures.* Routledge.
For smell in particular, you can look at *Aroma: The Cultural History of Smell* by Constance Classen, David Howes, and Anthony Synnott, 1994. For a very broad look at the senses overall there is the 6-volume set *A Cultural History of the Senses* (The Cultural Histories Series) edited by Jerry P. Toner, Constance Classen, Anne C. Vila, Richard G. Newhauser, David Howes, and Herman Roodenburg, 2015. Bloomsbury. The volumes cover the period 500 BCE to 2000 CE and deal with a panoply of topics, including the marketplace; religion and ritual; science and medicine; and literature and art.
Douglas Sharon's *Wizard of the Four Winds: A Shaman's Story*, 2015, documents an anthropologist's journey as a Peruvian curandero's apprentice. The original is actually quite old (1978), but there is plenty of exploration of the sensorium in both editions. Lionel Loong's *The Body and Senses in Martial Culture* (Loong 2016) might also be helpful. Ashley Montagu's *Touching: The Human Significance of the Skin* (3rd ed), 1986, is now somewhat dated and rather scattered in its approach, but it has a wealth of ideas for fieldwork.

The following works examine affective states in ethnography. Not all of them deal specifically or directly with the sensorium, but the two areas are often implicitly intertwined:

Skoggard, I. and Waterston, A. (2015). Toward an Anthropology of Affect and Evocative Ethnography. *Anthropology of Consciousness* 26/2: 109–120. (Introduction to a special volume on affect in anthropology).
Cvetkovich, A. (2012). *Depression: A Public Feeling.* Duke University Press.
Allison, A. (2013). *Precarious Japan.* Duke University Press.
Stewart, K. (2007). *Ordinary Affects.* Duke University Press.
Behar, R. (1997). *The Vulnerable Observer: Anthropology That Breaks Your Heart.* Beacon.

14

Performance

In many ways, performance can be seen as a part of ordinary life. We perform our social roles and use such performances to manage our relationships with others. Performance is also an essential element of the skilled performing arts. Similar to the process project (Chapter 11), for this chapter you will document a process. However, this time you will focus on a particular skilled performance, rather than a tangible product. You will document the process of your research participant planning, preparing for and presenting a public performance. This type of ethnographic research used to be restricted to specialists, such as ethnomusicologists, but is increasingly used as a tool for more general ethnographic fieldwork because of the ubiquitous nature of performance globally.

Learning Goals

1. *Document the process of preparing for and presenting a public performance in the arts or in related fields.*
   or
2. *Document public performance in creative ways, such as recording multiple performances of the same piece, analyzing audience reactions, or reflecting on the relationship between performance spaces and performances.*

The exercise for this assignment is similar to the Process Project (Chapter 11), except in this case your focus is on a skilled performer preparing for and performing a piece (loosely defined) as opposed to someone making a tangible object. For this project, the finished "product" is an ephemeral experience, a single performance – which is more elusive and challenging to document than recording the recipe for chicken soup and details about the cook. There are also some suggestions at the end of the chapter for more general possibilities involving the documentation of public performances. These are more focused on performance than a straightforward participant observer exercise, if working with an individual is impractical or unwarranted based on your fieldwork objectives.

Review the instructions for the Process Project and decide, in consultation with your instructor, whether to carry out this project as an alternative to the Process Project or in addition to it. The ideal for this project is to document how a person prepares for

Doing Field Projects: Methods and Practice for Social and Anthropological Research, First Edition. John Forrest.
© 2022 John Wiley & Sons, Inc. Published 2022 by John Wiley & Sons, Inc.

and performs a piece (the "product"), although the instructions contain a degree of flexibility because documenting all of this may involve more time than you have available, or may not be practical because of time constraints on the part of the performer.

There are some social scientists who argue that all life is a performance (e.g., Goffman 1956), but for practical purposes we can draw a line around certain kinds of performance, notably drama, music, and dance for focused attention. All three have their own anthropological specialties – ethnodramaturgy, ethnomusicology, and ethnochoreology respectively – each with its own specialists, literature, and professional journals and organizations. Working directly in these subspecialties requires a high degree of expertise, because of the technical knowledge involved. Without a firm grasp on music notation and music theory, for example, much of the analysis in ethnomusicology will be opaque to you. But, all is not lost. While you may not be able to understand the fine points of music theory, you can still have a satisfying discussion with a musician about the challenges involved in rehearsing for an upcoming recital. Or, you can select someone to work with, such as a preacher or juggler, whose performances are more easily understood by a novice. This project is not narrowly confined to the conventionally defined performing arts. My former college campus is the main center for conservatories of the arts within the State University of New York system, which means that students of all stripes have easy access to the inner workings of professionals in the performing arts. Anthropology majors can interview performing artists in training, and, under certain conditions, can observe classes and rehearsals, as well as attend performances. You might not have such a wealth of opportunities at your disposal on your campus. Nonetheless, you have plenty to work with if you expand your horizons sufficiently. Public speaking, religious ritual, and the like, all have performative aspects, including storytelling, that you can document in various ways. Furthermore, every town of any size has at least one dance studio and/or training facility for martial arts (and all martial arts have performative components). Think as broadly as possible. Big cities usually have places for street performers – musicians, mimes, jugglers, dancers – and if you expand your vision widely enough, you can think of a host of activities that fit the concept of performance. Discuss possibilities with your instructor.

Instructions

This project builds on a number of skills you have developed in past projects. First, select a person who works in the performing arts or in some allied type of performance. Your primary goal is to examine aspects of their process, including preparing for a performance, rehearsing, creating a new piece, or some other component of their preparation and performance. The guidelines are deliberately open here to give you the opportunity to investigate people who are performing artists specifically, or those who make presentations with a performative aspect, whether they are primarily aesthetic or not. A preacher, member of a debating team, or someone in any field related to public performance will work. Check with your instructor if you need extra guidance in getting started. The person you choose does not necessarily have to be a professional, but you should select someone with demonstrable skills in what they do (same as with the Process Project).

1. Select a performer and fieldwork methods

The first task is to choose the person you wish to work with and then you can decide which fieldwork methods you will need to use to carry out your investigation. Your choice of methods will also be influenced by your research question. As ever, the key to success is to narrow your goals. Do not approach a violin player and ask about preparing for and performing concerts in general or about music in general. Find someone who is working on a *specific* project – right now – and investigate what is involved in the preparation for, and execution of, that particular project. Suppose, for example, you are in contact with an oboe player who has a solo recital coming up, or perhaps your contact is a violin player getting ready for the performance of a concerto. You can approach the project in many ways depending on the circumstances. The oboe player's solo recital involves selecting pieces to play, deciding the order of the pieces, rehearsing them, and then performing them. The violin player does not have to decide what to play, but does have to take time to rehearse the piece, both alone and with an orchestra, and eventually has to perform for an audience. In both cases you should schedule at least one interview prior to the performance, and the directed questions for the interview will be determined at the outset by your research question.

Your research question is likely to be similar to the research question for the process project, but it need not be. I am particularly interested in dance ethnography because I was both a dancer and a dance instructor for many years, and many of my fieldwork experiences have involved the documentation of traditional dance in Europe and the United States (Forrest 1984; 1985, 1988b, and 1999). Therefore, when I attend dance events and talk to dancers and dance musicians, I often want to engage in a dialog concerning both technique and social meaning, because I am bringing my own experience in the dance world to my fieldwork. Often I ask dancers to instruct me in their techniques, and, in the process, I ask them about their training, the social significance of movements, and so forth. If you have specific training in performance relevant to your project, you can certainly bring it to bear in your investigations also, but such expertise is not a prerequisite for solid fieldwork. There are many avenues you can explore having to do with social status, personal identity, motivations of performers, and the like that do not require specialized knowledge in any performance field.

Apart from investigating your performer's process, you might also consider what is known as the "performer-audience connection" (where "audience" can be construed in the broadest terms to include people attending a concert or taking a martial arts class). You can, for example, ask your interviewee what an ideal audience response would be, and you can also talk to people at a performance or class. You can also include questions about audience response in your follow-up interview if you choose to do one. Interviewing audience members does create an issue of fieldwork ethics. You must be careful to inform people you talk to (at some point), that you are doing research. This can be done at the end of the conversation to avoid making it too formal at the outset, but it needs to be done somewhere along the way so that you have informed consent to use data collected in this way in your presentation. Another performer-audience project is outlined at the end of the chapter.

At this stage you should be comfortable with your interview technique, but you can also brush up by reviewing the interview project in Chapter 8. When setting up an interview with musicians, it is always a good idea to tell them to have their instruments with them (or plan the interview to be carried out in their practice space). They may not want, or need, to demonstrate passages to you, but without their instruments, they cannot. Talking in the abstract to a musician about rehearsal technique and the like is less useful than observing a demonstration from time to time during the interview. With an actor or singer, you are on safer ground because they carry their instruments with them. A dancer, likewise, can show you a great many things without need of special equipment. All the piano players I have ever interviewed have been quite happy to sit at the piano and talk, and then periodically turn to the keys and illustrate what they are talking about.

After the interview you may also attend the performance, and then you might want to schedule a second interview to discuss how the performer felt about the performance, all depending, of course, on your research question. The second interview should also be a directed interview, although you can leave plenty of opportunity for your interviewee to talk about anything related to the performance. Remember, your research question is your focal point, but it can change.

Developing a research question is likely to be an iterative affair, much like the analogous steps in the Process Project (pp 112–115). It is quite normal to begin this kind of fieldwork by simply picking someone of interest to you to investigate and letting your research question(s) evolve over time as you conduct interviews and observe practice sessions. Let's say you have a friend who is a jazz trumpeter. Perhaps you know something about jazz performance from past experience, so that you know that the heart of any performance is on-the-spot improvisation. Therefore, one of your first questions might be, "How do you practice or rehearse a performance which is, by its very nature, supposed to be spontaneous?" You might also ask, "How does an audience's response to your playing affect your performance?" From here you can ask for greater detail as illustration. Questions about the interaction between performer and audience could also apply to an actor or street performer. Your research question(s) will, thus, be refined as you learn more through interviewing and understanding the specifics of a type of performance.

My students covered a range of performers:

- jazz trumpeter
- script writer for a television series
- dancer for a post-modern dance company.
- actor preparing for an audition.
- guitarist in a rock band.
- juggler
- tai chi instructor
- professional DJ

2. Begin data collection

Once you have identified your research question and methods, it is time to begin your data collection. In most cases it is best if you have a finished "product" to document for this project, such as a recital, but time constraints may not allow for this eventuality. In an ideal world, being able to talk to your interviewee in the stage of preparing for an event, attending the event, and then assessing the event with your interviewee afterward will give you a complete picture. But there are many factors that can hinder the ideal. You will likely have to limit your objectives because of either your own time constraints or your interviewee's. Musicians preparing for a concert may not have the time to talk about their practice methods or may not want to have the process of rehearsal interrupted and dissected while it is occurring. You have to be flexible.

One solution is to contact your interviewee, say that you are going to attend the event in question, and then set up an interview, either before or afterwards, or both, depending on what is convenient, to talk about the event. Recall the questions from the process project (Chapter 11) suitably adjusted:

- Why did you learn this skill?
- Who taught you?
- Why is the skill important to you?
- When did you learn, and are you still learning?
- How long have you been doing it?

These are still useful questions, but they need to be augmented in light of the specific event your interviewee is preparing for, such as:

- What are/were your goals for this event?
- How will/did you judge success or failure?
- Is audience reaction important to you? If so, how?
- What are the most important aspects of preparation for this event?

Once again, you do not need to transcribe your interview(s) but you must listen to it/them at least once, when you are back home. Make a running log of subjects covered so that you can find particular topics (and salient quotes) quickly and easily when you are thinking about your conclusions and preparing your presentation. *Always be organized with your field notes.*

The Process Project, which has a similar structure to this project, combined interview technique with documentation of the skill using still photography. In this project, interviewing is also a key component, but videography is likely to be a better option for documenting key elements of performance than still photography depending on the kind of performance involved. Even verbal performances, including acting and preaching, cannot be fully captured using audio devices alone because you will lose all of the bodily movements involved. You might, for example, consider conducting a video, as opposed to an audio, interview. Review the instructions on video recording (pp 88–89) before proceeding. You may discover that audio or video recording of the actual performance is not permitted, in which case that component of the project will resemble the Participant Observer project.

3. Present your data

The general guidelines for presenting your data continue to apply with this project, but the mode of presentation will need to fit your data. Software, such as PowerPoint, or presentation apps such as Prezi, which allow the embedding of audio and video material in with typed descriptions, are probably your best option. You must first introduce your topic by discussing how you picked a performer, how you developed your research question, what methods you used to document the performance, as well as what difficulties arose in the course of research. Then lay out your data. Here your method of presentation is going to depend on what your data looks like. If you used videography, you cannot simply present everything unedited. You will need to narrow your focus to the key issues that you found, and edit your video into short segments for presentation, in much the same way as you selected key sections of an interview for transcription. Then summarize your conclusions, and reflect on ways you could improve your methods. Your instructor will probably have additional suggestions for presentation.

Additional Research Possibilities

The following are basic suggestions for fieldwork in the realm of performance that are directed more at actual performances than at the particulars of the performers. Discuss the specific details for such projects with your instructor if they appeal to you. These topics require adaptation of previous methods, such as Participant Observation (Chapter 9) or Mapping (Chapter 7), to the particulars of performance.

Multiple Performances

There is the possibility with the study of performance to focus on the performance itself, rather than the performer, somewhat akin to a participant observation exercise, but in a novel, comparative way by one person attending multiple performances of what can be thought of as the "same" event. Edward Gorey, the significantly eccentric illustrator and storyteller, is known to have had a fascination with the Nutcracker ballet such that he would attend performances whenever possible. One year he attended all 39 performances by the New York City Ballet, noting various differences each night and was later interviewed about the experience:

Tell me how anyone can sit through thirty-nine *Nutcrackers* in one season. Convince me.

At first I thought, my God, this is the most boring ballet in the history of the world. Then I began to go more and more. People say, oh nothing much happens in the first act, but the second act is lovely. For me it's the first act that's so marvelous. It's an aspect of Balanchine's genius that nobody has paid much attention to. That party is one of the most enchanting things ever set on the stage. The relations between the children and the adults, everything–are breathtaking. It's a Platonic party, the essence of every family party–the way it should be and never is, the party that no one has ever attended. Every year it gets a little bit better.

Naturally, one of the reasons for going to Nutcracker *is to watch the mice carry on–somebody's doing something crazy and new and different every night–and the tree grow, and the bed whiz around. And these days Shaun O'Brien, as Drosselmeir, gives a performance that holds the whole thing together; the instant he comes on you're riveted. The choreography for the Snowflakes is heaven. No one notices it because it's so pretty and they're busy watching the snow come down. And set back in time the way it is, it's nostalgic in a lost-world-that-never-really-existed way. Of course it's a very ambiguous ballet–frightening and funny and strange and beautiful–like most of George's work.*

(Wilkin 2001: 19–20)

Gorey was not a fieldworker, of course, and his motives were highly personal. But it is easy to imagine doing something similar as a fieldworker; perhaps not going to 39 performances of a ballet or play, but a significant number. The important issue here for this project is that the performance is in some sense the *same* each time. Gorey went to matinees, evening performances, performances on Fridays, Saturdays and Sundays, and noted changes in personnel, mood, and so forth – depending on these external factors. But it was always *Nutcracker*, always by the New York City Ballet, and always in the same theater – those factors were constant.

Some performances, such as showings of the *Rocky Horror Picture Show*, are routinely repeated on a regular basis because they have a cult following. If you are not familiar with Rocky Horror go here for details: (https://www.theguardian.com/culture/2016/oct/19/rocky-horror-picture-show-fan-rituals-fox-remake) Getting immersed in multiple showings of *Rocky Horror* could get complicated because there is a great deal of audience participation including the use of props (newspaper, lighter, toilet roll, etc.), which attendees bring, routine replies to dialog onscreen, and audience members dressing as one of the characters in the movie. The website http://www.rockyhorror.com/participation/showtimes.php gives details of showings near you (when movie theaters are open). Perhaps less entangling might be to go to numerous showings of the latest movie in a popular franchise, such as *Star Wars* or *Star Trek*. The problem here would be that movies in general are somewhat limiting when it comes to observation because the theater is dark, and it is hard to see much in the way of audience reaction (*Rocky Horror* excepted).

Audience Reception

Reception theory in literary studies was developed by Hans-Robert Jauss in the late 1960s and adapted into a theory of audience reception by social scientists in the 1970s and 1980s (see Further Reading). Reception theory is a component of communications theory in general and concerns the interplay between what a performer wants to project and what an audience receives and interprets. The ethnography of audience response was popular at one point because the nature of audiences and their behavior had historically been neglected as a component of anthropological analysis in favor of the technicalities of performances themselves. There have been exceptions, such as the fights, uproar, and general melee that broke out in the audience at the premiere of Diaghilev's *Rite of Spring* in Paris on April 2, 1913, which have since gone down in dance history as essential elements in the interpretation of the dance. Normally, though, audience response is given little attention. Yet, if the ethnography of performance is to be granted an equal place at the table with other anthropological topics, *all* of the contextual data must be recorded and analyzed, including how performances are received. To conduct such a study you need to combine some of the aspects of the main project in this chapter with components of participant observation (Chapter 9).

One half of the project entails collecting data on how individual performers view a particular performance they are giving, and the other half involves documenting how the performance was interpreted by its audience. As with the main project in this chapter, it is vital to choose a specific performance for analysis so that you do not slip into generalities. Pick a performance that you can attend and whose performers would be willing to participate in interviews at some point (before or after). A solo recital would work well, and parts of it would be quite similar to the main project described in this chapter. The main difference, in this case, is that your questions to the performer should be focused on what things the performer wants an audience member to pay attention to. If the performance involves a number of people you may have to be selective concerning which ones you can interview. The participant observation component has two elements. First, is noting audience reactions – laughter, clapping, silence, etc. – during the performance itself, and the second is talking to audience members after the performance to gauge their responses (following the same guidelines as for general participant observation).

Performance Spaces

The design and usage of performance venues is another contextual component of performance that is frequently overlooked. This topic can be as wide-ranging as your imagination and can involve many of the techniques you have already used, including mapping, participant observation, interviewing, and photodocumentation. There are a number of factors to consider, such as the size and placement of the performance area, size, placement, and type of accommodations for the audience, acoustics, lighting, and decor. Seeing the Bolshoi Ballet performing at the Bolshoi Theater in Moscow is a very different experience from seeing them perform the same pieces in a theater in London or New York. It is not simply that audience reception is noticeably different in the different venues; the physical features of the theater itself – decor, lighting, seating, etc. – add a significant dimension to the performances therein.

This project can be conducted in several different ways, and you should discuss your topic with your instructor for precise directions. One possibility is to document a performance space of your choice in two ways. Step one is to document the space by itself, without any audience members or performers present. Most places that sell tickets have, at minimum, a reasonably detailed map of the seating areas which can be used as a base map to expand to include other details, such as the dimensions of the performance space, the locations of exits and where they lead, decor, and any other relevant details that you observe. Along with a detailed map of the space, you can also create an album of photos to enhance your map. You can take photos of the view of the audience from the stage, and also the view of the stage from different seats (front, back, sides, center, balconies) in the audience. The second step is to attend a performance in the space as a participant observer exercise, but with a special focus on how the space itself contributes to aspects of the performance.

Another project, that would be too lengthy for a simple class exercise but might be suitable for a research thesis, is to follow a traveling company around to multiple venues and compare performances of the same piece in different locations. Such a project would, of necessity, involve more variables than the simple mapping of space. Geographic location, time of day, audience reception, and the like all play a part in shaping the nature of a performance, and would need to be taken into consideration. Nonetheless, the physical space used for the performance could be a primary focus, and performers could be interviewed on this topic specifically.

Further Reading

Much of the ethnography of performance is highly specialized (particularly in music and dance) and will not be much help in developing an adequate research proposal for your chosen topic unless you share the necessary technical skills. Nonetheless, there is plenty of scope for fieldwork projects using no more than standard ethnographic methods. The following might give you some general ideas for projects and their analysis:

Korom, Frank J. (2013). *The Anthropology of Performance: A Reader*. Wiley-Blackwell. (In this volume, note, in particular, Edward Shieffelin (1985) "Performance and the Social Construction of Reality"). There are also numerous articles included from folklorists who have been concerned with traditional music and dance practices for nearly 200 years. At first their interests were primarily concerned with collecting examples, but by the later twentieth century their focus had shifted to the social meanings of performances in general, especially those that fall outside the sphere of professionalism.

Turner, V. (1988). *The Anthropology of Performance* is one of Turner's last publications. It extends his well-established analysis of ritual, liminality, etc. into the domain of performance in general (including parades, public spectacles, etc.).

Royce, A.P. (1977). *The Anthropology of Dance*. Indiana U.P.

(2004). *Anthropology of the Performing Arts: Artistry, Virtuosity, and Interpretation in Cross-Cultural Perspective*. Altamira.

The first cited work is a bit dated but later editions have kept the work up-to-date, and some of the details are enduring. The second, more all-encompassing, work is probably more generally useful.

Williams, D. (2004) (2nd ed.) *Anthropology and the Dance: Ten Lectures*. Illinois U.P.

Schechner, R. (2011). *Between Theater and Anthropology*. University of Pennsylvania Press.

Lavenda, Robert H. (1988). "Minnesota Queen Pageants: Play, Fun, and Dead Seriousness in a Festive Mode." *Journal of American Folklore*. 101: 168–175.

Hamera, J. (2006). Performance, Performativity, and Cultural Poiesis in Practices of Everyday Life. In: *The Sage Handbook of Performance Studies*, (eds. D. Soyini Madison and Judith Hamera), 50–51. Sage Publications.

Guerrón-Montero, C.M. (2006). Can't Beat Me Own Drum in Me Own Native Land: Calypso Music and Tourism in the Panamanian Atlantic Coast. *Anthropological Quarterly* 79/4: 633–663

Wulff, H. (1998). *Ballet Across Borders: Career and Culture in the World of Dancers*. Berg

Marion, J.S. (2008). *Ballroom: Culture and Costume in Competitive Dance*. Berg.

Hutchinson, S. (ed.) (2013). *Salsa World: A Global Dance in Local Contexts* Temple U. P.

Reception theory is rather dated these days, but the following are useful resources:

Bennett, S. (eds.) (1990). *Theatre Audiences: A Theory of Production and Reception*. New York: Routledge.

Hohendahl, P.U. (1977). Introduction to Reception Aesthetics. *New German Critique* 10: 29–63.

Holub, R.C. (1992). *Crossing Borders: Reception Theory, Poststructuralism, Deconstruction*. Madison: U of Wisconsin P.

Holub, R.C. (1984). *Reception Theory: A Critical Introduction*. London: Methuen.

Jauss, H.R. (1982). *Toward an Aesthetic of Reception*. Trans. Timothy Bahti. Minneapolis: U of Minnesota P.

15

Life Histories (and Oral History)

In this chapter, you will practice the ethnographic fieldwork technique of collecting a life history through interviews. Life history interviews are useful to ethnographers because they help us appreciate an individual's agency throughout their life course. They illustrate how a person perceives and experiences their life in the context of their larger culture and society. Importantly, they also highlight the ways that change and continuity interplay and shape a person's life.

Learning Goals

1. *Record and effectively transcribe a life history from a single individual over an extended time period*
2. *Analyze its content critically.*

A life history, a particular subset or type of oral history, is a personal narrative recounted orally to someone else. It is, strictly, neither autobiography nor biography. It is autobiographical in the sense that it is a person's self-construction (and derives meaning and power from this fact). But it is told *to* someone and not simply created as a general work for universal consumption. Often the narrative would not exist in any preservable form were it not for the person that it is told to, and who that person is, is vitally important in the construction of the narrative. Life history interviews are a dialog between two people.

It is important to remember that life histories, while written and edited, are still essentially *oral* documents. Such oral documents have a long history. The oldest known so-called autobiography in English, for example – *The Book of Margery Kempe* (Windeatt 1985) – is really an oral life history, since Margery Kempe could neither read nor write, and, therefore, had to enlist the aid of a lettered priest to record and edit her oral narrative, around 1436. This text stands as a good example of the type in that it reveals several qualities that are unique to, and diagnostic of, the oral life history, including *authentic voice* and *personally constructed meaning*. A life history is never simply a neutral description of a life course (even when recounted to a completely indifferent transcriber), but always contains critically personalized elements.

The way in which a narrator constructs meaning in a life history is strongly influenced by the relationship between the teller and listener. Within this collaboration, the issue of who has initiated the narration (teller or listener) impacts the structure of meaning within the narrative. Conventionally within the social sciences it is the fieldworker who initiates the sessions, because of a desire to gather information. But, as in the case of Margery Kempe, some life histories have an inner compulsion built into them by their narrators – an Ancient Mariner effect, as it were – that governs their structure and meaning. The tale teller feels constantly obligated to seek out listeners and retell the life tale. Yet, whether the act of recounting a life history is initiated by the teller or listener, these texts are rarely, if ever, records of the objective facts of a person's life: they serve specific personal purposes.

Life histories, as subjectively legitimate understandings of life and culture, have become fundamentally valuable social documents in anthropology and the social sciences in general. Certain of these documents – e.g. *Black Elk Speaks* (Neihardt 1932), *Crashing Thunder* (Radin 1920), *Sun Chief* (Simmons 1942), *Son of Old Man Hat* (Dyk 1938) – have already achieved a kind of classic status within the discipline. There are many more that broaden and deepen our understanding of social systems from the individual's point of view (see e.g. Behar 1990, Crane 1987, 1999; Goodson 2009; Rosenthal 2018, Rosenwald and Ochberg 1992).

Beyond the employment of life histories in social science, there is also developing a body of theoretical insight into the nature of oral life histories themselves (see Angrosino 1989; Behar 1990; Bertaux 1981, Forrest and Jackson 1990; Freeman 1983; Hertz 1997; Linde 1993; Ochs and Capps 1996; Peacock and Holland 1993, Riessman 1990; Urban 1989), as a significant component of the general interest in reflexivity, metacommunication, and meaning that has evolved out of the postmodern critique of the fundamental materials of social science (Berg 2006, Clifford and Marcus 1986; Davies 1999, Ellis and Bochner 1996; Goodall 2000; Sanjek 1990). As part of this general re-evaluation of the agenda of social enquiry, attention is being devoted to the very methods of collecting and transcribing life histories as a concern related to, yet also significantly distinct from, general interview technique (see e.g. Crane and Angrosino 1984: 75–87; Crapanzano 1984; Ives 1974; Langness 1965; Langness and Frank 1981, Mishler 1995; Riessman 1993). What still needs to be better explored is the nature of the individual and subjective *relationship* between fieldworker and life history narrator, and how a life history emerges out of such a partnership (see, for example, Casagrande 1960, Shostak 1981; Kratz 2001; Riessman 1987 and 1993).

In the late 1960s and early 1970s in the United States it was common to ask, "What were you doing when you heard the news that JFK was shot?" These days, people occasionally do something similar for the events of 9/11. People my age in the United States (and elsewhere) remember exactly what they were doing when they heard the news of JFK's assassination, its impact on them and those around them, and what they did afterward. It is easy enough to document an oral history of the assassination by finding people who lived through the time and recording their narratives (e.g. https://www.youtube.com/watch?v=GvJnDyGnjxo). You get a very different kind of history that way from the kind that looks at primary sources that are written down. Oral history is lived history. Life histories are a species of oral history, with the same kind of immediacy, but with a different focus.

With life history, you are not looking for history on a grand scale, such as major battles, or political turning points, although these may enter the narrative. Instead, you are looking to document one person's life. Life history is a form of autobiography, told to a person rather than written down. There are a great many famous ones that have been published to popular audiences, such as *Autobiography of Malcolm X* (Haley 1965). In this project you do not have the time to document an individual's life history exhaustively. That exercise takes sustained effort for months or even years. You can, however, focus on a significant event in a person's life, or one segment of their life that has special meaning for them.

Make sure you choose your interviewee carefully, because this project requires sustained effort on your part and on theirs. Naturally, you should be interested in all of your projects, but it is understandable if you are not terribly excited about drawing maps or recording quantified data. Different methods attract different kinds of people. The important point is that graphs and maps do not get offended if you are not thrilled by them; a life history narrator, on the other hand, is not going to be happy with you if you nod off during an interview. You must choose a person whose life history interests you enough that you will pursue this project eagerly, and not only out of a sense of duty. My stern warning to my students was always (and is to you also), "If an informant's story does not interest you, *do not conduct an interview*." This is not simply a matter or practicality; it is a fundamentally ethical issue. I am not saying that the topic has to be earth-shatteringly interesting to you, but it has to hold more than superficial interest.

There are many other ethical issues at stake with life history interviews, and you should discuss them with your teacher should they arise. It is, for example, a bad idea to conduct an interview with someone whose story is going to trigger negative feelings in you, or generally make you feel uncomfortable. I would never interview an Argentine interrogator from the Dirty War, even though that period interests me, and it has had a profound impact on present-day Argentina. I do not want to know the mind of a torturer – even a rehabilitated one. I know of too many people who were tortured and murdered in Buenos Aires, and I still live with the fallout. Some people, more distanced from the culture than I, might be able to hold such an interview: I cannot.

On the other side of the coin, do not pursue a life history interview with someone who is going to be negatively impacted by the memories. Here you are probably on safer ground because people have a choice about what they reveal and what they conceal. You must be sensitive, though. Be aware of the possibility that a topic could be touchy, and always be prepared to stop the interview if your interviewee is uncomfortable. In fact, reassure them at the outset that the interview can stop at any time. Usually this will not be an issue, but be prepared.

Instructions

You will need to get absolute guidelines from your instructor concerning this project. I will outline how I set it up, but your class may vary. I laid out the life history project as follows:

- Choose an interviewee
- First interview

- Indexing and review
- Second interview
- Indexing and review
- Transcription
- Presentation

Go back and review the chapter on interviews (Chapter 8). The basic guidelines and methods outlined there, including types of interview, indexing, and transcription, apply here also.

1. Choose an interviewee

I am not going to suggest that your interviewee has to be somebody *amazing* (in italics). That is not the point of life history. If anything, you want to interview someone who is "ordinary." No one is "ordinary" of course, but what I am suggesting is that you should not go out of your way to find someone with a headline-grabbing story to tell. Quite literally anyone can work out for a life history project, as long as that person is comfortable talking at length. Also, you should choose someone who has a life story to tell – that is, someone who is old enough to have had a range of life experiences. But remember, you are not documenting a whole life – merely a component. Even so, the interview process will take time and you need to set it up effectively.

It is likely that you will have only a rough sense of a research question at the outset because you need not strictly be testing anything like a hypothesis in this project. You are seeking information and your general question is, "What happened?" This is enough to get you started. Naturally there might be a question in the background, such as "Do the history books tell the whole story?" but it is also reasonable in the case of life history to let your hypothesis develop in a dialectical fashion as the interviews progress and you analyze them. That is, you can start with a rudimentary research question, begin your interviewing, refine your question mentally as you proceed, take stock, do more interviewing, refine your research question further, and so forth.

Interviewing a parent or an older family member can have advantages and disadvantages. On the one hand they know you well and may be able to talk to you easily about life events. On the other hand, they may talk to you in telegraphic fashion about certain events, or assume that you already know certain things, which you may, but you still need them recorded for this project to be able to present them to readers who do not already know them. People that you are not so intimately connected to will probably not assume much knowledge on your part.

Interviewing a parent, which many of my students did, carries a potential benefit in that there are a great many components of their lives that occurred before you were born, that you may be interested in, but which they have never told you about. My father was an officer in the Royal Navy from 1935 through to the end of the Second World War, and he would occasionally come out with snippets of information about his experiences. But, I knew very little because he was not especially forthcoming – so much so, that I learned more about his life in the navy from my mother than from him. Yet, I knew that he had visited China, Japan, India, and Australia before the war, and was present at major incidents, such as the evacuation at Dunkirk. I knew nothing of the details growing up, and, by the time I was a professional anthropologist, he had died. All that knowledge is lost. I regret not having had the opportunity to get his life history recorded.

Choosing a complete stranger or a nodding acquaintance to interview has its benefits as well. With them there should not be the same awkwardness that can arise with a family member. It is a much more formal affair. But it can, nonetheless, easily become intimate. It all depends on the topic. Your key to fruitful interviews is to select someone who has a story to tell that you want to hear (of course). Chances are that you will end up with a flood of data. Some people will tell you that they are not good speakers, but all you need to do is assure them that you are not looking for a polished speech. You will guide them, and all they have to do is talk in the same way that they talk to friends. But, only guide them as needed.

My students did two, hour-long, interviews on two separate occasions, which meant that they had to clear their own schedules, and had to set up two different appointments. They did not need to be conducted on days that were many days apart (although they could be). The students did, however, need time to review and index the recording of the first interview and use that review to prepare questions for the second interview.

2. Conduct the first interview

The first interview should be undirected. All you need to do is ask an open-ended leading question and then listen, interjecting as little as possible ("Let's start at the beginning. How did you end up being a soldier in Vietnam?"). Of course, most people need prompting every so often, and will not just talk and talk without some kind of feedback. However, in an undirected interview your job is to stay in the background as much as possible. From time to time you may need to push things forward with questions such as "What happened next?" or "What did that feel like?" but when someone is on a roll, all you have to do is nod, and make short comments ("Yes," "I know," "Really," etc.) to show that you are interested and paying attention. These are the kinds of things you should be able to do naturally by this point if you have had previous experience with interviews.

Unless it is absolutely necessary, do not get involved in a discussion. If your interviewee asks a question, you should answer it, of course, but do not get carried away. Also, if the interview goes badly off topic, find a way to bring it back. By "off topic" I do not mean that if your informant is talking about, let's say, growing up in Mississippi, and that was what you wanted to know about, but then starts talking about a school trip to New York. The content has changed, but it is still life history information. That's fine. It might lead somewhere interesting. But if the topic changes to current affairs or the weather, subjects which have nothing to do with life history, then you need to steer things back on course – *gently* ("Yes, the storms were brutal last night. I was very nervous. Now – can you tell me a bit more about what happened after you …").

Make sure that your recording begins with you making a simple statement that includes the interviewee's name, the date and time, and some brief mention of informed consent. ("I have set the recorder going, and before we start I want to say that I am here with (name) on (date) and we are going to be discussing (topic) which I am recording for an essay I am writing. You are OK with this?"). You can be lighthearted with this part so that it does not seem like a labored duty that clouds the beginning of the interview, but it is essential.

This interview should be around an hour, and not much longer. If you wear your interviewee out the first time through, it may be fun at the time, but it may make setting up a second interview difficult. You want your interviewee to be happy to do a second interview rather than feel that the first was exhausting, and not worth repeating. Remember, you are leading the enterprise in general. It is much better to cut things off midstream and return to them at a later date, than to leave your interviewee with the feeling that there is no more to say. This means that you need to keep an eye on the time. You may be enjoying the interview, but this kind of work takes a toll on you too, and you need to be clear-headed at all times. When an hour is up, find a gentle way to wrap things up, and set up the next interview.

3. Index and review

As soon as it is convenient after the first interview, listen to your recording of it all the way through. This task is important for two reasons. First, you need to index the interview for future reference (see pages 83–84). Second, you need to be developing questions for your next interview, which will be, in part, a directed interview. Also, if you have not established a specific research question, now is the time to start shaping one. Putting together a list of directed questions is essential before starting the second interview, and may help you in finding greater direction and focus for your research question. You may find, as is often the case, that a particular thread stands out in the first interview leading you to concentrate on that subject more in the second interview by asking specifically targeted questions. Let's say you chose to interview a veteran from a foreign war. At the beginning, and during the first interview, you may have had only the vaguest research questions in mind based on your own limited knowledge and preconceptions, such as "How does war change people?" or "How do people overcome fear in highly stressful situations?" Then, as the first interview progressed, you found a theme unexpectedly jumping out at you, such as food on the battlefield or the various ethnicities in a company, leading you to refine your focus for the second interview. Therefore, you can ask such questions as, "How did the nature of battlefield food affect morale?" or "Did ethnic differences disappear or heighten under fire?" From the answers to these questions you can generate more general hypotheses (although still limited and qualified) on, say, the possible impact of diet on stress or how ethnicity plays out under different circumstances.

We call this an **"iterative"** approach to hypothesis development that was not normally possible in previous projects because they are mostly one-shot deals. An iterative approach is a back-and-forth progression. You gather some data, ask what it means, develop a question based on the data, look at the answer and see if it (a) confirms your idea, (b) contradicts your idea, or (c) suggests a different question. You proceed in steps (iterations) like this until you have a firm hypothesis, and have accumulated relevant data. This is one of the possible methodologies of long-term fieldwork (but not the only one). This procedure mimics the **hypothetico-deductive** model in natural science (see p 35), but it is a poor mimic, and is not rigorously secure.

4. Conduct the second interview

Armed with your questions, conduct your second interview. This time you do not have to be quite so fussy about time constraints, although you should be sensitive to your interviewee's capacity to continue. For the second time around, one hour (or shorter) is fine. If it goes longer, also fine. You could open with a small recap, and you should have your index of the first interview with you as a reminder of what you covered. If you left off in the middle of things in the first interview, that is where you should start the second. Then you can proceed to your questions.

Because this is a directed interview you should approach it differently from the first. In the first you could be content to let your interviewee talk without interruption, and you could afford to let awkward pauses hang in the air. Sometimes pauses get filled with surprising new directions. In a directed interview you need to have a firmer grip on the wheel. By all means let your interviewee complete an answer to your question for as long as it takes, but do not let the subject matter drift.

During the interview be aware of the iterative process. Do not think that your initial list of questions is all that you need to carry out the interview. Be fully prepared to ask questions that have not occurred to you before, and be willing to lead the interview in a new direction if it seems fruitful to you.

5. Index and review

As with the first interview, listen to the full recording as soon as you can, and completely index topics covered. This second time you should still be concerned with questions raised by the interview, but they should now be in the form of hypotheses (loosely defined), or speculations, concerning the nature of your information. For example:

- HIV/AIDS fundamentally changed gay culture in New York City in the 1980s
- People living below the poverty line do not form an homogenous culture
- Physical disabilities can carry social advantages
- Sometimes children want their parents to divorce

Go back over both interviews and decide what material can be incorporated in your presentation, around a finalized research question.

6. Transcribe

I asked my students to transcribe around 15 to 20 minutes of interview material that addressed their research question. When I first taught field methods, I did not give adequate instructions on the length of transcription, and one student turned in 80 pages: essentially her entire interview. It was impressive and I was suitably astounded. It not only captured her interviewee's authentic voice, such that you could virtually hear him speaking, it was an incredibly rich treasure of information. Her project alone convinced me of the value of undergraduate life histories. But an 80-page life history is more worthy of a semester-long project than a simple exercise. Discuss this component with your instructor.

When selecting passages for transcription, keep your research question in the forefront. Transcribe those sections that best exemplify what you were seeking to discover. It could be one single passage, or two, or several. Do not, however, transcribe snippets from here and there at random. Make sure that each passage explores a key topic in some detail. Choose a transcription method that suits you from the possibilities described in Chapter 8, and also discuss the exact nature of this part of the project with your instructor. You will have much, much more data than you can reasonably present for a single project of this nature. What you will inevitably discover is that hand transcription of parts of a life history involves a kind of listening you have likely never done before. You listen to every word, every turn of phrase, every nuance. In the process you may gain insight for your research question, or change your research question completely.

Here is an excerpt from one of my students' interviews with an African-American who was born in South Carolina and moved to Brooklyn, NY, with his family as a boy. Note the authentic voice, and the advantages and disadvantages of the transcription method (W is the interviewee and L is my student). At the time described here, W was a small boy in Brooklyn making money by shining shoes and delivering packages:

W: I was a working motherfucker – but that's from tips – and then the boys in the neighborhood started robbing me – you know yo man – yo yo homeboy – yo country boy – come here – I know you making all the money man – I saw you with the box over there in front of the bank – I saw you with the carriage man – give me an old nickel – I was dumb enough to reach in my pocket – I had so much motherfucking change I didn't know where to get it – I had both pockets full of change – I'd be down there looking for a – looking for a nickel – [strikes table] – stepping on me – and take it all –

L: oh they'd just slap your hand to make you ...?

W: yeah – yeah – I'd be dumb enough to be down there looking – trying to find a nickel – I'd have quarters and dimes and shit – I'd give them two or three nickels – cause I had a handful – I'd be standing back – they used to say – "yo yo" [strikes table] they'd hit my hand like that – and they'd go [shhh sound] – like that – "yo Mick get that change" and everybody'd be scrambling – and I'd say "whoa wait that's my money" – and they'd just get it and run off and say "ah fuck you" – you know – and I'd say "oh shit" – then I started telling my mom about them taking my money – she said "boy I don't tell you to be no fighter – but I cannot shine shoes with you – I will not carry packages with you – said – "if you can't – if you can't handle it – then you don't have to go out and shine the shoes – and you don't have to carry packages – but I'm not going with you – and if you're going to get your ass whipped – and get your money took – stay home – cause when Monday come – we're going to send you to school – but we're not going – I'm not going with you – to carry your – loaded shine box – and I'm not going to push your fucking – package cart – and watch your money – I don't have the time – you know – if you can't do that – leave it alone" – so I said "I ain't going to leave this alone – I'm going to get straight" – and I got straight – I took a lady – I told a lady about it – a lady lived on Lewis Avenue – and Kosciusko Street – uh – uh – she said "why are you so nervous?" – I said "because them boys are going to get me" – she said "what boys? you mean the ones that hang on the corner of DeKalb in the summer?" – she said "look – you don't fight them?" – I said "no because – I don't know" – I told her I was from the country and shit – she said "I don't give a shit where you come from" – she said "you fight them son of a bitches – you got a right to work – you got every goddamn right in the world to work" – and I said "but there's a whole bunch of them" – and she said "well I don't give a shit" – said "you try to avoid them" – she said "let me give you something" – said "I'm going to give you a quarter – bring your – bring your cart in my gate" – I put the cart in the gate – she said "take that" I had a – a throw board – she said "pick it up" – you know the mat for the baby – mattress and all – she said "pick that shit up – I picked up a big old [?] – she said "put these bottles down in there" – she said "I'm not paying you in bottles" – she said "I'm paying you in fighting material" – she said "they ask you for a goddamned quarter or a penny or a nickel or a dime" – said "you just get down up under this board and get busy" – said "cause you got a right to work" – said "now if you've got to leave and stop early" said "you stop early" – but throw these fucking bottles" – said "I'm not giving you… "– cause back in them days – a bottle was – a penny for a little bottle and – three cents for a big bottle – something like that – yeah yeah – penny for a little bottle – penny for a small bottle – and – three cents for a big bottle – like beer bottle was three cents – she says "I'm not telling you – you take these bottles and take them to the store" – she gave me about twenty five bottles – she said "when you see them approaching you" – said "don't you budge until they get within firing range" [laughs] – she said "when they come" said "you know what they coming for" – said "how many times?" – I said "I don't know so many times I'm ready to quit" – she said "don't you quit" – said "keep working" – said "when they come to you" – said "you just reach down in front of this – when they say – when they get close enough to say 'yo man – give me an old nickel' – said "you say 'I've got it right up under here'"– said "you reach up under there with both hands" – said "when you come out don't aim – just throw" – and I said "damn" you know – "if I do this they're going to kill me" right? – "if I hit somebody in the head with a bottle – when they see me next week – I'm going to be dead – this woman's telling me how to get killed" – she says "I'm – I'm telling you how to survive boy" – said "now you go – don't go back" – said "now – look" – said "I be late" – she always come in the store late – like about six thirty seven o'clock – that'd be about dark – she said "this time you go home anyway" – said "now when I finish you off you don't go back to – Somers Avenue – go down Lewis" – she said "but they'll be looking for you – they'll cut you off at the pass" – and she was right on the money – she said "but when they get within range of you – when they say 'yo yo my man – let me have a nickel – say "oh oh I've got it up under here" – said "when you come out" – said "that one in the front – do the best you can – blast" – and I was a country boy I could throw a rock – she said "well now you can throw a bottle you're in New York now motherfucker" – and goddamn it I did just what that woman said – and you know what them motherfuckers told me? – I was scared to go back to work – right? – cause I figured man all them motherfuckers – I fired them motherfucking bottles – I lit their ass up with them bottles – right – and I said "oh shit" – I went home and told my mama about it – and she said "well you got all your money" – I had pockets full of change – she said "well you got all your money."

7. Prepare your presentation

By now your method of presentation should be second nature. Describe the process whereby you selected an interviewee and why, and how you conducted the interviews. Describe also all the complications that arose and what, if any, research questions you began with. Next, present your transcriptions, indicating time, place, and location. Do not include any analysis in this section; this is your raw data. If you are presenting to a class you might also include some direct clips from your voice recordings that match your transcriptions, so that your interviewee's actual voice can be heard and compared with the transcription. There are also ways that you can do this for presentation to your teacher only. Finally, lay out your conclusions based on your transcriptions and your research question(s).

Drawing conclusions from limited data is fraught with difficulties, and is often the hardest part of any fieldwork project. Two hours of interview material is a great deal of information, which may be confusing and complicated even if you have managed to narrow your focus over time to a small area of inquiry. Conclusions do not hit you over the head; you have to search for them. Bear in mind also that your interviews represent the viewpoint of one person only concerning a small part of their life. In scientific terms, such information is called "anecdotal," and it cannot be used on its own to make sweeping generalizations. It may be highly idiosyncratic. Even so, it may provide an avenue for further study, and, certainly, it can be used to draw limited conclusions concerning a person's life trajectory.

If you have formed a tightly cogent hypothesis in the course of interviewing, one conclusion can be that your hypothesis was confirmed or denied. Such an outcome is rare, however. More likely, you have a tangle of information with no obvious central point to build out from. Let us return to the example of a set of interviews with a veteran of a foreign war for an example. Perhaps you have a collection of short stories, emerging from your questions, showing how the habitual tensions involving ethnicity in civilian life were typically downplayed under battlefield conditions, but resurfaced during respites in hostilities. You do not have enough data from this limited sample to draw any major conclusions about the relationship between social stress and ethnic tension, but you do have enough of a head start to pursue the topic with further, more targeted, research. Your conclusions for this project will be, of necessity, tentative and limited, but your goal is to draw together the overall themes that you discern in the interviews. Think of the interviews as the oral equivalent of a book you have read and enjoyed. When you have finished the book, what lessons do you take from it? Why did you enjoy it?

Further Reading

Some well-known examples of life histories have been noted already in this chapter, and you may well be aware of many others. A thorough critique of the life history method in anthropology ran alongside the overall concern in the discipline about the legitimacy of ethnographic writing in general, launched in the 1980s. Look, for example, at exchanges such as this one:

Runyan, W.M. (1986). Life Histories in Anthropology: Another View. *American Anthropologist*. 88/1: 181–183.

Crapanzano, V. (1986). Crapanzano's Response to Runyan. *American Anthropologist*. 88/1: 183–185.

By now you should be well aware of the pitfalls of any interview method, including the multiple ways in which the status of the fieldworker can influence the interviewee's narrative, the blurred objective/subjective distinction, the vagaries of memory, the biases injected into analysis by the fieldworker, and so forth. The following readings address these issues, and more, and can help strengthen focus in the field:

Goodson, I. (2009). The Story of Life History: Origins of the Life History Method in Sociology. *Identity: An International Journal of Theory and Research.*

Rosenthal, G. (1993). Reconstruction of life stories: principles of selection in generating stories for narrative biographical interviews. *The Narrative Study of Lives* 1/1 : 59–91.

Bertaux, D. (ed.) (1981). *Biography and Society: The Life History Approach in the Social Sciences.* Sage.

Chamberlayne, P. et al. (eds.) (2000). *The Turn to Biographical Methods in Social Sciences.* Routledge.

Jolly, M. (ed.) (2001). *The Encyclopedia of Life Writing. Autobiographical and Biographical Forms.* Routledge.

Stanley, L. (1992). *The Autobiographical I: The Theory and Practice of Feminist Autobiography.* Manchester University Press.

16

Charting Kinship

In this chapter, you will gather kinship data and develop a kinship chart. Charting kinship is a classic ethnographic technique that was common in early ethnographic research. These anthropologists found it useful because, in part, family and kinship are the foundational organizing structures of non-industrialized cultural groups. Kinship charts can be useful to ethnographers today for a variety of reasons. Kinship and kinship terms play a significant role in all cultures.

Learning Goals

1. *Gather kinship data accurately*
2. *Present the collected information clearly on a kinship chart using anthropological kinship notation*

By the time you get around to studying field methods you will probably be aware of the historic importance of kinship studies in anthropology. You may also be aware of the numerous approaches that anthropologists have taken to kinship over the years. Nowadays, the importance and significance of kinship studies are constantly being re-evaluated, and long-established conventions are continually questioned (see e.g. Carsten 2000). This project steers clear of most of the keen debates, but you may find yourself questioning older traditions of kinship study, and their relative value, within anthropology, nonetheless. If you are interested in new departures for kinship studies and the whole notion of what "kinship" is, you could consult works such as Kath Weston's *Families We Choose: Lesbians, Gays, Kinship* (Weston 1991), or those in the Further Reading section. In recent years kinship studies have slipped in importance within anthropology, but this project, when used creatively, can bring back renewed vigor to them. When starting this project try to clear your mind of the technicalities of Iroquois kinship systems, or cross-cousin marriages, or other kinship studies that you have been introduced to, and focus instead on the multi-varied data that a kinship chart can convey.

A kinship diagram is a visual presentation of mental (or written) information, and, just as with mapping, there are multiple ways to record and display the data depending on what you want to convey to an audience. Genesis 10 in the Bible, the so-called Table of Nations, is an elaborate accounting of the kinship of Noah's three sons and their descendants laid out verbally (as is all the information on kinship throughout the

Bible). It is unlikely that what Genesis is recording is legitimate kinship information in a classic sense. Rather, it is a depiction of the relationships between all the nations known to the author characterized in kinship terms. Kinship is not just about ties of blood and marriage.

As a simple experiment in what you can do with "kinship" information, look at Genesis 10 and figure out different ways in which you could present the data contained in it visually. You could make a classic kinship diagram using traditional symbols, or you could be more creative. You could, for example, plot the various descendants on a map of the world – focusing on Europe, Asia, and Africa – and then find ways to show the "kinship" ties between these individual locations. This map will help show how the writer of the chapter saw the relationships between cultures and geographic regions of the known world in kinship terms. Such an exercise may also spark new ideas for you in terms of broadening your concept of what kinship studies are, or what their wider potential is.

You may well be familiar with, and comfortable with, conventional kinship diagrams and their special symbols. If so, some of the introductory material here will be redundant for you. Read it anyway, and also discuss methodology with your instructor because there are some alternatives to the conventional symbols used here that may be useful to you, and, also, some that you may not be familiar with.

Originally, kinship charts were drawn by hand. Today, there are several computer applications available that can aid in this process. SILKin is probably the best because of its flexibility, but it does require strong computing skills to install (including having Java 7 or higher), and, like similar apps, it is oriented toward genealogical diagrams by default and requires some tinkering to shift it into a mode that is more useful for general ethnographic information. You can find it here https://software.sil.org/silkin

There are others including:

Kinship Diagram Maker https://kinship-tree-diagram.pdffiller.com
Creately (Kinship) https://creately.com/diagram/example/iga4qm20/Kinship
Lucidchart https://www.lucidchart.com/blog/make-a-kinship-diagram-online
Visual Paradigm https://online.visual-paradigm.com
You can also find links to, and evaluations of, numerous kinship apps, from basic to professional, here: https://www.kinsources.net/editorial/tools.xhtml

Check with your instructor about the pros and cons of different apps including ones not listed. You will almost certainly find it easier to collect or note kinship data using pencil and paper first, and then translate the data into a finished diagram using a computer app. Widely available kinship programs do not have the steep learning curve that CAD apps do, but they are not always helpful with ethnographic needs. Some people find that simple presentation or illustrating software such as Microsoft PowerPoint or Adobe Photoshop work just as well.

Instructions

1. **Identify your ego**

For this exercise you will draw a **kindred** chart and analyze patterns within it. You will find other possibilities for the project at the end of the chapter. To start this project you must first decide who you want EGO to be. This is the person you will be collecting data on. A kindred chart is a specialized kinship diagram with one person as the focal point – labeled EGO, which technically means "me," but in this case means the reference point for labeling all the other kin in the chart. You could draw a chart of related people and label each person on the chart with their names (see, for example, Figure 16.2). This can provide valuable ethnographic and consanguineal information, but it is not a kindred chart because to be a kindred chart the relationships between the people on the chart must be labeled from a focal point. Without a focal point it is not a kindred chart. You could have, let's say, a woman labeled Anna Jones, and a man in another part of the chart labeled Tom Smith, but there is no way of knowing from the chart what the relationship is between them, that is, what they call one another, except in very general terms. If you have one individual labeled as EGO, you can still put all the names of the people on the chart, but you can now add their kin terms. So, if Anna Jones is EGO's mother's mother, you can label her "grandmother," and if Tom Smith is EGO's mother's brother's son, you can label him "cousin." You cannot label their relationship to each other, though, only to EGO. Drawing a kindred is a limited kinship exercise – deliberately.

2. **Generate a research question**

To start this project you must first decide who you want EGO to be. This is the person you will be collecting data on. You must also decide on a research question, which can be difficult at the outset, and may have to remain somewhat vague until you get into the meat of the project. The central aim of this exercise is to find patterns in the kindred you draw, so, like the mapping project, the most basic question is, "Are there any discernible patterns?" The simplest way to get the feel for this project is to draw your own kindred using yourself as EGO. The crucial issue with this project, whether you are doing your own kindred, or working with another person, is that it is to be done *from memory*. The goal is to chart the kinship information in a person's head, not what can be discovered through additional research.

3. **Draft your chart**

For practice working on drawing your own kindred, start with a large sheet of paper, squared if possible, (taping smaller sheets together if need be), and begin by placing yourself in a suitable location on the page. Place yourself roughly in the middle if you have children or your cousins have children. Place yourself more toward the bottom, but in the middle from right to left if there are few, if any, children in the generation below you. Work in pencil, because, with the best intentions in the world, you will need to erase and redraw segments.

Once you have marked yourself on the page, mark down your siblings (if any), using standard anthropological symbols. Figure 16.1 will remind you of the basics, although sometimes you need to get creative. Try to keep siblings in order of birth from left to right if possible (do not worry if it is not possible). In your case, mark your siblings in from left to right in descending birth order, putting yourself/EGO in the correct place. If you have half-siblings or step-siblings, things can get complicated, so just begin with full siblings. Then mark on your parents. Then work outward from there. Figure 16.2 shows the rough beginning of a very detailed kindred of seven generations that I recorded over a period of several months.

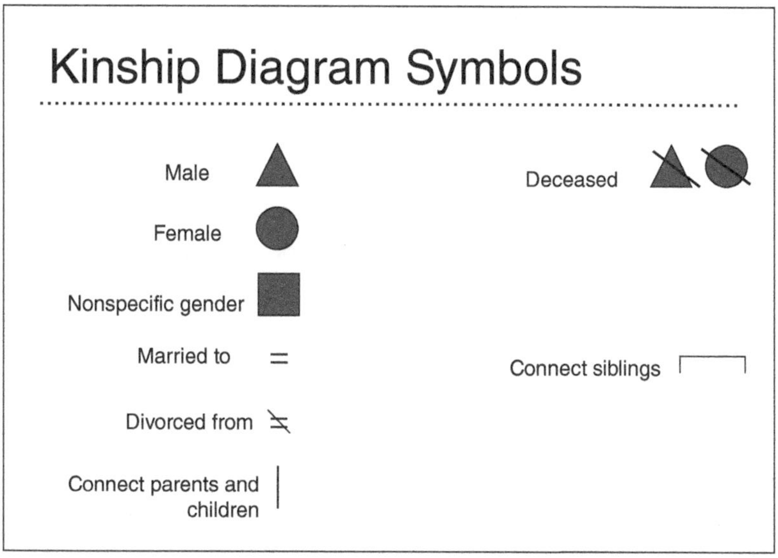

Kinship Diagram Symbols

Male ▲

Female ●

Nonspecific gender ■

Married to =

Divorced from ⚊

Connect parents and children |

Deceased

Connect siblings

Figure 16.1 Standard Kinship Symbols.

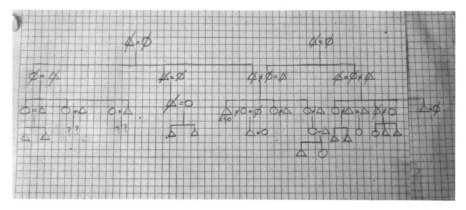

Figure 16.2 Sample Kindred (Abbreviated).

When I started recording this kindred, my initial research question was, "How does formal kinship terminology differ from actual usage?" I have always been troubled by kinship studies that use the formal kinship terms of a culture and then draw major conclusions from them when I know that formal terms and actual usage can be markedly different. In China, for example, it is common for people who grew up under the one child policy to refer to their first cousins using the standard Chinese words for "brother" or "sister" (and they call their children "niece" and "nephew") because they have no biological siblings, yet they desire that relationship. Hence, they treat first cousins as siblings. But, a standard kinship diagram of kin terms in China will show only the Chinese terms for cousins. Rather more commonly than in the United States, the Chinese also typically refer to their parents-in-law as "mummy" and "daddy" (in Chinese of course – and using the relevant diminutives). I have also marked on the chart the fact that the person does *not* know some information. A larger kindred (Figure 16.3) shows that this person has much greater, and more detailed knowledge of matrilateral kin than patrilateral kin. Why is that, do you think?

On Figure 16.3 I have marked the names that EGO typically uses, which is sometimes a kin term and sometimes a first name (marked [name]). In recording the data, EGO told me several names for each person: (1) formal kinship term (2) birth name (3) name EGO normally uses. These could all be noted on the diagram.

I chose first to examine what parts of the kindred were clear in memory, and what parts were vague. The conclusions are not startling. EGO knows more about the segments of the kindred he interacts with a great deal (sisters), than about the segments he rarely interacts with (cousins). To some extent geography is an issue, but not immensely so. When EGO lived in close proximity to his maternal cousins he still interacted more with his sisters, who lived farther away, and paid more attention to what was happening with them and their children than to his cousins. Location suggests another possibility for diagramming this kindred, however. I could use colors to demark the regions where each member of the kindred lives. Just using labels would be a mistake because colors show patterns more effectively. (I might leave deceased people uncolored.)

Probably to indicate location I would use one distinctive color per country, but then would use different shades of that color for different regions within that country. You would then see that the patrilateral kin are, on the whole, tightly clustered in northern Argentina, but the matrilateral kin are scattered all over the world. Why might that be, do you think? You will also notice that all the matrilateral kin in ego's generation and the generation above have been divorced at least once, and none of the patrilateral kin has been divorced. Why? These are the kinds of questions that were prompted by the kindred chart itself. They had not occurred to me before I drew it. I knew all the information, but I had not organized it in my head until then.

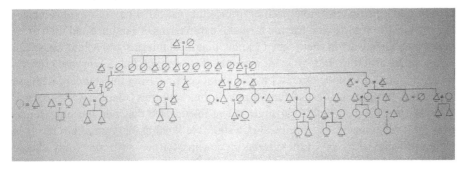

Figure 16.3 Detailed kindred.

How you add symbols to your kindred chart is going to be determined in large part by what your research question is. You might decide to chart residence patterns, religious affiliation, jobs, hereditary illnesses, or whatever else interests you. Even if you are going to chart someone else's kindred for your project, you should start with your own for practice. The first thing that will almost inevitably surprise you is what you cannot remember, or where you have no knowledge to begin with. That always prompts a good first question. Why is your knowledge/memory strong in some areas and weaker in others?

In the sample case, his knowledge of his mother's kin is much, much more comprehensive than his father's kin for two reasons. First, his father died when he was quite young and in consequence he had little opportunity to ask about his family. His mother, on the other hand, was fond of pulling out a collection of family photos in spare moments and talking about her relatives – especially because for most of his childhood he lived at a great distance from these people and never communicated with them. Second, his father's kin almost all live in Argentina, and he has lived in the United States most of his life. He visits Argentina occasionally and, once in a while, cousins visit him in the United States; but person-to-person contact is rare. On the other hand, he sees his maternal kin quite often, even though they are widely scattered, because he regularly visits their hometowns on business and because his sisters have tight bonds with many of these kin. Location might also be a clue to patterns of marriage and divorce. In Argentina, which is a predominantly Catholic country, divorce is possible but still frowned upon. This is where the majority of EGO's patrilateral kin live, whereas his matrilateral kin live in predominantly Protestant or secular regions where divorce is commonplace. Remember, though, that such an initial conclusion is purely speculative because it is based on an extremely narrow dataset.

Drawing someone else's kindred is much more difficult than documenting your own, and may have to be done in stages. You cannot be dragging around a giant sheet of squared paper to create the chart in a single session. You will have to draw segments of the chart on separate sheets, and then piece them all together at the end. The process is akin to the mapping project: you start off with some rough charts as your notes, and then convert them to a finished chart later. When I did my doctoral fieldwork, I drew dozens of small, rough kinship charts as I visited different residents of the community which I then put together to form a giant chart. On it I indicated which members were born in the village and stayed, those who were born in the village and moved out in adulthood, and those who were born outside the village and moved in in adulthood. I also marked lines of inheritance of property on the chart. The results were not surprising, but clear to see. (Figure 16.4). Those people who inherited land in the village stayed and those who did not, left. Those who stayed, married people who had been born outside the village. Note that this is not a kindred chart: there is no EGO marked (and not all the people on the diagram are related to each other), but it gives you an idea of how kinship charts can work to display information clearly and succinctly.

4. **Produce a finished chart**
Once you have gathered all your kinship data in rough form, make a single chart for presentation using either one of the computer apps listed above, or by drafting by hand

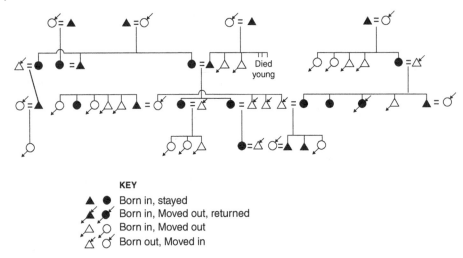

KEY
▲ ● Born in, stayed
◭ ◉ Born in, Moved out, returned
△ ○ Born in, Moved out
⟁ ♂ Born out, Moved in

Figure 16.4 Residence and Kinship in Tidewater.

neatly. Decide how you want to label the chart based on the information you wish to convey. Figure 16.4, for example, uses shading and arrows to indicate residence patterns which are then explained in a key. The goal is to make the central data marked on the chart immediately obvious. On this chart, black represents people who inherited land, and it is obvious that this was the single biggest factor in whether a person stayed in the village or left.

Your finished chart is your ultimate goal for presentation. You should precede it with a discussion of how you decided on your informant and on your research question. You should also detail the problems you had in that process, as well as in collecting your data, and creating your chart. Subsequently you can discuss how producing kinship data in visual form aids in seeing relationships and patterns clearly.

Additional Suggestions

Although drawing a kindred and indicating patterns on it is the baseline project here you need not feel limited to that one idea. As I have already indicated, there are multiple lines of attack possible besides a kindred chart. Geneticists, for example, take great interest in kinship diagrams for diagnostic, and other, reasons. You may be familiar with the kinship chart of queen Victoria of Great Britain who was a carrier of the recessive gene for hemophilia (see https://hy382aq.wordpress.com/2018/10/09/queen-victoria-and-hemophilia) What is interesting about this chart is that, tracing the lineage back, the trait stops with Victoria. As with all royal bloodlines, there are exhaustive data on Victoria's ancestors stretching back 17 generations and includes all of her collateral descendants. No one prior to Victoria, nor any of their descendants, had hemophilia. But, Victoria must have inherited the gene from someone! One logical possibility is that Edward, Duke of York, who is recorded as her father, was not actually her biological father, and that she was, in fact, illegitimate (making her ineligible to inherit the crown) – that is, she inherited the gene from her actual biological father.

In my own matriline I have always been intrigued by the steady progress of social mobility. My maternal great-grandfather was a shepherd and his line as far back as I can record were shepherds or farm workers. As a young man he left shepherding and took up employment as a gardener, eventually being promoted to head gardener, at a manor house. His daughter (my grandmother) began employment as a maid in the manor and progressed up to being a housekeeper. Her daughter (my mother) was first a shop assistant, but then enlisted in the WAAF as a plane spotter during the Second World War. After the war, when my family migrated to South Australia, she attended a teacher training college, and became qualified as a primary school teacher. At each generation, my matriline ascended one rung up the social ladder. Meanwhile, the other descendants of my great-grandfather remained relatively immobile socially. Why? I can link various lines in my matriline to historical events (such as two world wars), geographic relocation/stability, choice of marriage partners, and so forth, and can display all this information on a kinship diagram.

In the United States some families take great interest in carrying out extensive genealogical research. My wife's kin have an unusual family name – Blincoe (also spelled Blinko, Blencow, etc.) – and some people in the United States have gone to extraordinary lengths to trace various lineages back to a knight, Adam de Blencowe, who fought with Edward III of England against France at the Battle of Crécy (August 26, 1346), and was awarded land for his service near Penrith in Cumbria that became a manor and the village of Blencowe. They also maintain a website, http://www.blencowefamilies.com, and hold family gatherings every other year. Why is such genealogical information important to some people?

Alex Haley, who recorded Malcolm X's life history in *The Autobiography of Malcolm X*, went on to produce *Roots: The Saga of an American Family*, which reputedly tells the story of Kunta Kinte, an eighteenth-century Mandinka man from The Gambia who was captured as an adolescent, sold into slavery in Africa, and transported to North America where he had children whose descendants eventually produced Haley. The book was hugely successful, 46 weeks on *New York Times* Best Seller List, including 22 weeks at number one. One obvious reason for the book's popularity is that African-Americans in general can barely trace their lineages back to the time of slavery, let alone beyond, whereas people of European heritage whose forebears migrated to the United States of their own free will have a much easier time of it. Even so, why does it matter to these people?

In both Argentina and New Mexico, where I have done fieldwork, there is a common pattern within certain families to establish their genealogical bona fides as descendants of Spanish conquistadores, somewhat similar, perhaps, to the Daughters of the American Revolution (DAR) tracing their ancestry back to Revolutionary War soldiers. Why are these links important, and what do they mean for people in the contemporary world?

Do not feel in any way constrained by the instructions given here; their purpose is to get you started thinking about the value of kinship research, not to limit you. Consult with your instructor about possibilities, and try to find avenues of research that engage your interest and that resonate with issues of cultural significance. Older kinship studies in anthropology tended to focus on patterns of marriage, alliance, political and social power, exchange, inheritance, and so forth, but you should feel free to branch out in any direction that is of relevance to you or to today's world.

Further Reading

The anthropological study of kinship has tended to drift with the tides, with the popular theories of the day shaping their analysis. Its prominence began with Lewis Henry Morgan's discovery of patterns of kinship among the Iroquois that differed from Euro-American norms, which he followed up by studying a range of Native American groups. His *Systems of Consanguinity and Affinity of the Human Family* (Morgan 1871) was foundational for decades, even after his model of cultural evolution faded into oblivion. Subsequently, functionalism had its day in the sun, then structuralism, and now things are in flux as Marxist, post-colonial, feminist, GLBTQ+, and post-modern critics all weigh in on the deficiencies of classic kinship studies.

Starting in the 1960s, David Schneider began questioning the importance of consanguineal relationships in social organization that until that point had largely remained unchallenged (Schneider 1984). His critique did soften the supposed centrality of consanguineal ties to social organization worldwide, but it did not undermine the need for kinship studies completely: he merely shifted the focus away from outmoded theories. Linda Stone's anthology, *New Directions in Anthropological Kinship* (2001), contains articles that expand the scope of kinship studies. Likewise, this review article examines the current diversity in outlooks: https://www.annualreviews.org/doi/10.1146/annurev.an.24.100195.002015

The main point that modern theorists want to get across is that kinship is not as neat and tidy as was once thought. Neither is it constrained within a narrow range of topics. Take a look at *Social Bonding and Nurture Kinship: Compatibility between Cultural and Biological Approaches* by Maximilian Holland for a comparative view of kinship studies as contemporarily conceived by anthropologists, evolutionary biologists, and psychologists in relation to bonding, identity, and social behavior.

17

Digital Ethnography (1) Social Media

This project examines social media in a broad way. Social media encompass various apps, platforms, techniques (visual and verbal), and styles. You have the opportunity to choose which of these many approaches you wish to examine, or you may conduct a number of different exercises. You can also choose between numerous possibilities within the social media world, such as cancel culture, influencers, online communities, selfie culture, and more. The emphasis in these exercises is on contributing an ethnographic perspective on the "social" nature of social media.

Learning Goals

1. *Understand the precise* social *nature of social media*
2. *Explore ways to document these media ethnographically.*

All media are social insofar as media communicate or express some*thing* some*where*. And by media, we include not only mass media or the Internet, but other technologies and aesthetic expressions that mediate our relationships with one another and the world. The social theorist Raymond Williams (1983 [1976]) considers the history and etymology of the word "media" in his entry of the same name in *Keywords: A Vocabulary of Culture and Society*. The use of "medium" predates "media." A medium is "an intervening substance or agency." Language, then, is a medium. So, too, is *Fountain*, the readymade created by Marcel Duchamp in 1917 that represented a new form of artistic expression and changed the Western art world in incalculable ways. Now let's jump forward – a lot – to social media in the sense likely most familiar to you.

Social media are ubiquitous in the modern world, such that the majority of people with smartphones, tablets, and/or laptops spend significant time during the day checking their apps. Defining social media adequately can be tricky, but for the purposes of this project we can use the 2019 *Merriam-Webster* definition: "forms of electronic communication (such as websites for social networking and microblogging) through which users create online communities to share information, ideas, personal messages, and other content (such as videos)." In the United States the 10 most popular platforms as of this writing (in descending order) are:

Doing Field Projects: Methods and Practice for Social and Anthropological Research, First Edition.
John Forrest.
© 2022 John Wiley & Sons, Inc. Published 2022 by John Wiley & Sons, Inc.

1. Facebook
2. YouTube
3. WhatsApp
4. Instagram
5. TikTok
6. Reddit
7. Snapchat
8. Twitter
9. Pinterest
10. LinkedIn

If you have any familiarity at all with these platforms, you will know that they differ markedly in content and style, and their users vary widely demographically. Facebook and YouTube are the far and away leaders; yet they are radically different from each other and from other platforms. Facebook allows subscribers to upload text, photos, videos, or links to websites, and users get to choose how big or small their list of friends/followers is. YouTube, on the other hand, features only videos, although commenting and networking functions remain; and the rise of livestreaming has made more real-time interactions possible.

Instagram, Snapchat, and TikTok are overwhelmingly more popular with the 18- to 25-year-old demographic in the United States than the other platforms, and each has its own favored style. Instagram, when launched, was primarily a straightforward image sharing app, but now has hashtags like Twitter to attract like-minded users, and these users have created "trends" through these hashtags. Trends vary – they are trends, after all – but one simple, ongoing example involves highlighting a specific day of the week to attract material, such as #SelfieSunday, #MotivationMonday, #TransformationTuesday, #WomanCrushWednesday, #ManCrushMonday, and #ThrowbackThursday (mirroring TBT on Facebook and other social media). Instagram also now has an "Explore" tab that displays popular photos, photos taken at nearby locations, and trending tags and places, curated content, as well as the ability to search for locations, concerts, sports, and other live events and, like all other social media, an algorithmically curated page of the "best" Instagram Live videos currently available.

TikTok, known in China as Dǒuyīn (抖音), is a video-sharing service used to create short music, lip-sync, dance, comedy, and talent videos of between 3 and 15 seconds, and short looping videos of between 3 and 60 seconds. Launched in 2017 for iOS and Android in most markets outside of mainland China, TikTok became available for the US market only in 2018. TikTok and Dǒuyīn have almost the same user interface but no access to each other's content. TikTok came to general public attention in June 2020 when users engaged in a ticket-reserving effort to inflate projected, and depress actual, attendance at President Trump's June 20, 2020, campaign rally in Tulsa, Oklahoma, and also posted other content satirizing or criticizing Trump and his actions.

A considerable number of TikToks are challenges – trending songs and topics taken up by users who post their own efforts, such as choreographed dances or carefully lip-synced responses to popular memes. These in turn generate additional content in a number of ways, such as reaction videos. TikTok has also become widely used for various forms of activism. People do not simply post their own political views; they engage those of others, often in carefully constructed arguments and rebuttals – a form of edutainment or infotainment popularized by, among others, satirical news shows such as *Full Frontal with Samantha Bee* or late-night comics like Stephen Colbert.

One characteristic of TikTok is its recursivity. To offer one generalizable example of a reaction video (generalizable in that this both refers to a specific example and stands in for others): a white woman posts a TikTok in which she espouses racist views, then an anti-racist white woman posts a TikTok in which she reacts in real time to the first woman's comments. That reaction video may then itself be taken up by other users: a Black woman then posts her own reaction to the original white woman's reaction video to the original post. Then – there always seems to be another then in meme cultures – another Black woman posts *her* reaction to the previous Black woman's reactions to the white woman reacting to the racist commenter. This is a five-layer TikTok cake, six if we count the user who comes across it.

In addition to TikTok, there are a great many other Chinese social media platforms such as WeChat, Weibo, Renren, Douban, and Diandian, all serving much the same functions as Facebook, YouTube, Twitter, and such – all of which are banned in China. The Chinese apps are, in turn, banned in the United States and Europe because of their use for surveillance by the Chinese government. There are ways to circumvent the ban, although gaining access to such apps usually involves Chinese-language skills, and most posts (not all) are in Chinese. Even so, some limited participant observation is possible if you are interested. WeChat is the most accessible to English speakers, and is the most easily available.

These platforms, and those that follow, share one essential characteristic: whatever amount of control users may have, or believe themselves to have, their engagement is fundamentally shaped by unseen, unaudited algorithmic processes. An algorithm is like a recipe – ingredients plus instructions plus output. In social media, as in many other contexts today, *we* are collectively the ingredients, everything we do on- *and* off-line generates quintillions of bytes of data *every day* (a quintillion is 1 followed by 18 zeroes or 10^{18} – it would take 210,000 years for a quintillion gallons of water to flow over Niagara Falls). The internet studies scholar John Cheney-Lippold (2017) has written about how "we are data," a notion that refers not only to the material realities of contemporary data harvesting, but to profound metaphysical questions about human agency – the capacity to make intentional choices and to effect change in the world. All of the data we produce every day are the ingredients that go into algorithms designed to produce particular outputs, such as increased engagement and consumption.

These methods are related to, but also distinct from, traditional advertising. In the latter, demographic and other data are used to create ads for large numbers of people. In the algorithmic era, collected data are tailored for much smaller groups of people, even for individuals – you may have heard the term "micro-targeting." These techniques take into account an array of factors: where you live, how much you earn, and even your personal style, as well as, by proxy, things like your race and sexual orientation. These data are not only used to market to you what you want, but to predict what it is you might not yet know that you want. Consider this example: you have a cat that you post pictures of on Instagram, as well as friends whose cat posts you like, and you recently joined a cat training group on Facebook (they exist, and good luck). Additionally, you are in your 20s and living in Hell's Kitchen in New York City, which likely means you have a tight budget. What follows will be unsurprising. Soon, you begin to see ads on your Instagram feed for more cat-related goods, like specially designed scratching posts, influencer-endorsed CBD for cats, and elaborate, locally constructed cat bridges ideal for small spaces that you can install yourself on the walls of your home and purchase using an affordable payment plan. These outcomes result from the data: you like cats a lot, but your cat might have some behavior problems you want to remedy, and the previous goods are remedies other people your age, living in your neighborhood have purchased. And luckily, this locally sourced product – sustainable consumption matters to you – is affordable, only $49.95 per month for six months.

Social media are social, and we can also say that they are anti-social. The business models of all the major social media companies, as well as Google, not only draw us into a public of shared interests or connect us to friends and family, they also depend on the underbelly of human behavior. The spread of misinformation and disinformation, for example, generates ad revenue for these companies because the content of particular messages is less relevant than the scale of their circulation. Eyes on screen, time on device, conspiracy theories and hate speech likewise yield returns, as the more people see and engage content, the more ads they will encounter, and the more data they produce, the better to tailor future ads. Conspiracies and outrage, it turns out, are big money. Thus far, social media companies have failed to meaningfully address the concerns of researchers, tech privacy and security groups, and policy figures in addressing and remedying their current practices.

Online Communities

Like culture, "community" can be a loaded term. The political scientist and historian Benedict Anderson's *Imagined Communities* underscores that all communities are imagined; they are complex arrangements that help nations cohere through shared identities that are produced through factors such as the standardization of language, media addressed to specific populations, and the cultivation of nationalism. All communities work this way, whether we consider them at the micro- or macro-level. Whether we consider the culture of an apartment building or a nation, not all of the inhabitants will know each other, but they will be connected by other means, such as sharing concerns about the building's upkeep, by speaking the same language, or in the ways they identify with what it means to be Navajo or Nigerian. Queer studies scholar Michael Warner (2002) uses the term "public" in lieu of community. "Community" for him, as well as for many anthropologists and interdisciplinary scholars, can imply that people are more homogenous than they think they are. Using terms like "a public" or "publics" remind us that what we often think of communities are comprised of people who may be connected in a variety of ways, such as national identity or race or sexuality, but do not, and cannot, know (all of) each other. A phrase like "As American as baseball and apple pie" signals a shared national identity, but what "American" means differs radically depending on your social location. America means different things for older white men, recent immigrants, women, the disabled, and so on.

In a public comprised mostly of strangers, what becomes of interest to the researcher are the forms of sociality the more-or-less strangers engage in with one another.

"Stranger sociality" is a concept that has proven useful in the analysis of an array of social interactions; one example of this is the study of gay male sex publics linked to cruising, centuries old sets of practices of pursuing and engaging in anonymous sex (Humphreys 1999). Networked cultures are comprised of intimates, intimate strangers, and, let's face it, strange intimates.

So, while the term "community" is used here and elsewhere in this book as a recognized, common shorthand, it is important to keep the above in mind as a reminder that there are no communities or cultures that are entirely coherent or identical with themselves. Online publics come in a seemingly infinite number of forms and scales: there are the millions of people who use dating apps, who watch the videos of their favorite influencers, and there are also the small neighborhood news Facebook groups and those raucous extended family WhatsApp groups. The list goes on, and on. This is to say, that while social media are a meta-cultural phenomenon that cuts across every sphere of social life – politics, economics, art, etc. – they are also comprised of many, perhaps innumerable, publics and subcultures.

One of the well-documented effects of the growth of social media has been the ability of people who hold marginal, minority beliefs to post comments online and to build a network of like-minded individuals. Building such a network was next to impossible in the days before social media. If you wanted to circulate your ideas about the earth being flat or how the moon landings were faked, or how aliens had landed at Area 51, you had to spend time and money to produce the relevant documents and circulate them, and even then the chances of reaching a wide audience were slim. With a social media account, you can broadcast your ideas with little effort, and attract a following. This is true for the conspiracies above, as well as for social movements, discussed below.

One critical historical note here: while many readers may think of online communities as very recent phenomena, resulting from the greater degree of interactivity of Web 2.0, in fact, their roots have existed in forms we would recognize since at least the early 1980s. Usenet is one such example, operating from 1979 until 2011. danah boyd (2011) and Nicole Ellison (Steinfeld, Ellison, and Lampe 2008) outline the early history of social networking sites as we know them, beginning in 1997 with sixdegrees.com, a site whose name underscores another important feature of social media; in addition to being able to find people with whom to connect, you can choose to display those connections to others, thereby potentially expanding your own network or simply demonstrating your status and influence.

Because of the complexity of social media, you have numerous choices when it comes to the focus of this project. In fact, it is even possible to construct a whole semester's worth of projects by selecting from the following choices.

Online Community Project Instructions

Identify an online community or public. For example, you might choose a Facebook group, or subscribe to a subreddit of interest to you – you can find them on virtually any topic. Fanfiction.net might also prove a promising space, with decades' worth of fanfiction about virtually anything, along with much spirited discussion. As always, pay close attention to any patterns you observe. What shape do the interactions take in the threads?

Threads can be a fertile ground for investigation because the various forms of social media spawn comment threads of different kinds, and the various types of postings yield different responses. How these threads play out is determined in part by content and in part by the available audience. On Facebook, for example, you can limit who sees your posts to your friends only, and, in so doing, you can limit the kind and number of comments on a post, so that if you hold an especially strident political view, you can post a poignant meme or statement in line with your views and expect comments to be mostly supportive. If, on the other hand, you post a video on YouTube in the same vein, and with your viewing set to "Public," you can expect a wide range of opinions expressed, and these opinions may (d)evolve into arguments between commenters. You might choose other communities, as well, such as an online gaming community, for which there are also specific exercises below, although here it is a distinct exercise.

As you undertake your project, ask whether there are regular contributors of stature? How do users typically interact with one another, and if so, what are the characteristic elements of these interactions? Are there linguistic shorthands, stated or implicit rules to these interactions? How social is the platform or site? Anti-social? Keep in mind, too, the importance of situating your chosen site historically. When did it come about and how has it changed?

How deeply you can research online communities will be limited by time constraints, and you should consult your instructor concerning this limitation. You could, for example, observe an online group intensively for (say) three weeks, or you could take notes and analyze interactions much less intensively but for an entire semester – while also carrying out other projects. You probably have an online community presence anyway, so this approach would not be difficult. However, to be successful this project must involve a community that is new to you.

When completed, you can present your research in a number of ways, and it is extremely valuable to draw on characteristic elements of the platform or site you have chosen when presenting your findings – and you might bear this fact in mind as you conduct your research. For example, you might create a Facebook group specific to this project and invite classmates to respond to your research questions. Or you might write a short piece of fanfiction in a reflexive, auto-theoretical vein to communicate your findings.

Selfie/Self-Instructions

Many of you will likely associate the selfie – the ubiquitous digital self-portrait – with social media. Social media in many ways are exemplars of stranger sociality. After all, it is likely that you are not intimate with every person whose posts you like. This does not mean you are not connected to them, and they to you. Indeed, they depend on you for their status and often, depending on their level of recognition, their income.

When you post a selfie, you enter into relationships with your intimates, strangers, and intimate strangers. Like all representational genres, selfies generally adhere to a set of formal qualities regarding composition, lighting, angles, and, of course, context. In the following assignment, you will study these qualities, as well as how they are produced and reproduced. A dating profile picture is not the same as a group photo at a sports event or tourist site.

For this exercise, you will study conventions of selfies, focusing on the following genres: self-portrait of the face, self-portrait of the body, outdoors, and eating. Consider what and how each of these communicate something about an important element of the visual economy of networked culture. That is, what are the aesthetic conventions that govern the selfie? You may have heard about some tips about how to take the most flattering selfie from lighting to how one should hold one's phone or contort one's body to highlight one's physical assets. Model your efforts on tips like these and the endless archive of selfies you have come across and produced yourself.

In addition to working with the above conventions, you should reflect anthropologically on the cultural significance of self-presentation in the age of the selfie. What sorts of things do selfies communicate, not just about particular people, but about cultures more broadly? For example, sticking one's tongue out or giving the peace sign express particular things – a spirit of playfulness, or it can instrumentally provide a means to deal with the perennial problem of what to do with one's hand(s). When considering issues such as posture and gesture, you can also relate them to demographic factors such as age, gender, ethnicity, and social status.

So now take your own selfies! Take more than one (as with *all* photodocumentation – take a lot of photos). Attend, then, especially to the process of taking selfies. Feel free to post them in a variety of places to see what kinds of responses you get.

Smartphone Bootcamp Instructions

Social media are also a rich field for autoethnography, as well (see Chapter 5). How do *you* use social media and why? There are apps that can do some preliminary checking for you, such as Moment (iOS) or BreakFree (iOS, Android), which are geared toward breaking smartphone addiction and developing mindfulness about our use of technology. The above apps are helpful in tracking your daily usage, but an autoethnographic approach will dig deeper. Start with one of these apps to give you some initial ideas, but then be more self-investigative.

The following exercises borrow from several sources, including the Moment app, the WNYC podcast series "Bored and Brilliant" and "Infomagical," as well as exercises tested for many years in classes.

You do not need to complete all of the items below, but some are highlighted as especially important and, be forewarned, likely to challenge you. A standard initial research question can be, "What patterns do I see in my social media usage?" but this broad entryway needs to be narrowed early in the proceedings: "What patterns are surprising?" "What patterns might I change and why?" "What do my patterns teach me about myself and other users?" And "how are my own and others' engagements with their phones situated more broadly in our culture"? etc. This last question asks that you step back and adapt the role of a more detached observer. In this way, you will recall that it is important to see patterns but also to reflect on their specific cultural significances. Apps or programs designed to help you to be more organized and efficient, for example, reflects the cultural value that working should be optimized (that being more organized and more efficient is a desirable social outcome). Asking why, then, will help you to move toward linking patterns and underlying assumptions to particular cultural sites.

Again, feel free to pick and choose, though we urge to select at least a week's worth of exercises, especially the ones that seem most daunting.

1. No photo day. For some of you this will be quite easy, but others might miss the chance to take a golden hour selfie.
2. Keep your phone in a bag. When you move about your daily business, rather than keep your phone in your hand or elsewhere on your body, put it in a purse or backpack when you go for a walk or undertake an errand.
3. Tidy your phone. This exercise is inspired by Marie Kondo, the Japanese decluttering guru.First, go through the apps on your phone and ask yourself "does this app bring me joy?" (That is a version of Kondo's signature philosophy). Or, just identify the apps you don't use and delete them. You can always download them again. Once you've deleted apps, make folders to put them in – health, finances, social media, etc. You likely have some already. Try to put everything into a folder, although you may wish to keep a few apps visible. Finally, move all of the folders off your home screen and on to the second page of your device's screen. Now, when you unlock your device, you will see only the home screen. Why do all of this? Well, often you may find yourself bored, simply swiping through pages of apps. This exercise will help you to pause and consider which app you really want to open. Another effective technique is to use the global search function of your phone to open the app you actually want to open, rather than look for one you might.
4. Turn off notifications for any app you don't use regularly. There's a reason notifications ping and are displayed in red. They're designed to capture your attention and to keep capturing it. The apps are designed, as mentioned above, to maximize engagement. Those notifications are part and parcel of that effort. Notifications interrupt your attention, and it is very hard to return to a task at hand after being interrupted – it takes about 25 minutes to become immersed in a task and every ping interrupts that flow and, moreover, can function to decrease your overall performance through the impact of notifications on our physiology. For those of you who might say, "yes, but I'm really good at multitasking," you are almost certainly not! Researchers have repeatedly demonstrated the myth of multi-tasking. You may try to do several things at once, but it is unlikely you are doing them as well as you otherwise might. For those applications that you keep notifications on for, consider what kind of notification you really need. Do you need to have pings and banners, for example, or can you make do with badge notifications only?
5. Make a folder labeled "TIME WASTERS" and put everything in there that drops you into the rabbit hole of scrolling, swiping, and liking. (Goodbye TikTok!).
6. Rather than using a time-wasting app on your phone, delete the app and then force yourself to use a web browser to access it. This will help you to pause when you open Twitter or TikTok. In addition, accessing some of these sites via browsers provides limited functionality, so you may not be able to use them as you normally do – a boon in many instances.
7. Do not sleep with your phone. Having your phone in bed is a bad idea, anyway, and is correlated with poorer sleep and increased anxiety. Many of you may protest, "but I use it for my alarm." You can put your phone in a dresser drawer (or across the room) – as long as it is out of arm's reach. Or simply buy an old-fashioned alarm clock.

8. Alter when you first pick up and finally put down your phone (if you do). For example, if you tend to pick up your phone when you eat breakfast, try waiting until after breakfast. Do the same in the evening, gradually moving up the last time you use it.
9. Delete your most used app for a day. This is a challenging one, especially if you are a frequent poster to social media.
10. Call someone and have a conversation with them that lasts at least 7 minutes. Texting offers a kind of buffer with which we can manage our interactions with one another. But today, call someone.
11. Go on a walk without your phone. This is likely to be one of the most anxiety-provoking exercises for you – if not *the* most. While you walk, pay attention to the environment around you, to sights and smells, as well as whatever discomfort you might feel.
12. Take a day off – *no* texts, voice memos, or TikTok challenges. Simply tell your most intimate friends in advance that you're taking a one-day tech-free vacation. If you really worry about something terrible happening – zombie apocalypse maybe? – then keep your intimate friends in your favorites. That way, if the zombies do attack, their second warning calls will still make it to you.

There are many ways you might report this project. While you could choose to keep an analog journal in the spirit of the exercises, using a social media platform would be both suitable and effective. In so doing you can both report your findings and exemplify them at the same time. One example is to create your own data visualization of your use patterns, as well as your feelings about the exercises. The designers Georgia Lupi's and Stefani Posavec's *Dear Data* archives postcard-sized hand-drawn data visualizations they exchanged for a year on a variety of topics. You can adapt their methods for your project. Choose a combination of variables, such as time spent on device, the app you used most frequently, how early you begin using your phone, or your feelings about the boot camp challenges. Then you will choose something to represent a variable. Perhaps you will choose red dots for your time spent on your phone and then vary the size for the amount of time and draw them according to a logic of your choosing. Perhaps you put all of the big circles at the bottom and the smaller ones on top of the page. Or you can chart your use over time, using an x axis to mark the duration of your exercise. In the end, you will have an image that might give you other kinds of insights into your smartphone use. It is easier than you might think. Look at some examples from their book here: http://www.dear-data.com/theproject.

Influencers

An influencer is a person who has achieved a particular degree of fame online and is thereby able, or thought to be able, to affect their followers' views and behaviors. The term "influencer" gained popularity beginning in early 2000s. In early research, scholars dubbed these people "micro-celebrities" (Senft 2013). The bonds between a person, or public, to influencers are what are called parasocial relationships. A parasocial relationship is characterized by an identification with a public figure in which a person believes their relationship to that figure to be an intimate one. However, it is nearly universally a one-sided relationship; no matter how much an influencer addresses "you," you are not really their friend, even if they like a response you may have posted about them. While this may seem an obvious point, consider whether your own relationships with influencers, if you have them, comport with this definition.

Influencers are an important part of today's Internet cultures. Most, by definition, have made some kind of niche for themselves. For example, influencers might perform forms of care and intimacy in recommending beauty routines or encourage their audience to take on activist causes. Then, too, there are influencers such as Natalie Wynn (aka ContraPoints), Kat Blaque, Oliver Thorn, and Lindsey Ellis who are best known for their video essays, carefully and often artfully constructed expositions and arguments about a vast range of topics. Wynn and Thorne, for instance, are philosophers who tackle a variety of issues, including especially controversial ones, in their videos, such as gender identity, cancel culture, and abortion. As you undertake this exercise, think not only about beauty gurus' make up routines, but their discourses about self-care, identity, and politics (Abidin 2015, 2019). The same goes, of course, for any other figure you may choose. Keep in mind too that parasocial relationships/audiences developed with influencers are also complicated by the commercialization of influence. Influencers often receive financial or other support from companies whose products they promote; others may seek to obtain their influence by paying consultants or even paying for followers.

Influencer Instructions

First, identify and follow an influencer, if you do not already. You can pick any kind of influencer – a beauty guru, a gaming expert, a famous drag queen, or a video essayist for example. Engage their content while also paying close attention to the ways that they and their users interact with one another. How often, for instance, does the person post materials, and to what degree do they respond directly to their audience? What hashtags do they use? Do they promote products and, if so, how do they integrate the promotion into their content? In what other ways do they solicit the financial support of their audiences? Are their posts political in nature? It might prove especially fruitful to pick a particularly controversial influencer. In that way, you might consider in even more detail the parasocial relationships between consumers and creators. This is an observational exercise that will help you to piece together a more holistic, if always incomplete, portrait of not just an individual influencer but the digital cultural landscape in which they are situated.

Cancel Culture

What has been dubbed "cancel culture" emerged from call out culture on Black Twitter, "the meta-network of culturally connected communities on the microblogging site" (Clark 2015). Scholars have underscored the ways such practices are rooted in Black and queer traditions of dragging and reading – think of the crushing quip that expertly dresses down an offender. Call out and cancel culture refer to phenomena in which ordinary people use social media to hold others to account, usually, but not only, public figures, for engaging in speech and behaviors deemed racist, sexist, ableist, and so on. Cancel culture's origins in Black Twitter began with efforts to hold the R&B star R. Kelly accountable for decades' worth of claims by women about their abuse at Kelly's hands: #MuteRKelly. As a loosely collective effort that responds to and assesses the behavior of others in moral terms, a key element of the phenomenon is public shaming, which can focus on individuals as well as those who enrich and empower them. Call-out and cancel culture are typically, and sometimes derogatorily, tied to the progressive left, although one finds similar techniques employed by the right.

One way to understand calling out or cancelation is to consider it a form of boycotting, although with some important differences. Take, for instance, the #MeToo movement, in which victims of sexual assault spoke out against sexual violence. Activist Tarana Burke first used the hashtag #MeToo in 2006, although it did not enter into widespread circulation until 2017. #MeToo especially shook media industries, with the disgrace of Harvey Weinstein being only one of many examples. Depending on when you might read this, you may recognize some of these high-profile cancelations. With media cultures, however, everything is dated in quick order, so here are only three. By the time you read this, many more will surely have been added to the list.

> Author J.K. Rowling – for making and defending comments widely viewed as transphobic.
>
> Talk show host Ellen Degeneres – for revelations that she had created a long-standing toxic work environment.
>
> Influencer Shane Dawson – for videos in which he made sexually inappropriate comments about then 12-year old Willow Smith, among other things.

You will notice that the above are all established, wealthy celebrities. Although they have been widely criticized and groups and individuals may withdraw their support from them, they are unlikely to lose very much, at least financially. This raises important questions about cancel culture and its relation to power and privilege. While #MeToo, to take one example, has achieved some degree of success, other efforts at cancelation are more ambiguous. The stakes are higher for those less powerful public figures, as well as everyday people, for whom cancelation might cause greater harm. And to be clear, cancelation *can* cause harm, even if we believe the cancelation warranted, as when a celebrity loses endorsements for promoting conspiracy theories or a public servant fired after it has been discovered they engaged in racist speech. There are the "Karens," too, originally referring to Black women, but now a widespread vernacular usage referring to white women also, who, among other things, seek to police the behavior of other people (usually loudly and distinctively), documented in widely circulated videos and memes. There are many examples, as well, of mistaken cancelations or of cancelations for long past behavior for which an individual has already made amends. Sometimes no apologies, however sincere, may mollify the cancelers.

Cancel Culture Instructions

In this exercise, you will select (1) an example of cancelation (or an attempt at it) and (2) representative contemporaneous discourses about the cancelation. Anthropology's holistic nature means there are a number of ways you might proceed. For example, you might focus on the specific kinds of language used or social postures players adopt when they accuse someone of wrongdoing, confess to wrongdoing, and/or apologize. If you compare your example to others, you will find common patterns. You might also choose to focus even more narrowly on one of those patterns. For instance, critiques of cancel culture frequently raise the issue of free speech, suggesting that cancel culture chills speech. Whatever you do, make sure to situate your choice historically. Who was canceled and for what? How is this event situated in relation to other cancelations? Approach this assignment like a sleuth; your anthropological perspectives will be attuned to the phenomena as emergent, as still taking shape as a cultural formation. Here is an example that might help you get started:

Jeffree Star is a makeup artist and cosmetics mogul, who has been engaged in numerous controversies and survived several cancelations. You might focus on a particular one, such as his documented use of racist slurs and his subsequent apologies. How did these instances of racist speech come to light? In what ways did he apologize, and how were the apologies received? How have the controversies impacted his stature and influence? And how does his case resemble those of others, or not?

#Activism

Since the earliest networked publics like the global discussion system Usenet's talk.politics forum, people have used the Internet's capacity to connect people across distances to create, support, and broaden activist causes. In recent years, you have undoubtedly come across various forms of online activism. The focus here is on hashtag activisms. This is a very small sampling with which you may already be familiar, along with some brief parenthetical context:

> #BlackLivesMatter
> (a wide-encompassing social justice movement that has particularly challenged police violence and the carceral state)
>
> #IdleNoMore
> (focuses on indigenous efforts to protect tribal territories from exploitation)
>
> #MeToo
> (survivors of sexual harassment and abuse share their stories, as well as challenge the widespread impunity of sexual assault)
>
> #UmbrellaRevolution
> (pro-democracy protests in Hong Kong that fought against mainland Chinese efforts to quash dissent in the island)

There are many, many more examples – too many to list here. Of paramount importance to remember at the outset is that social movements have always been networked. Those fighting for change have used whatever media technologies have been available: from pamphlets and books to community radio and the hashtag. Today's online activisms represent a historical shift, presenting fewer, or different, as we'll see shortly, barriers to political engagement and the ability to circulate one's ideas on a vast scale (Lingel 2017). Of course, the Internet, as so many scholars have shown, is not an equal playing field. In the United States, for instance, "digital divides" persist, typically most impacting communities of color and ethnic minorities, rural areas, and the poor. Elsewhere, as in mainland China, the government engages in vigorous policing of activism, including online, which is one reason the country censors its Internet (although savvy people can bypass many restrictions by using proxy services like virtual private networks and other means).

While it is clear that a hashtag like #BlackLivesMatter has served as a rallying cry and ideological anchor, it is more difficult to assess the *exact* degree to which the hashtag has shifted public discourse and policy. This is not unique to Black Lives Matter, of course. Like many cultural phenomena, it can be difficult to pin down a hashtag's social impacts with precision. Black Lives Matter is a social movement, of which the hashtag comprises only a part, so we might know about how different groups of Americans felt about the Black Lives Matter movement at different moments during 2020, but not the role the hashtag played (although critical data scientists might have more to say). What we do know, however, is that the hashtag played an important role in making the phrase "Black Lives Matter" resonate powerfully not only in the United States, but around the world and has sparked broader awareness of anti-Black racisms.

An ongoing critique of #HashtagActivisms is that they do not necessarily mobilize individuals to engage in direct political activism, whether street protests or local community organizing. The simplicity and ease of producing, liking, or retweeting hashtag politics have led to the rise of the term "slacktivism" to describe the ways hashtags and memes, among much else, do not clear the bar of doing "real politics."

#Activism Instructions

At whatever moment you may be engaging this text, there will be numerous political movements around the world using hashtags to spread awareness about them. Pick at least one. First, what social issue does the hashtag address? And how is it situated in relation to other hashtags past and present? For example, as noted above, R. Kelly's cancelation began on Black Twitter and profoundly influenced the rise and spread of #MeToo. Trace the hashtag, its first uses and by whom, and how awareness of it has spread. Work to identify as well how that awareness has effected change, or not. Anthropologists look to history, economics, and politics simultaneously. So, once more, this exercise is one centered on you working to create a complex portrait, and so is primarily observational in nature.

Further Reading

Boyd, D. (2011). White flight in networked publics? How race and class shaped American teen engagement with Myspace and Facebook. In: *Race After the Internet* (ed. L. Nakamura and P. Chow-White). Routledge.

Surowiecki, J. (2004). *The Wisdom of Crowds*. Anchor Books.

Watts, D.J. (2003). *Six Degrees: The Science of a Connected Age*. London: Vintage.

Agozzino, A. (2012). Building a personal relationship through social media: A study of millennial students' brand engagement. *Ohio Communication Journal* 50: 181–204.

Schoen, H., Gayo-Avello, D., Takis Metaxas, P., Mustafaraj, E., Strohmaier, M., Gloor, P. (2013). The power of prediction with social media. *Internet Research* 23 (5): 528–543.

Donovan, J. (2018). After the #keyword: Eliciting, sustaining, and coordinating participation across the occupy movement. *Social Media + Society* 4 (1).

For selfies in particular there is a network of researchers which can be found here: http://www.selfieresearchers.com/

Abidin, Crystal. 2019. "Yes Homo: Gay Influencers, Homonormativity, and Queerbaiting on YouTube." *Continuum* 33 (5): 614–29. https://doi.org/10.1080/10304312.2019.1644806.

—-2015. Communicative Intimacies: Influencers and Perceived Interconnectedness. *Ada*, 8, 1–16

"Algorithms in Culture: Big Data & Society." n.d. SAGE Journals. Accessed December 31, 2020. https://journals.sagepub.com/page/bds/collections/algorithms-in-culture.

Amrute, S. (2014). Proprietary freedoms in an IT office: How Indian IT workers negotiate code and cultural branding. *Social Anthropology* 22 (1): 101–17. https://doi.org/10.1111/1469-8676.12064.

Anderson, B. (1993). *Imagined Communities: Reflections on the Origin and Spread of Nationalism*. New York: Verso.

Barassi, V. (2015). *The Ethnography of Digital Activism. Activism on the Web*. Routledge. https://doi.org/10.4324/9781315870991-2.

Boellstorff, T., Maurer, B., Bell, G., Gregg, M., and Seaver, N. (2015). *Data, Now Bigger and Better!*. Prickly Paradigm Press.

Bonilla, Y. and Rosa, J. (2015). #Ferguson: Digital protest, hashtag ethnography, and the racial politics of social media in the United States: #Ferguson. *American Ethnologist* 42 (1): 4–17. https://doi.org/10.1111/amet.12112.

"Bored and Brilliant: BOOT CAMP | Note to Self." n.d. WNYC Studios. Accessed August 30, 2020. https://www.wnycstudios.org/podcasts/notetoself/episodes/bored-and-brilliant-boot-camp.

Bouvier, G. (2020). Racist call-outs and cancel culture on twitter: The limitations of the platform's ability to define issues of social justice. *Discourse, Context & Media* 38 (December): 100431. https://doi.org/10.1016/j.dcm.2020.100431.

Barassi, V. (2015). *Activism on the Web: Everyday Struggles against Digital Capitalism* 1st edition. New York: Routledge.

Brown, A.M. and Crutchfield, J. (2017). Black scholars matter: #BlkTwitterstorians building a digital community. *The Black Scholar* 47 (3): 45–55. https://doi.org/10.1080/00064246.2017.1330109.

Burton, O. (n.d.) "Black Lives Matter: A Critique of Anthropology." Society for Cultural Anthropology. Accessed December 31, 2020. https://culanth.org/fieldsights/black-lives-matter-a-critique-of-anthropology.

Cheney-Lippold, J. (2017). *We Are Data*. New York: New York University Press.

Gray, M. (2009). *Out in the Country: Youth, Media, and Queer Visibility*. New York: New York University Press.

Humphreys, L. (1999). Tearoom trade. In: *Public Sex/Gay Space* (ed. W. Leap), 29–54. New York: Columbia University Press.

Jackson, S.J., Bailey, M. (2020). Brooke Foucault Welles, and Genie Lauren. *#HashtagActivism: Networks of Race and Gender Justice*. Illustrated edition. Cambridge: The MIT Press.

Johnson, H. (2017). #NoDAPL: Social Media, Empowerment, and Civic Participation at Standing Rock. Faculty Publications, October. https://digitalcommons.lsu.edu/libraries_pubs/28.

King, T.J., Giles, D.B., Meher, M., and Gould, H. (2020). Anthropology and #MeToo: Reimagining fieldwork. *The Australian Journal of Anthropology* 31 (3): 274–87. https://doi.org/10.1111/taja.12371.

Lingel, J. (2017). *Digital Countercultures and the Struggle for Community*. Cambridge, MA: MIT Press.

Lupi, G., Posavec, S. and Popova, M. (2016). *Dear Data*. Illustrated edition. New York: Princeton Architectural Press.

Majorities Across Racial, Ethnic Groups Express Support for the Black Lives Matter Movement (2020). *Pew Research Center's Social & Demographic Trends Project* (blog). June 12, 2020. https://www.pewsocialtrends.org/2020/06/12/amid-protests-majorities-across-racial-and-ethnic-groups-express-support-for-the-black-lives-matter-movement/.

McGlotten, S. (2013). *Virtual Intimacies: Media, Affect, and Queer Sociality*. Albany: SUNY Press.

Pipyrou, S. (2018). #MeToo Is Little More than Mob Rule // vs // #MeToo Is a Legitimate Form of Social Justice. *HAU: Journal of Ethnographic Theory* 8 (3): 415–19. https://doi.org/10.1086/701007.

Seaver, N. (2017). Algorithms as culture: Some tactics for the ethnography of algorithmic systems. *Big Data & Society* 4 (2): 2053951717738104. https://doi.org/10.1177/2053951717738104.

Senft, T. (2013). Microcelebrity and the branded self. In: *A Companion to New Media Dynamics* (ed. J. Hartley, J. Burgess, and A. Bruns), 346–54. Malden, MA: Blackwell.

Warner, M. (2002). Publics and Counterpublics. *Public Culture* 14 (1): 49–89.

Williams, R. (2003). *Television: Technology and Cultural Form*. New York: Routledge. https://www.routledge.com/Television-Technology-and-Cultural-Form/Williams/p/book/9780415314565.

Williams, B. (2013). *Virtual Ethnography*. Oxford University Press. https://doi.org/10.1093/obo/9780199766567-0107.

18

Digital Ethnography (2) Online Gaming

This project is a digital version of participant observation involving Massively Multiplayer Online Role-Playing Games (MMORPG). MMORPGs involve the creation of a cultural space in the digital world that is quite separate from the everyday world. Participants can craft a persona that is unlike their own, they can perform actions that they cannot do in daily life (such as killing enemies), and they can repeat actions, or start again, when one approach fails. Your task is to document the social world of the gamer, and to note how the digital world differs from the everyday.

Learning Goals

1. *Experiment with participant observation in a virtual world.*
2. *Understand the social dynamics of online gamers.*

This project is another participant-observation exercise, but this time your "event" will involve a Massively Multiplayer Online Role-Playing Game (MMORPG). There are many possibilities, but there are two hard-and-fast rules. First, the group must be new to you. If you play *World of Warcraft* every waking moment when you are not in class, then it is off limits (much like the participant-observer provisions in Chapter 9). Second, there has to be a genuinely socially interactive component to the platform. MMORPGs could be a problem depending on which you pick.

Currently there are numerous games to choose from. The most popular are:

World of Warcraft
Eve
Final Fantasy XIV
Rift
Blade and Soul
Trove
Runescape
Star Trek Online
Albion Online
Lord of the Rings Online
Star Wars: The Old Republic

Doing Field Projects: Methods and Practice for Social and Anthropological Research, First Edition.
John Forrest.
© 2022 John Wiley & Sons, Inc. Published 2022 by John Wiley & Sons, Inc.

Archeage
Guild Wars 2
Neverwinter

Most of these are pay-to-play games, but some are free, and most have free introductions.

MMORPG communities have developed their own sub-cultures with unique slang and metaphors, as well as an unwritten list of social rules and taboos. Social rules exist for such things as invitations to join an adventuring party, the proper division of treasure, and how a player is expected to behave while grouped with other players. An MMORPG's rules might be different from others. As such MMORPG cultures can be investigated using suitably adjusted participant-observation. While it may be reasonable to compare participant-observation online to roughly equivalent events offline, and to thereby follow analogous guidelines for research, online research does present challenges. You might consider some spaces in an MMORPG, such as a marketplace, to be akin to Sunday services in a giant cathedral or attendance at the Olympic Games where no informed consent is required because the "event" is open to all comers and is public. However, ethnographers of digital spaces, among others, have pointed to the complex ways that categories of public/private are constructed in online "town squares." A marketplace in *World of Warcraft* or a public chat channel where anyone can contribute at any time may differ from what you discuss in a private chatroom with fellow adventurers while adventuring. In any case, your participant observation should help you to learn the norms and conventions of whatever game you have chosen. When in doubt, let your fellow gamers know that you are undertaking research and why, and acquire their consent to record or otherwise document their experiences. Finally, you should examine the Terms and Conditions of any group before you subscribe (the screen you usually click "I Agree" on without actually reading what you are agreeing to). Make sure that participation for research purposes is allowed.

Instructions

Decide what game you want to be involved in. Many of them allow you to create your own persona online, and these have considerable potential for research. You should, however, familiarize yourself with sociological research that has been done already, and there are a few suggestions at the end of the chapter. Nick Yee's Daedalus Project is online and will give you plenty of ideas for research questions particularly when it comes to online personas.

Alongside the issue of the game you choose is the issue of which technological interface you choose to go online with. There is clearly a fundamental difference between playing an MMORPG on a smartphone and playing on a desktop with a 30-inch flat-screen monitor and surround sound. You can experiment with different interfaces (if you have the technology) and see which one you like the best, and/or which one suits the platform best. (This issue is covered more fully in Chapter 19 (HCI), where you are freer to deal with applications you are familiar with.)

Your research question (as always) has to be your guide. Many questions have been asked and answered by researchers: Why do people become addicted to online gaming? Why do people choose online personas that differ from their personas in the physical world? What roles do race or gender identity, among others, play in online interaction? If you look online through the kinds of questions that have been asked before, you will be able to avoid the most obvious and build on the work of others. Try to take a "meta" tack in thinking about those asked-and-answered-questions. For example, you might consider how specific discourses that frame extended game play as addiction emerged and gained traction, or the ways changing real-world politics appear in games. In other words, what might it mean to ask how "addiction" functions as a cultural shorthand for behaviors that do not match up with normative ideas about what is play and what is work? Or, you may come across statistics that tell you that 51% of "women" playing an MMORPG, as expressed in their avatars, are controlled by men, but what does that survey actually say about gender in the game? Does it matter, and if so, how so, that a cisgender man is playing an Orc priestess? What about a non-binary person playing a female paladin? Lean into the nooks of those asked and answered questions, and you will find fruitful space for yet more questions.

The project can be enormously time-consuming and you will have time constraints of your own to be concerned about. You have to set yourself limited goals that can be accomplished in the time you have available. With all of the above in mind, choose your platform and your research question. Although time can be your enemy in this exercise, it can also be your friend. Unlike many other projects in which you have to search for a person to work with or an event, and then take the time to visit and document, you can start on this project immediately, and you can work on it when you have time during the day

The first part of your presentation of this project should be an explanation as to why you chose a particular platform, what your research question was, and any useful preliminary information, including what your reader needs to know about the platform to understand what it entails. The second part, the presentation of data, needs careful thought. The data must be digested in some fashion. If you have sat at the keyboard for several hours per day for a solid week participating in a game, you may have a mountain of data that is generally illustrative of your methods and/or that directly addresses your research question but needs to be digested. Part three summarizes your findings and draws conclusions based on your research question. One creative way you might present your research is as a short video documenting highlights from your game play—in the past such films were called machinima (machine + cinema), though now you are much more likely to find walkthrough and "flex" videos in which creators guide other users through the game and show off their own skills. Perhaps you could create a walk-through guide that explores not only how to play the game to newcomers (or "noobs") but why this play matters anthropologically.

Further Reading

To get some idea of the possibilities of this project you can look at Nick Yee's "An Ethnography of MMORPG Weddings" on *The Daedalus Project*, www.nickyee.com/daedalus/archives/000467.php. www.nickyee.com/daedalus/archives/000467.php

There's also Griffiths, M. and Hussain, Z. (2008). Gender swapping and socialising in cyberspace: An exploratory study. *CyberPsychology and Behavior* 11: 47–53 and two books by Turkle, S. (2009). *Simulation and its Discontents*. MIT Press, and *Alone Together*, Basic Books (2011).

Nicholas, M.J. (2011). *The Reality of Friendship Within Immersive Virtual Worlds*. Springer Science+Business Media.

Schroeder, R. and Axelsson, A. (2006). The psychology of MMORPGs: Emotional investment, motivations, relationship formation, and problematic usage. In: *Avatars at Work and Play: Collaboration and Interaction in Shared Virtual Environments*. London: Springer-Verlag.

Castronova, E. (2006). *Synthetic Worlds: The Business and Culture of Online Games*. University Of Chicago Press.

Jøn, A.A. (2010). The development of MMORPG culture and the guild. *Australian Folklore: A Yearly Journal of Folklore Studies* 25: 97–112.

Dyer-Witheford, N. and de Peuter, G. (2009). *Games of Empire: Global Capitalism and Video Games*. University of Minnesota Press.

Jenkins, H. (2004). Game Design as Narrative Architecture. In: *First Person: New Media as Story, Performance, and Game*, 118–30. MIT Press.

Gray, K.L. (2012). Deviant bodies, stigmatized identities, and racist acts: examining the experiences of African-American gamers in Xbox Live. *New Review of Hypermedia and Multimedia* 18 (4): 261–276.

(2018). Gaming out online: Black lesbian identity development and community building in Xbox Live. *Journal of Lesbian Studies* 22 (3). https://www.tandfonline.com/doi/abs/10.1080/10894160.2018.1384293?journalCode=wjls20& https://www.tandfonline.com/doi/abs/10.1080/10894160.2018.1384293?journalCode=wjls20&

Taylor, T.L. (2006). *Play Between Worlds: Exploring Online Game Culture*. MIT.

Boellstorff, T., Nardi, B., Pearce, C., and Taylor, T.L. (2012). *Ethnography and Virtual Worlds: A Handbook of Method*. Princeton University Press.

Boellstorff, T. (2015). *Coming of Age in Second Life: An Anthropologist Explores the Virtually Human*. Princeton University Press.

McGlotten, S. (2012). Breaching barriers between work and play. In: *Fantasy media in the classroom: Essays on teaching with film, television, literature, and video games* (ed. E. Dial-Driver, S. Emmons, and J. Ford), 123–137. Jefferson, NC: McFarland Press.

Nardi, B.A. (2010). *My Life as a Night Elf Priest. An Anthropological Account of World of Warcraft*. Ann Arbor: University of Michigan Press.

Sundén, J. and Sveningsson, M. (2012). *Gender and Sexuality in Online Game Cultures: Passionate Play* (1st ed.) New York: Routledge.

19

Digital Ethnography (3) Human–Computer Interaction

This project investigates the ways in which people interact with digital technology in general (keyboards, touchpads, headsets, etc.), and the ways in which this type of interaction differs from person-to-person interaction. There is also the possibility of exploring specialized interfaces, particularly virtual and augmented reality systems. You may also examine the ways in which computer interfaces encourage human errors.

Learning Goals

1. *Understand the ways in which human interactions with computer technologies affect individual and group behavior.*
2. *Explore the potential benefits and harm in human–computer interface.*

According to the broadest anthropological definition of "technology," the words "tools" and "technology" are synonyms. Our tools enhance our physical capacities. Bicycles and cars allow us to go farther and faster than our legs allow us; telephones and radios project our voices over greater distances than we can accomplish by shouting; telescopes and microscopes let us view objects that our eyes alone cannot see clearly; computers store our memories and expand our minds. The transformation of our technology over time has played a powerful role in the transformation of our species, to such a degree that it is impossible to separate tool from human.

It is important, however, as Raymond Williams (2003 [1974]) argued, to avoid deterministic perspectives about the relationship between technology and society; technologies do not necessarily drive social changes, nor do they simply appear as symptoms of them. Technologies emerge, or not, as the result of a complex set of historical, economic, political, and cultural factors. A technology might be stumbled upon as an accidental discovery, but none will develop in a vacuum. As the example of Charles Babbage's work suggests, just because something can be built does not mean that it will be built. In the early nineteenth century, Babbage invented his Difference Engine, the first modern computer. However, due to lack of funding, he never completed it. Babbage was largely forgotten, his work unfamiliar to the computer scientists and engineers who pioneered modern computing after the end of the Second World War. After his rediscovery, the Science Museum in London completed a working model of his machine, using only nineteenth-century materials and methods. Again, this is to say that Babbage's computer *could* have been built a hundred years before the first modern computers, but it wasn't – technology does not "evolve" in a linear fashion.

Human–Computer Interaction (HCI) is a complex field of research where qualitative field research can play a part. In this project this interaction can be broken into two distinct areas of analysis. First is the human–computer interface. This is the physical component of HCI – the actual technology, such as keyboards, touchpads, and controllers, that allows interaction between humans and computers. Second is the human–computer interface in which the relationship between a computer and a person, or many computers and many people, becomes entangled to such a degree that it may be hard to tell where one begins and the other ends. Conjure up these familiar images: a person, perhaps yourself, is curled up around their phone on the couch, while another stares intently at a computer screen, eyes reflecting the light of the device, unable to hear you speaking to them. Where is the line between person and computer?

One straightforward way to approach this fieldwork project is to consider observing people using different interfaces. Bear in mind that all of the peripherals of the computer's central processing unit (CPU) are interfaces – and by "computer" is meant not only desktop or notebook computers, but smartphones, gaming consoles, wearables, and smart home devices. From a human standpoint, these interfaces include both input and output devices. You may relay your needs to the CPU via a keyboard, touchpad, controller device, microphone, or mouse, and the CPU replies to you via a monitor, speakers, haptic feedback, printers, and much more. Think of your interaction with a computer as analogous to interacting with another human – but also radically different. You have your senses, such as sight and hearing, for input, a brain to process the input, and a voice, face, and limbs to provide output. Your interaction with another person is going to be influenced by how that other person receives and responds to your input. Because computers and humans have different ways of getting input and providing output, their interaction with one another is not like the interaction between two humans.

There was a time when computer input was all handled by punch cards and output by line printers. This method made HCI very slow and cumbersome. When keyboards replaced punch cards, and monitors replaced line printers, things not only moved faster, there was more that the human–computer interface could accomplish – *together*.

For example, back in 1970, when mainframe computers used punch cards and line printers, John Conway invented the *Game of Life* for computers (Gardner 1970). If you have not come across *Life* before you can find numerous apps online to play it, such as https://curlie.org/Computers/Artificial_Life/Cellular_Automata/Conway%27s_Game_of_Life. When the game was played in the 1970s, the generation of the output was slow and laborious (turnaround times sometimes being hours), and input required considerable programming skills, the availability of a punch card machine, and access to a mainframe computer. The game was, therefore, an arcane pastime for the privileged few. Now, with the ability to use a touchpad for input and a monitor for output, plus fast processing times, the entire nature of the game has become both streamlined and democratized. Herein lies one avenue of investigation for your project. How does the input/output technology in use influence the personal and social dimensions of computing? This path could involve observation of users' actions and behaviors, or more technical questions such as the ease of usage and the development of User Experience (UX). It might also involve interview questions concerning users' own understanding regarding their interactions with an interface or device. As such, the project can involve elements of previous projects, including proxemics, participant observation, process analysis, interviews, and performance. (The smartphone boot camp in chapter 17 might also prove useful for reference.)

You may also choose to investigate failures in HCI, which can have disastrous consequences, as in the case of the Three Mile Island disaster (Rogovin 1980). It is extremely easy to put trust in a computer's output without questioning its validity or accuracy because of (sometimes unwarranted) trust in the computer's abilities, the belief that a computer is not influenced by human foibles such as emotions or the capacity to deceive (or forget), and so an element of trust is warranted. But computers may fail in other ways: hardware and software. For two decades, for instance, a wide array of researchers has increasingly considered the disparate social impacts of technologies, including the ways human biases can be encoded into hardware and software. To provide one of many examples: facial recognition software performs incredibly well -- for white men with much higher error rates for women and people of color (Benjamin 2020, Buolamwini and Gebru 2018).

Instructions

An HCI fieldwork project is neither easy to conceive nor to execute, even though you may have considerable experience with digital technology, because the technology is changing all the time, and there are so many different facets to HCI. Bear in mind that this project does not concern the use of computers for social interactions. That topic is covered in the Social Media project (Chapter 17). Here we are concerned with the direct interactions between humans and computers themselves and is, therefore, inherently autoethnographic or reflexive. Your first decision will be what kind of computer interface you want to focus on: input/output for desktops, laptops, tablets, smartphones, or some other dedicated technology. Within that decision there are other factors to consider given the range of peripherals available, including voice activation and communication, webcams, virtual reality, handheld devices, keyboards, touchpads, etc. Therefore, the initial question to resolve must be which interface you want to study. This decision narrows down the next questions which concern what kind of human–computer interactions you wish to concentrate on. The following are sample suggestions for projects.

Virtual Reality and Augmented Reality

Virtual reality and augmented reality computer systems are related, but distinct, concepts. In a virtual reality environment, the user's senses, especially sight and sound, are completely taken over by the hardware and software so that all the user's experiences are computer generated. In an augmented reality environment, some of the user's sensory experiences are computer generated and some of them are natural. Using augmented reality, a user can go through a natural environment and overlay components that are not real. You could, for example, walk through a building fitted with special goggles that allow you to see the real walls, floors, and ceilings, but you can add items to those components through virtual imaging. So, you could change the colors of the walls, hang paintings or curtains, and add furniture of your choice.

For this project you can select either virtual reality or augmented reality as your focus. Either way, the project is an excellent opportunity to experiment with autoethnography via participant observation (see Chapter 9). One way or another, you will have to have the actual experience of virtual or augmented reality to be able to understand what they can accomplish and what the experience is like. The simplest exercise would be to find a place offering a virtual reality experience and sign up for it. Take part in the experience and document it. This kind of project would be autoethnographic because you are the sole participant and sole observer, so you would be documenting the event as *you* experienced it. It might be possible to get a digital recording of the experience; otherwise, you will have to rely on the same methods used in a conventional participant-observer procedure (Chapter 9).

If you are able to find someone to help you with augmented reality, the project can combine some of the aspects of the process project (Chapter 11) with participant observation. You might work with a realtor, perhaps, who has some ability to use augmented reality. Or, as with the virtual reality project, you may decide to experiment on your own. There are, for example, augmented reality GPS apps known as heads-up displays (HUD), that display projected information concerning directions, speed, warnings, etc. directly on to your windshield so that you can still see the road, but it is overlaid with the information you need to navigate safely (https://www.youtube.com/watch?v=KWs9ucwO4Vo). The question you might consider in this case is whether augmented reality while driving provides you with too much information, and whether or not this information is helpful or distracting. Finally, many social media applications include augmented reality filters you can use while taking photos or videos. When in doubt, there is always https://www.youtube.com/watch?v=KWs9ucwO4Vo *Pokémon Go!*

Other Human-Computer Interactions

There are numerous other domains of HCI research that are detailed here: https://en.wikipedia.org/wiki/Human%E2%80%93computer_interaction. Affective or emotional computing, for example, is being developed for several practical purposes. One is research into ways that computers can detect, and respond to, emotions in users using various visual, auditory, and other bodily stimuli. Another is the development of computers that can project human emotions in their output. Then there is the developing field of brain–computer interfaces (BCI). These and other areas of HCI could be fruitful areas for qualitative research, if you have the available resources.

Because an HCI project has numerous possibilities, the way that you present it is highly variable. If you have approached it using the project as an observer or as a participant will influence the kind of data you have, as will a process approach versus a participant-observer approach. Likewise, your initial research question is going to be highly specific to the HCI you select. Nonetheless, at some level you should be asking about the strengths and weaknesses of the interface, what influences it has on the process you are investigating, and how it could be improved. The degree to which a fieldworker is able to participate and/or observe HCI experiences is determined by the nature of the experience, as already noted. Adding your thoughts on this side of the project is also important.

Further Reading

Literature on HCI is surprisingly old (and deep), because mainframes were being used in research and business long before the age of the personal computer. If you investigate further you will discover that specifically ethnographic fieldwork studies are not in the forefront. As early as 1976 James Carlisle was interested in how the use of computers was affecting top management decisions (*"Evaluating the impact of office automation on top management communication"*), and in 1983 Stuart K. Card, Allen Newell, and Thomas P. Moran produced *The Psychology of Human–Computer Interaction*. Since then the field of HCI has been flooded with studies such as the following which tend to straddle all of the social sciences. See if anything is of interest or sparks an idea:

Friedman, B., Kahn, Jr., P.H., and Borning, A. (2006). *Value Sensitive Design and information systems. Human–Computer Interaction and Management Information Systems: Foundations*. https://vsdesign.org/publications/pdf/non-scan-vsd-and-information-systems.pdf https://vsdesign.org/publications/pdf/non-scan-vsd-and-information-systems.pdf

Wickens, C.D., Lee, J.D., Liu, Y., and Gordon Becker, S.E. (2004). *An Introduction to Human Factors Engineering* 2nd ed. Upper Saddle River, NJ: Pearson, Prentice Hall.

C. Marlin Brown, *Human–Computer Interface Design Guidelines*. Intellect Books, 1998. 2–3.

Posard, M. (2014). Status processes in human–computer interactions: Does gender matter? *Computers in Human Behavior* 37: 189–195.

Posard, M. and Gordon Rinderknecht, R. (2015). Do people like working with computers more than human beings? *Computers in Human Behavior* 51: 232–238.

Grudin, J. (2007). A moving target: The evolution of human–computer interaction. In: *Human–Computer Interaction Handbook* (2nd Edition) (ed. A. Sears and J.A. Jacko). CRC Press. (2007).

Myers, B. (1998). A brief history of human–computer interaction technology. *Interactions* 5 (2): 44–54.

Carroll, J.M. Human Computer Interaction: History and Status. Encyclopedia Entry at Interaction-Design.org

Carroll, J.M. (2010). Conceptualizing a possible discipline of human–computer interaction. *Interacting with Computers* 22 (1): 3–12.

Sara Candeias, S. and Veiga, A. The dialogue between man and machine: The role of language theory and technology. In: *New Language Technologies and Linguistic Research, A Two-Way Road* (ed. S.M. Aluísio and S.E.O. Tagnin). Cambridge Scholars Publishing.

More specifically social scientific analyses of HCI include:

Nass, C., Fogg, B.J., and Moon, Y. (1996). Can computers be teammates? *International Journal of Human-Computer Studies* 45 (6): 669–678.

Nass, C. and Moon, Y. (2000). Machines and mindlessness: Social responses to computers *Journal of Social Issues* 56 (1): 81–103.

Posard, M.N. (2014). Status processes in human–computer interactions: Does gender matter? *Computers in Human Behavior* 37: 189–195.

Alper, M. (2017). Chapter 5 "Augmenting Communication with New Media and Popular Culture: What Does It Mean to Communicate with an iPad?" From Giving Voice: Mobile Communication, *Disability*, and Inequality. Cambridge, MA: MIT Press.

Benjamin, Ruha. 2020. *Race After Technology*. Medford, MA: Polity. https://inforrm.org/2020/03/01/facial-recognition-is-spreading-faster-than-you-realise-garfield-benjamin/

Buolamwini, J. and Gebru, T. (2018). Gender Shades: Intersectional Accuracy Disparities in Commercial Gender Classification. In Conference on Fairness, Accountability and Transparency, 77–91. PMLR. http://proceedings.mlr.press/v81/buolamwini18a.html.

20

Digital Ethnography (4) Online Meetings/Classes

This project is another digital participant-observation exercise, this time involving the various apps used in meetings and teaching. Use of online apps for meetings and classes has been available for many years both because they can be time and money savers for businesses, and because they can expand the reach of teachers and other professionals. With the arrival of COVID-19, these applications have become enormously widespread. Here you have the opportunity to examine the advantages and disadvantages of using digital media in comparison with face-to-face meetings.

Learning Goals

1. *Examine and critique multiple methods of conducting meetings and classes online.*
2. *Use participant-observation to document online meetings and/or classes.*

The use of digital technology to facilitate meetings has been around in one form or another for quite some time. It is expensive and time-consuming to have executives of multinational corporations fly country to country to meet to discuss business, not to mention the problems associated with jet lag, staying in hotels, and the thousand different ways in which such gatherings are inconvenient for all involved. Similarly, having shortlist candidates for a job fly to a conference center for an hour for a preliminary interview is a waste of time and resources for all involved when an online meeting could do the same job as, or more, efficiently. Even before the internet was routinely available to the general public, businesses were finding ways to conduct meetings online in one fashion or other.

Online teaching has also been a growing phenomenon for many years. For most of the twenty-first century, universities and colleges have been expanding their offerings via the internet to satisfy an ever-growing body of students who, for one reason or another, cannot or do not wish to attend classes in person, but who can plug into online classes. For over 50 years, higher education has been offered in a variety of ways to people who have full-time jobs and, therefore, do not have the flexibility to attend lectures and classes to advance their education, but do have time on evenings and weekends to participate. Then, too, there are many who have been de facto excluded from attending brick-and-mortar institutions, such as people with disabilities.

Doing Field Projects: Methods and Practice for Social and Anthropological Research, First Edition.
John Forrest.
© 2022 John Wiley & Sons, Inc. Published 2022 by John Wiley & Sons, Inc.

The UK's Open University (O.U.), founded in 1969, began its distance learning opportunities using primarily television and radio lectures and demonstrations with some in-person work as needed. The O.U. was able to switch much of this in-person teaching to online services, slowly, as increasing numbers of people had access to personal computers and the internet. The O.U.'s contemporary descendants are local community college's all online programs, as well as massive open online course providers (MOOCs) like Coursera or the Khan Academy. Many public libraries in the United States also provide access to learning platforms such as LinkedIn Learning that feature courses on hundreds of topics, from video editing to how to set up a music business.

There has also been a surge in interest over the past decade or so in using the internet for large-scale academic conferences via webinars and other online resources, making it possible for scholars from around the world to meet and exchange ideas without leaving their homes. These were starting to increase in popularity before the COVID-19 pandemic, but since the outbreak they have expanded their reach and influence considerably. The pandemic has, likewise, filled an increasing need to offer instruction online for schools and universities that cannot provide in-person instruction. In turn, educational software has grown to meet the need, and there are a number of apps available now for teachers, such as:

EasyClass https://www.easyclass.com/#
Google Classroom https://classroom.google.com/
Vedamo https://www.vedamo.com/
Showbie https://www.showbie.com/
ClassDojo https://www.classdojo.com/
Educreations https://www.educreations.com/

There are also plain meeting/webinar apps such as:

Zoom https://zoom.us/
Connectwise Control https://www.connectwise.com/software/control
Blue Jeans https://www.bluejeans.com/mobile
Webex Meetings https://www.webex.com/
Team Viewer https://www.teamviewer.com/en/
Go To Meeting https://www.gotomeeting.com/
Google Meet https://meet.google.com/

These apps are gaining ground all the time, yet the nagging question that hovers over their use concerns how to use them in such a way they can approach the feeling of intimacy and connectedness of in-person meetings. When international buyers and sellers meet in person, for example, they do not only sit around a table and negotiate deals. They also go out to drink and have dinner together and, in so doing, cement personal bonds. Likewise, when large groups of people meet to watch a political rally or football game, there is a collective energy developed by participation together that is absent in distance broadcasting. It is more difficult for these kinds of collective experiences of belonging to group encounters to happen online, although not impossible, as the rise of Zoom happy hours or dance break lunches during the pandemic attests.

On the other side of the coin, online meetings can achieve a number of things that in-person ones cannot. For example, I am deaf in one ear and hard of hearing in the other. I cannot easily understand what a person is saying unless I can see their mouth moving and they are speaking loudly and distinctly. In large in-person meetings this problem is a considerable nuisance. I often have to ask the person sitting next to me to repeat something a speaker has said. With an online meeting I have no such difficulty. I have ear buds or headphones that amplify voices sufficiently and I can see a speaker's mouth most of the time. The same kind of compensation can equally apply with people whose eyesight or mobility is challenged.

In this project one of your tasks is to consider the forms of intimacy online spaces afford and produce, and how these intimacies are distinguished from those in real-world spaces. As elsewhere, comparing online and offline meetings will be fruitful; however, it is additionally useful to take those observations as a platform for thinking deeply about what it is we mean by "intimacy." Does it refer to being intimate with others, with a nation, with oneself? Is it about feeling connected or a sense of belonging? Is it about familiarity? Intimacy is not a taken-for-granted pre-cultural thing – what it describes has been shaped by history, and it is being made and remade all of the time. Thus, we should say that there is no one intimacy, but *intimacies*. A comic example will serve: casual Fridays aside, in most business contexts, there are norms of professional dress and comportment. During the pandemic, however, these norms governing degrees of intimacy between employees and supervisors began to break down. Cats jumping on computers and children with tantrums can be equalizers.

Instructions

This project is a participant-observer exercise, but before you get started with a specific research question, you should familiarize yourself with some of the apps listed here (as well as any others that you come across). Your university or school may have its own version of meeting software, for example, and you should try that out as well. Maybe during the pandemic you took classes online, or maybe you are taking some now. Or maybe you have experience with social meetings or webinars. Whatever your platform and experience, your twin opening research questions are:

- What are the affordances of online classes vs. in person meetings?
- What sorts of intimacies can be cultivated online, offline, and at their intersections?

Online classes and meetings also suggest specific questions. For example, "How does whether your face is always visible to all the other members of the class affect how you participate?" "Where is your focus typically?" Digital ethnography is a perfect opportunity for you to experiment with reflexive anthropology. That is, you observe outward but you also search inward, and report on both (see Chapter 21 for more details).

A crucial question that should hover over any online research is: "How does a machine interface alter, enhance, or limit interaction with others?" This question has been analyzed by sociologists and psychologists, but in this project you are raising the question reflexively: that is, "How does a machine interface alter *your* modes of interaction?" This need not be your main research question, but it needs to be in the mix somewhere. Human–computer interface is the topic of a separate exercise (Chapter 19).

I am not a big fan of online teaching, but for several years our university's administration encouraged us to design and teach at least one seminar per semester online, with students being able to sign into class from across the United States. The platform's basic setup was reasonably standard: a screen with individual windows showing the head and shoulders of each of the participants on webcams. I controlled the windows, and could make mine, or that of any of the participants, full screen at any time I wished, or I could enlarge one window and make all the others proportionally smaller. I chose to keep all the windows the same size throughout the seminar because I like to see my students' faces when I am talking to them so that I can gauge their reactions. My method was the digital equivalent of sitting in a circle. I felt that when teaching online, students seemed to rarely get distracted. Maybe having a webcam trained at your face, and having your image beamed back at you, creates a degree of self-consciousness that simply sitting in a classroom lacks. Or, it could mean that you have to develop the skills necessary to appear to be paying attention when you are not, so that no one will notice.

Some students and teachers had not participated in online teaching prior to the pandemic. Their experiences with teaching remotely differed significantly from mine and from each others'. In many cases students do not keep their cameras on. While it might be tempting to view this as an excuse for students to multitask or zone out, other factors can be at play too. Many students, for example, lack the necessary equipment like a working camera or a stable internet connection. The pandemic worsened already existing disparities like these; even students from previously financially stable households found themselves without an internet connection due to a caretaker's job loss. Then, too, there was "Zoom fatigue." Looking at screens all day, much less performing for the camera with the self-consciousness touched on above, proves exhausting mentally and physiologically.

Consequences of the pandemic will include new relationships with online meetings, like new norms (athleisure wear) or etiquettes ("can everyone keep themselves muted, please?"), and they will also include practices that respond to the wearing down that comes with these kinds of virtual intimacies, like Zoom disco parties or remote reiki.

You may have the opportunity to interview fellow participants online if you like, same as with in-person participant-observation, but standard rules apply. You need to get informed consent before proceeding, spelling out who you are and what the interview will be used for.

There are numerous ways to present your findings, but for all the digital projects it makes sense to use the technology that you have been exploring. You could, for example, set up a webinar and, in part, show your findings by example, as well as playing clips and projecting other materials you have collected. You might also make suggestions, based on your observations, for the ways in which online technology could be exploited better. Rather than thinking of an online class or meeting as being little more than a teacher and students doing much the same things as they do in a regular class, you could experiment with new ways to present materials, hold discussions, and so forth. Thus, you could demonstrate your findings by holding an experimental class in the format that tests your ideas. This is your opportunity to be creative. The key question to be answered is how the anthropological theory you have learned, and your experience with other fieldwork projects, add a dimension to your analysis beyond what can be learned through observations that anyone could make. How does online participant-observation differ from in-person fieldwork, for example? Does it differ? And how might these differences matter for an anthropologist's inevitably intimate entanglements with their informants and field sites?

Further Reading

There are not many resources that deal specifically with the *ethnography* of online meetings and classrooms, and many of the relevant studies are dated. There is, however, a growing body of educational investigations concerning online teaching, and the following is a sampling:

Cook, K.C. and Grant-Davie, K. (eds). (2005). *Online Education: Global Questions, Local Answers*. Baywood Publishing.

Wilcox, K.E., Sarma, S., and Lippel, P.H. (2016). *Online Education: A Catalyst for Higher Education Reforms*. MIT Online Education Policy Initiative.

Fraser, K. (2014). *The Future of Learning and Teaching in Next Generation Learning Spaces*. Emerald Group Publishing.

Hew, K.F. and Cheung, W.S. (2012). *Student Participation in Online Discussions: Challenges, Solutions, and Future Research*. Springer.

Lai, K.W. and Hong, K.S. (2015). Technology use and learning characteristics of students in higher education: Do generational differences exist? *British Journal of Educational Technology* 46 (4): 725–738.

Ito, M., Baumer, S., Bittanti, M., Boyd, D., and Cody, R. (2009). *Hanging Out, Messing Around, and Geeking Out: Kids Living and Learning with New Media*. MIT Press.

Livingstone, S. and Sefton-Green, J. (2016). *The Class: Living and Learning in the Digital Age*. NYU Press. https://www.jstor.org/stable/j.ctt18040ft

21

Winding Down and Gearing Up

Now that you have completed the projects here – or some of them at least – it is time to look back and reflect on what you have learned, as well as consider the path forward. You are ethically required to keep copies of all your field notes and findings in a safe place, so now is a good time to make sure that everything that you have recorded in the course of these projects is carefully indexed, filed, and stored permanently in a safe place, such as a thumb drive, cloud storage, or, preferably, both. Redundancy is a wise precaution. You may think of these projects as beginners' exercises with limited merit; however, they do have value beyond their pedagogical objectives. If you worked individually with an interviewee, be sure to provide a copy of your final report or presentation to them as well.

Recall that there are major differences in the projects in this book and experiments that you have to perform for an introductory lab section in biology or chemistry or physics. The "experiments" in an introductory physics lab are not designed to help you overturn Newton's laws of motion or optics. You perform them to confirm Newton (or Maxwell or whomever), and you use Newton's formulas to calculate results. If your results do not confirm Newton, you have done something wrong and you have to conduct the experiment again until you get it right. Newton's laws are foundational, even though they have undergone radical modification over several hundred years. Anthropological research is a horse of a very different color.

There are many reasons that the fieldwork projects you completed in this book do not replicate lab experiments in the physical sciences. For one thing, anthropology does not have a series of laws (or theories) that are considered foundational. There are some reasonably solid guiding principles, but even these norms are repeatedly contested. Second, anthropological fieldwork at the beginner stage, while under the (distant) supervision of an instructor, is usually conducted alone. Student fieldworkers do not have a lab assistant at hand to help when things go wrong, or when they have questions in the middle of a project. You need a level of self-confidence and self-awareness to guide you through rough patches. Third, and most important, every project in this book has the potential to produce new and interesting data. That is not to say that you necessarily did produce such data, but field projects certainly have that capacity. This is not the case when you drop zinc into hydrochloric acid. If you do not get hydrogen gas and zinc chloride as a result, you did something wrong. The results are predictable, and the experiment is designed to show you what is already known about chemical displacement. Fieldwork is always a leap into the unknown. For this reason

Doing Field Projects: Methods and Practice for Social and Anthropological Research, First Edition.
John Forrest.
© 2022 John Wiley & Sons, Inc. Published 2022 by John Wiley & Sons, Inc.

alone you must preserve your field notes. You should also return to them periodically. As you develop intellectually, you will see new things in what you have recorded.

For the moment, your first step should be to take out your Self-Study and examine it carefully. How would you write it differently now? Was it a fair assessment of your abilities given your subsequent fieldwork experiences? Did you learn anything new about yourself by doing fieldwork? You might also consider doing the seven-day observational study again (pp. 40–43) to see if your skills have improved. Fieldwork is always a two-way street: you learn something about others, and you also learn something about yourself. It should be clear now that we cannot have anything even approximating objective fieldwork. What we can do is interpret data in the context of who the fieldworker is, rather than be swallowed up in a black hole of postmodern nihilism. There are things we cannot know, but there are things we can get closer and closer to knowing by developing better methods of observation and self-analysis.

You should revisit all of your projects and maybe even rework some of them. As a concluding project you might reflect on which ones were your favorites, and why, and which were your least favorite and why. By doing so you will grow in your understanding of fieldwork in general, and also develop an increasing awareness of what you can contribute to anthropology. Assessing yourself in this way is also a good step on the way to considering what is next for you. Maybe a senior thesis or extended project that requires fieldwork? Would you like to pursue graduate study in anthropology later? If so, training and experience in fieldwork will become much more intense. The training offered here is a good foundation for that work, but it is just a start. Most of my students did not become professional fieldworkers (4 out of approximately 3000), but a great many of them took fieldwork methods with them into their training as social workers, doctors, clinical psychologists, chefs, architects, lawyers, and ... you name it.

One thing that worries me deeply is the growing mountain of data in anthropology as the profession turns out more and more ethnographers. Morally, we must ask the questions, "What is the purpose of all this fieldwork?" "Why am I doing fieldwork, and what do I hope to gain?" These are minor versions of the question, "What is the point of anthropology?" This latter question does not get asked often enough, even though we all have stock answers for introductory lectures. Answer the question truthfully – Why are *you* studying anthropology? Certainly, part of your answer will be that you gain personal satisfaction from the study. You probably also believe that you can make a contribution to human knowledge. Without those elements, the enterprise is pointless. Is there more?

There are many academic fields where fulfilling your personal goals does not entangle you in moral dilemmas. You can spend your whole career solving puzzles in pure mathematics without engendering the tiniest ruffle in the world. Not so with fieldwork. Fieldwork makes a difference in the world. It may not always be an earth-shattering difference, but it is a difference – and sometimes, unfortunately, it can be a harmful difference.

What Can Anthropology Do?

What social ills in the contemporary world are you most concerned with? – racism? police brutality? gun violence? economic inequality? gender disparities? homophobia? rights of the disabled? immigration and xenophobia? or something else? For every social problem in the world today there are anthropological studies that confront the issue, and I will append some sample, recent readings at the end of the chapter to get you started. One of your next steps can be to research the anthropological literature on an area that concerns you, and then decide if/how you are able to contribute to the discussion.

Both the mainstream media and social media are filled with ill-thought-out, quasi-solutions to complex social issues. Bad ideas cannot be censored in a nation that values free speech, but it is important to add an informed and reasoned voice into the mix to give people some choice. Well-spoken and knowledgeable anthropologists can rise above the noise and can make a difference in the world.

Think of how physicians work. First, they need extensive training in anatomy and physiology, and then they need some hands-on experience with patients under the direction of a supervisor. Before they can cure patients, they must learn how to diagnose them accurately, and then they need a broad knowledge of treatments. Now think of anthropologists as something like cultural physicians. First, you need to learn the basics of how cultures work (the anatomy and physiology). Then you need to gain practical experience of cultural situations with the help of your instructor. That area is what this book is concerned with: the equivalent of a physician's internship. Different cultural problems require different methods to diagnose them, and the projects in this book lay out an array of specialties to deal with those issues. Then comes the hardest nut of all to crack – implementing solutions to problems that have been diagnosed.

There is always the possibility that an anthropologist will misdiagnose a social problem, or will propose a solution that only makes things worse. There are numerous examples of good intentions gone wrong in the ecological world, which ought to give us pause. For example, The Nile perch (Lates niloticus) was deliberately introduced into Lake Victoria in the 1950s as a food source. It has since become one of the worst predatory species in the world, catastrophically disrupting the lake's ecosystem and the people who rely on it. Its introduction has led to the extinction or near-extinction of several hundred native species, and many local people have thereby been displaced from their traditional occupations in the fishing trade, and have become economic refugees. The introduction of Nile perch has also had additional negative ecological effects on shore. Nile perch have a high fat content, and, therefore, cannot be sun-dried, but must be smoked to avoid spoilage. This has led to an increased demand for firewood in a region already hard-hit by deforestation, soil erosion, and desertification. Intervention in social situations can be similarly disastrous.

One of my colleagues, before he was a graduate student, worked on several community projects in rural Nepal, and one village where he worked was plagued with multiple diseases that were caused by contaminated water in the community well. City-based engineers proposed replacing the well (supplied by an artesian basin) with indoor plumbing carrying clean drinking water from a local filtration plant. My colleague, along with other consultants, was troubled by this approach because, while it would clear up the water-borne disease issue, it would create a new problem in that it would fragment the village in multiple ways. The community well was a major meeting place where villagers daily exchanged information, resolved conflicts, or just hung out together. Indoor plumbing would have disrupted this critical social function of the well by isolating all of the households. Stop for a minute, and consider how you might resolve the problem of having infected water without disrupting village culture.[1]

Applied anthropology has been a potential specialty within the discipline for many decades and is even considered a fifth subfield by some American anthropologists. But the active involvement of anthropologists in social engineering of various kinds has had an uneven history. Ruth Benedict's *The Chrysanthemum and the Sword* (1946) is an old example of the use of ethnography to promote military goals for national purposes. The ethical issues involved in such projects are immense, and have resurfaced repeatedly, especially in the twenty-first century during conflicts between the United States and Afghanistan and Iraq (see, e.g., Price 2004; 2008, 2011, 2016). Even under ostensibly benign circumstances, anthropological knowledge based on fieldwork is a two-edged sword. Data about a population can always be used to benefit or to exploit those people. In the first half of the twentieth century, British social anthropology was primarily conducted in regions under British colonial control, and by the 1940s was increasingly funded by the British government whose attempts at colonial reform required more and more data from their colonies. https://www.cairn.info/revue-histoire-des-sciences-humaines-2002-1-page-161.htm#

Max Gluckman (1911–1975), who founded the so-called Manchester School of British social anthropology, was born and educated in South Africa before he moved to England and received training in anthropology from R.R. Marett, while also being heavily influenced by Radcliffe-Brown and Evans-Pritchard. In both his personal experience and in his fieldwork in South Africa he knew the evils of apartheid, racism, rampant urbanization, and labor exploitation firsthand. As such, he saw it as the principal mission of social anthropology to confront these evils. Both in his published works and in popular radio lectures, Gluckman sought to educate the public on the negative consequences of racism and colonialism. By the 1980s, his critique, and that of others, had evolved into a greater understanding of the implicit, though not necessarily intentional, ethnocentrism of anthropology that had emerged from its own colonialist baggage. Gluckman saw it as the moral duty of anthropologists to engage with indigenous communities and to right the wrongs of the past imposed upon them by the colonial system.

Another endeavor that sought to overturn the legacy of colonialism, but still deeply problematic, was the Cornell Peru Project, begun in 1952 and continuing until 1966 (see https://pdfs.semanticscholar.org/06b8/918fcad46db3c67063695a302264fed3f7d9.pdf). Cornell University had been engaged in multiple projects concerning agricultural research and modernization worldwide for some time under the rubric of "Cultural Applied Science," so that when the hacienda in Vicos in Peru became available, Cornell's anthropology department rented it with a view to making improvements to the lives of the inhabitants (based on anthropological theory). As Alan Holmberg notes:

> In 1952, as part of a research program in Cultural Applied Science, Cornell University, in collaboration with the Indigenous Institute of Peru, arranged to rent Vicos, a publicly owned hacienda on which previous observational studies

---

1 HINT: #1 Replacing the old well is necessary. #2 Indoor plumbing will disrupt community activities. Therefore, what will provide clean drinking water for the village while maintaining the communal functions of a well?.

had been made, for an initial period of five years. Broadly speaking, the purpose of embarking on this experience was twofold: on the theoretical side, it was hoped to conduct some form of experimental research on the processes of modernization now on the march in so many parts of the world; on the practical side, it was hoped to assist the community to shift for itself from a position of relative dependence and submission in a highly restricted and provincial world to a position of relative independence and freedom within the larger framework of Peruvian national life.

(Isbell 2009: 21)

This experiment was one of the earliest attempts at applying anthropological theory to social reform, and I will leave you to read about the results. In short – as you can probably guess without reading further – the end product was not great, not awful.

Activism using anthropology runs into all manner of ethical, legal, and practical problems but, with care, you can use your fieldwork experience to find solutions to concerns you may encounter in everyday life. The first thing you must do is gather data on the problem that you perceive and ask key questions: Is the problem a concern to others beside yourself? What are the dimensions of the problem? What fieldwork methods would be best for gathering data? From gathering data you must move to suggesting solutions, which is the tricky part. There could be practical considerations, such as costs, that may prohibit or limit change; or there may simply be official resistance to change (a social issue that requires skill in diplomacy alongside ethnographic data). You also have to consider the possible negative consequences of the changes that you are suggesting.

The best solutions to social problems are generated from within the culture, in consultation with outside helpers, rather than simply being imposed from above by "those who know." For example, a colleague of mine was once asked by the elders in a Diné (Navajo) village to work with a contracted architect who was designing a new school. The first draft plans presented by the architect had classrooms with multiple ground-level windows which the elders disliked. They explained that they wanted plenty of light in the classrooms but did not want people passing by to be able to see in. So my colleague, drawing on his knowledge of Diné culture based on participant observation studies, acted as an intermediary between the elders and the architect to produce plans that met both conventional architectural standards and traditional community values.

Around 15 years ago, when a new president was hired at my college, my fieldwork students wanted to use the opportunity to pitch for some innovations and adjustments to campus life. Everyone complained about food services on campus, but it did not take long to dismiss this topic from our list because this was an area that involved complex contractual obligations between the college and vendors which could not be altered without major negotiations. The contracts alone were thick legal documents that we had neither the time nor the expertise to analyze. On the other hand, there was a common complaint that the library hours were too short. Participant observation revealed that for most of the semester the complaint was baseless; at 10 p.m. when the library closed it was typically empty. However, at closing time during the exam period at the end of the semester, the library was packed. Therefore, my students showed their data to the new president and suggested that the hours be extended for the weeks before and during finals. The president agreed to extend the hours to 1 a.m., and, when this proved a huge success, extended them to 24 hours a day during the period in later years. There was a financial cost, of course, but the president agreed, based on my students' data, that the cost was worth it for the benefit derived.

Next Steps

While the discipline of anthropology seems to be on firm ground after 100 years of growth, critiques of its theory and methods in recent years, from both philosophical and practical points of view, have hit their marks with increasing accuracy. At the tail end of the twentieth century into present times there has emerged an undercurrent of discontent with ethnography as a means of producing useful knowledge to the point where a small, but vocal, minority is calling for an end to anthropological inquiry altogether. John Comaroff summarized the issue as follows:

> The "End of Anthropology" has been predicted many times and for many different reasons – among them, its disappearing object of study, its political imbrication in colonialism, the loss of its distinctive concepts, and the effects of globalization in diffusing its received subject matter. And yet, both institutionally and discursively, the discipline is very much alive, producing new species of knowledge, new theoretical discourses, new empirical interests, new arguments. How, in light of this, do we read the history of its present? By what means is its "end" to be avoided, its future(s) assured? Where should it go from here, empirically, methodologically, theoretically?
>
> (Comaroff 2010: 524)

Comaroff's points are well taken. The days of an anthropologist traveling off to some hard to access region, thinly populated by the members of an isolated culture to be studied and written about, are long past. Not only is the very idea of "studying" a culture anathema in modern times because of its colonialist implications, but also, cultural isolation – if it ever existed at all – is very much a thing of the past. The "remote" village in the highlands of Borneo you are contemplating for specialized ethnographic analysis may turn out to be the latest site for a new Starbucks or KFC. Even so, pessimism about the usefulness of ethnographic methods has its limits. A McDonald's in Long Banga in the Sarawak rainforests, or in Once barrio in suburban Buenos Aires, while being symbolic of the global spread of US capitalism, is not the same kind of cultural phenomenon as one in White Plains, New York, and careful fieldwork will reveal this reality.

Pursuing the projects in this book should have taught you, at minimum, that qualitative field methods are invaluable in engendering and preserving cultural knowledge. There is no substitute for a life history documenting the lived experience of, say, growing up the daughter of African-American sharecroppers in Mississippi in the 1960s, or of a Hasidic Jew in Brooklyn in the 1990s. There is no equivalent to participant observation to appreciate the experience of being a Central American asylum seeker living in squalor in a Mexican migrant camp, waiting for years for your asylum hearing with

US immigration officials. The official histories and media reports do not capture life on the ground in the same kind of way.

Ethnographic fieldwork will likely never be superseded as a data gathering instrument because of its well-honed, and constantly updated, methodology. Nevertheless, it is likely that additional research strategies will be included into the canon and existing strategies will be adjusted. For instance, more recently, there is a resurgence in interest in art-based and story-telling methodologies among researchers with an express anti-colonial framework. Other researchers advocate for methods that are rooted in Indigenous or Black **epistemologies** and **ontologies** (see Straits et al. 2019; Fish and Counts 2020). These methods are designed, in part, with the goal of actively resisting colonialism and racism. Although there is certainly some overlap with activist approaches, these emerging fieldwork techniques are grounded in articulated decolonial, anti-imperialist and anti-racist politics and perspectives that intentionally center the voices and struggles of Black, Native and Indigenous people, women of color, and other marginalized groups. Other emerging strategies include studying the process of positionality and knowledge production and analyzing collaborative research projects with an eye for how ethnography can be designed, and used for justice and liberation (see https://nomadit.co.uk/conference/spa2021/p/9690 and references below).

So ... what is next for you? Like any type of education, learning fieldwork techniques is transformational. You emerge at the end of the experience a little different, a little changed. How do you think this experience has shaped the way you view the world and your abilities to understand it? Where will you take this training? Whether you hit on medicine, social work, journalism, politics, business, teaching, or writing, or, perhaps, graduate study in anthropology, I am certain this training in fieldwork can be helpful to you. It is my fervent hope that whatever path you travel in the future you carry your ethnographic knowledge with you to help you on your journey.

Further Reading

The principal journal of applied anthropology in the United States is *Human Organization* and in the UK is *Anthropology in Action*. You can search them for areas of interest. There is also:

"Lessons from Vicos" by Billie Jean Isbell https://pdfs.semanticscholar.org/06b8/918fcad4 6db3c67063695a302264fed3f7d9.pdf, which gives a comprehensive analysis of the Cornell project in Peru.
Or, you might look at Charles Hale's (2001) "What Is Activist Research?" https://liberalarts.utexas.edu/anthropology/_files/PDF/Hale.pdf

There are online groups and resources involved in activist anthropology such as:

https://thefamiliarstrange.com/2019/04/22/activist-anthropology/
http://www.americananthropologist.org/2017/03/27/activist-anthropology-a-conversation-between-daniel-m-goldstein-and-keisha-khan-y-perry/
https://www.reddit.com/r/Anthropology/comments/2n9ptl/can_someone_explain_to_me_how_activist/

https://culanth.org/fieldsights/what-does-anthropology-sound-like-activism

Sallie Han and Jason Antrosio
Open Anthropology
"Enough: Anthropologists Take On Gun Violence."
Volume 6, Number 1
2018
https://www.americananthro.org/StayInformed/OAArticleDetail.aspx?ItemNumber=22601

Jason Antrosio and Sallie Han
Open Anthropology
"Race, Racism, and Protesting Anthropology
Volume 3, Number 3
2015
https://www.americananthro.org/StayInformed/OAArticleDetail.aspx?ItemNumber=13103

The Anthropology of Police
Kevin G. Karpiak and Garriott, W. (eds) 2018

Taylor & Francis (2021). *Burning at Europe's Borders: An Ethnography on the African Migrant Experience in Morocco* by Isabella Alexander-Nathani Oxford University Press.

(2012). *Intimate Migrations: Gender, Family and Illegality among Transnational Mexicans* by Deborah A. Boehm New York University Press.

(2017).*Writing the World of Policing: The Difference Ethnography Makes* edited by Didier Fassin University of Chicago Press.

(2019). *Mamma Might Be Better Off Dead: The Failure of Health Care in Urban America* by Laurie Kaye Abraham, University of Chicago Press.

References Cited

Abidin, C. (2015). Communicative Intimacies: Influencers and Perceived Interconnectedness. *Ada* 8: 1–16.

Abidin, C. (2019). Yes Homo: Gay Influencers, Homonormativity, and Queerbaiting on YouTube. *Continuum* 33 (5): 614–629. https://doi.org/10.1080/10304312.2019.1644806.

Adams, T., Holman Jones, S., and Ellis, C. (2021). *Handbook of Autoethnography*, 2nd ed. New York. Routledge.

Albro, R., Marcus, G., McNamara, L.A. and Schoch-Spana, M. (eds). (2011). *Anthropologists in the SecurityScape: Ethics, Practice, and Professional Identity*. Walnut Creek, CA: Left Coast Press.

Armbruster, H. and Lærke, A. (eds). (2008). *Taking Sides: Ethics, Politics, and Fieldwork in Anthropology*. New York and Oxford: Berghahn.

Armstrong, R.P. (1971). *The Affecting Presence: An Essay in Humanistic Anthropology*. Urbana, IL: U. Illinois Press.

Angrosino, M.V. (1989). *Documents of Interaction: Biography, Autobiography, and Life History in Social Science Perspective*. Gainesville, FL: U. of Florida Press.

Ayi, B., Harrell, S., and Lunzy, M. (2007). *Fieldwork Connections: The Fabric of Ethnographic Collaboration in China and America*. U. Washington Press.

Barnes, R.H. (1984). *Two Crows Denies It: A History of Controversy in Omaha Sociology*. Lincoln, NE: U. Nebraska.

Behar, R. (1990). Rage and redemption: Reading the life story of a Mexican marketing woman. *Feminist Studies* 16 (2): 223–258.

Benedict, R. (1946). *The Chrysanthemum and the Sword*. Boston, New York: Houghton Mifflin.

Bestor, T.C., Steinhoff, P.G., and Bestor, V.L. (eds). (2003). *Doing Fieldwork in Japan*. U. Hawaii Press.

Berg, B.L. (2006). *Qualitative Research Methods for the Social Sciences*, 6e. Boston. California State University

Bertaux, D. (1981). *Biography and Society: The Life History Approach in the Social Sciences*. Newbury Park, CA. Sage.

Boas, F. (1887). Museums of Ethnology and their classification. *Science* 9 (228): 587–589.

Boas, F. (1927). *Primitive Art*. Oslo: H. Aschehoug & Co.

Doing Field Projects: Methods and Practice for Social and Anthropological Research, First Edition. John Forrest.
© 2022 John Wiley & Sons, Inc. Published 2022 by John Wiley & Sons, Inc.

boyd, D. (2011). White Flight in Networked Publics? How Race and Class Shaped American Teen Engagement with MySpace and Facebook. In: *Race after the Internet*, (eds. L. Nakamura and P. Chow-White), New York: Routledge.

Bradburd, D. (1998). *Being There: The Necessity of Fieldwork*. Washington D.C.: Smithsonian.

Briggs, J. (1970). *Never in Anger: Portrait of an Eskimo Family*. Cambridge, MA: Harvard U.P.

Buolamwini, J. and Gebru, T. (2018). Gender Shades: Intersectional Accuracy Disparities in Commercial Gender Classification. In *Conference on Fairness, Accountability and Transparency*, 77–91. PMLR. http://proceedings.mlr.press/v81/buolamwini18a.html. (accessed 3 Jan 2021).

Carsten, J. (ed). (2000). *Cultures of Relatedness: New Approaches to the Study of Kinship*. Cambridge U.P.

Casagrande, J.B. (ed). (1960). *In the Company of Man: Twenty Portraits of Anthropological Informants*. New York: Harper.

Cerwonka, A. and Malkki, L.H. (2007). *Improvising Theory: Process and Temporality in Ethnographic Fieldwork*. U. Chicago Press.

Cheney-Lippold, J. (2017). *We Are Data*. New York: New York University Press.

Clark, M.D. (2015). Black twitter: Building connection through cultural conversation. In: *Hashtag Publics: The Power and Politics of Discursive Networks*, (ed. N. Rambukkana), 205–217. Pieterlen and Bern: Peter Lang Press.

Clifford, J. (1997). *The Predicament of Culture: Twentieth-Century Ethnography, Literature, and Art*. Cambridge, MA: Harvard U.P.

Clifford, J. and Marcus, G.E. (eds). (1986). *Writing Culture: The Poetics and Politics of Ethnography*. Berkeley, CA: U. of California Press.

Comaroff, J. (2010). The End of Anthropology, Again: On the Future of an In/Discipline. *American Anthropologist* 112: 524–538.

Crane, J.G. (1987). *Saba Silhouettes: Life Stories from a Caribbean Island*. New York: Vantage.

Crane, J.G. (ed). (1999). *Statia Silhouettes*. New York: Vantage.

Crane, J.G. and Angrosino, M.V. (1984). *Field Projects in Anthropology*, 3e. Prospect Heights, IL: Waveland.

Crapanzano, V. (1984). Life Histories: A Review Essay. *American Anthropologist* 86: 953–960.

Davies, C. (1999). *Reflexive Ethnography: A Guide to Researching Selves and Others*. New York and London: Routledge.

DeWalt, K.M., DeWalt, B.R., and Wayland, C.B. (1998). Participant Observation. In: *Handbook of Methods in Cultural Anthropology*, (ed. H.R. Bernard), 259–299. Walnut Creek, CA: AltaMira Press.

Diamond, S. (1972). Anthropology in Question. In: *Reinventing Anthropology*, (ed. D. Hymes), 401–429. New York: Pantheon.

Dumont, J.-P. (1978). *The Headman and I: Ambiguity and Ambivalence in the Fieldwork Experience*. Prospect Heights, IL: Waveland.

Durkheim, E. (1915 [1912]). *The Elementary Forms of the Religious Life*. trans. J.W. Swain. London: Allen & Unwin.

Dwyer, K. (1999). *Moroccan Dialogues: Anthropology in Question*. Baltimore: Johns Hopkins U P.

Ellis, C. and Bochner, A.P. (eds). (1996). *Composing Ethnography: Alternative Forms of Qualitative Writing*. Lanham, MD: Rowman.

Ellis, C. (2004). *The Ethnographic I: A Methodological Novel about Autoethnography*. Walnut Creek: AltaMira Press.

Emerson, R.M., Fretz, R.I., and Shaw, L.L. (2011). *Writing Ethnographic Fieldnotes*, 2nd ed. U. Chicago Press.

Emerson, R.M., Fretz, R.I., and Shaw, L.L. (2001). Participant Observation and Fieldnotes. In: *Handbook of Ethnography*, (eds. P. Atkinson, A. Coffey, S. Delamont, J. Lofland, and L. Lofland), 356–357. Thousand Oaks, CA: Sage Publications.

Faubion, J.D. and Marcus, G.E. (eds.). (2009). *Fieldwork Is Not What It Used to Be: Learning Anthropology's Method in a Time of Transition*. Ithaca, NY: Cornell U.P.

Fish, J. and Counts, P.K. (2020). Justice for Native People, Justice for Native Me: Using Digital Storytelling Methodologies to Change the Master Narrative of Native American Peoples. In: *Cultural Methodologies in Psychology: Describing and Transforming Cultures*, ed. Kate C. McLean. Oxford University Press. DOI:10.31234/osf.io/y2w3v.

Forman, S. (1993). *Diagnosing America: Anthropology and Public Engagement*. Ann Arbor, MI: U. Michigan Press.

Forrest, J. (1984). *Morris and Matachin: A Study in Comparative Choreography*. University of Sheffield, Centre for English Cultural Tradition and Language Publications #4.

Forrest, J. (1985). Here We Come A-Fossiling. *Dance Research Journal* 17: 27–34.

Forrest, J. (1988a). *Lord I'm Coming Home: Everyday Aesthetics in Tidewater, North Carolina*. Ithaca, NY: Cornell UP.

Forrest, J. (1988b). Who Calls the Tune? New Methods for Exploring the Relationships Between Dances and their Music. *Folk Music Journal* 5: 448–468.

Forrest, J. (1999). *The History of Morris Dancing (1458-1750) University of Toronto Press, 1999*. (U.S. & Canada): James Clarke and Co., 1999. (Great Britain)

Forrest, J. (2006). *Horizons of the Sacred: Mexican Traditions in U.S. Catholicism*, Timothy Matovina and Gary Riebe-Estrell, and, *Dancing with the Virgin: Body and Faith in the Fiesta of Tortugas, New Mexico*, Deidre Sklar. *Reviews in Anthropology* 35: 139–154.

Forrest, J. and Blincoe, D. (1995). *The Natural History of the Traditional Quilt*. Austin, Texas: U Texas Press.

Fortes, M. and Evans-Pritchard. E.E. (eds.) (1940). *African Political Systems*. Oxford: Oxford University Press.

Forrest, J. and Jackson, E. (1990). Get Real: Empowering the Student through Oral History. *Oral History Review* 18 (1): 29–44.

Frazer, J.G. (1890). *The Golden Bough: A Study in Comparative Religion*. 2 volumes. New York and London: Macmillan.

Freeman, D. (1983). *Margaret Mead and Samoa: The Making and Unmaking of an Anthropological Myth*. Cambridge, MA. Harvard U. P.

Gardner, M. (1970). Mathematical Games – The fantastic combinations of John Conway's new solitaire game "life". *Scientific American* 223 (4): 120–123.

Gardner, P.M. (2006). *Journeys to the Edge: In the Footsteps of an Anthropologist*. St Louis, MO: U. Missouri Press.

Geertz, C. (1973). *The Interpretation of Cultures*. New York: Basic Books.

Geertz, C. (1990). History and anthropology. *New Literary History* 21 (2): 321–35

Geertz, C. (1990). *Works and Lives: The Anthropologist as Author*. Stanford U P. Stanford, CA.

Goffman, E. (1956). *The Presentation of Self in Everyday Life*. New York: Doubleday.
Goodall, H.L. (2000). *Writing the New Ethnography*. Lanham, MD: AltaMira.
Goodson, I. (2009). The story of life history: Origins of the life history method in sociology. *Identity: An International Journal of Theory and Research* 1 (2): 129–142
Griffith, R. (1953). *The World of Robert Flaherty*. New york: Duell, Sloan, and Pearce.
Haley, A. (1965). *Autobiography of Malcolm X*. New York: Grove.
Hall, E. (1966). *The Hidden Dimension*. Garden City, New York: Doubleday.
Hannoum, A. (2011). The (Re)Turn of the Native: Ethnography, Anthropology, and Nativism. In: *The Anthropologist and the Native: Essays for Gananath Obeyesekere*, (ed. H. Seneviratne), 423–444. London: Anthem Press. 10.7135/UPO9780857289919.020.
Harrison, A.K. (2009). *Hip Hop Underground: The Integrity and Ethics of Racial Identification*. Philadelphia, PA: Temple U.P.
Hayano, D. (1979). Auto-ethnography: Paradigms, problems and prospects. *Human Organization* 38 (1): 99–104.
Hertz, R. (ed.) (1997). *Reflexivity and Voice*. Thousand Oaks, CA.
Herzfeld, M. (1987). *Anthropology through the Looking- Glass: Critical Ethnography in the Margins of Europe*. Cambridge. Cambridge U P.
Honigmann, J.J. (1976). *The Development of Anthropological Ideas*. Belmont, CA: Dorsey Press.
Howes, D. (ed). (1991). *The Varieties of Sensory Experience: A Sourcebook in the Anthropology of the Senses*. U. of Toronto Press.
Hurston, Z.N. (1935). *Mules and Men*. Philadelphia: Lippincott.
Hurston, Z.N. (2018). *Barracoon: The Story of the Last "Black Cargo"*. New York: Amistad.
Humphreys, L. (1999). Tearoom Trade. In: *Public Sex/Gay Space*, (ed. W. Leap), 29–54. New York: Columbia University Press.
Hymes, D. (1972). The Use of Anthropology: Critical, Political, Personal. In: *Reinventing Anthropology*, (ed. D. Hymes), 3–79. New York: Pantheon.
Hymes, D. (1976). Louis Simpson's The Deserted Boy. *Poetics* 5: 119–155.
Hymes, D. (1977). Discovering Oral Performance and Measured Verse in American Indian Narrative. *New Literary History* 8: 431–457.
Ingold, T. (1991). Fieldwork projects in undergraduate anthropology. *Anthropology Today* 7 (2): 22–23.
Isbell, B.J. (2009). Lessons from Vicos. *Anthropology in Action* 16: 41–54.
Ives, E.D. (1974). *The Tape Recorded Interview: A Manual for Field Workers in Folklore and Oral History*. Knoxville: U. Tennessee Press.
Jay, R. (1972). Personal and Extrapersonal Vision in Anthropology. In: *Reinventing Anthropology*, (ed. D. Hymes), 367–381. New York: Pantheon.
Kedia, S. and Van Willigen, J. (2005). *Applied Anthropology: Domains of Application*. Westport, Conn: Praeger.
Kratz, C. (2001). Conversations and Lives. In: *African Words, African Voices: Critical Practices in Oral History*, (ed. L. White, S. Miescher, and D.W. Cohen), 127–161. Bloomington, IN: U. Indiana Press.
Langness, L.L. (1965). *The Life History in Anthropological Science*. New York: Holt, Rinehart, and Winston.
Langness, L.L. and Frank, G. (1981). *Lives: An Anthropological Approach to Biography*. Novato, CA: Chandler and Sharp.

Leach, E. (1954). *Political Systems of Highland Burma*. Cambridge, MA: Harvard U P.

Linde, C. (1993). *Life Stories: The Creation of Coherence*. Oxford. Oxford University Press.

Lingel, J. (2017). *Digital Countercultures and the Struggle for Community*. Cambridge, MA: MIT Press.

Low, S.M. and Merry, S.E. (2010). Engaged Anthropology: Diversity and Dilemmas An Introduction to Supplement 2. *Current Anthropology* 51 (Supplement 2).

Malefijt, A.D. (1974). *Images of Man: A History of Anthropological Thought*. New York: Random House.

Malinowski, B. (1961 [1922]). *Argonauts of the Western Pacific: An Account of Native Enterprise and Adventure in the Archipelagoes of Melanesian New Guinea*. New York: Dutton.

Malinowski, B. (1967). *A Diary in the Strict Sense of the Term*. Routledge and Keagan Paul. Milton Park, UK.

Marcus, G.E. (1998). *Ethnography through Thick and Thin*. Princeton, NJ. Princeton U. P.

Maréchal, G. (2010). Autoethnography. In: *Encyclopedia of Case Study Research*, (eds. A.J. Mills, G. Durepos, and E. Wiebe), Vol. 2: 43–45. Thousand Oaks, CA: Sage Publications.

Marriott, A. (1953). *Greener Fields: Experiences among the American Indians*. Springfield, OH: Crowell.

Mingming, W. (2002). The Third Eye: Towards a Critique of 'Nativist Anthropology'. *Critique of Anthropology* 22 (2): 149–174. https://doi.org/10.1177/03075X02022002850.

Mishler, E.G. (1995). Models of Narrative Analysis: A Typology. *Journal of Narrative and Life History* 5 (2): 87–123.

Morgan, L.H. (1851). *League of the Ho-dé-no-sau-nee, or Iroquois*. Rochester, NY: Sage & Brother.

Morgan, L.H. (1871). *Systems of Consanguinity and Affinity of the Human Family*. Washington DC: Smithsonian Contributions to Knowledge.

Morgan, L.H. (1877). *Ancient Society*. Chicago: Charles Kerr.

Murphy, Y. and Murphy, R.F. (1974). *Women of the Forest*. New York: Columbia U.P.

Neihardt, J.G. (1932). *Black Elk Speaks*. New York: William Morrow.

Ochs, E. and Capps, L. (1996). Narrating the self. *Annual Review of Anthropology* 25: 19–43.

Olivas, H., O.L. (2018). *Danzar la frontera: procesos socioculturales en la tradición de danza azteca en las Californias*. México: El Colegio de la Frontera Norte-Juan Pablos Editor.

Parreñas, J.S. (2018). *Decolonizing Extinction: The Work of Care in Orangutan Rehabilitation*. Durham, NC: Duke U.P.

Peacock, J. and Holland, D. (1993). The narrated self: Life stories in process. *Ethos* 21 (4): 367–383.

Pike, K.L. ([1954, 1955, 1960] 1967). *Language in Relation to a Unified Theory of the Structure of Human Behavior*, 2e. The Hague: Mouton.

Powdermaker, H. (1967). *Stranger and Friend: The Way of an Anthropologist*. London: Secker and Warburg.

Price, D. (2004). *Threatening Anthropology: McCarthyism and the FBI's Surveillance of Activist Anthropologists*. Durham, NC: Duke University Press.

Price, D. (2008). *Anthropological Intelligence: The Deployment and Neglect of American Anthropology in the Second World War*. Duke University Press.

Price, D. (2011). *Weaponizing Anthropology: Social Science in Service of the Militarized State*. Petrolia, CA: AK/CounterPunch Books.

Price, D. (2016). *Cold War Anthropology: The CIA, the Pentagon and the Growth of Dual Use Anthropology*. Duke University Press.

Rabinow, P. (1977 & 2007). *Reflections on Fieldwork in Morocco*. Berkeley, CA: U. California Press.

Richardson, M. (1990). *Cry Lonesome and Other Accounts of the Anthropologist's Project*. Albany, NY: SUNY Press.

Riessman, C.K. (1987). When Gender is not Enough: Women Interviewing Women. *Gender and Society* 1: 172–207.

Riessman, C.K. (1990). Strategic Uses of Narrative in the Presentation of Self and Illness. *Social Science and Medicine* 30: 1195–1200.

Riessman, C.K. (1993). *Narrative Analysis*. Qualitative Research Methods Series #30. Newbury Park, CA. Sage.

Rivers, W.H.R. (1906). *The Todas*. New York: Macmillan.

Robben, A.C.G.M. and Sluka, J.A. (eds). (2012). *Ethnographic Fieldwork: An Anthropological Reader*, 2e. Chichester: Wiley-Blackwell.

Rogovin, M. (1980). *Three Mile Island: A Report to the Commissioners and to the Public*. Vol. I. https://web.archive.org/web/20101130124554/http:/threemileisland.org/downloads/354.pdf.

Rosaldo, M.Z., Lamphere, L., and Bamberger, J. (eds). (1974). *Woman, Culture, and Society*. Stanford U.P.

Rosaldo, R. (1986). From the Door of His Tent: The Fieldworker and the Inquisitor. In: *Writing Culture: The Poetics and Politics of Ethnography*, (ed. J. Clifford and G.E. Marcus), 77–97. Berkeley, CA: University of California Press.

Rosenthal, G. (2018). *Interpretive Social Research. An Introduction*. Göttingen: Universitätsverlag Göttingen.

Rosenwald, G.C. and Ochberg, R.L. (eds). (1992). *Storied Lives: The Cultural Politics of Self-Understanding*. New Haven: Yale U.P.

Sanford, V. and Angel-Ajani, A. (eds). (2006). *Engaged Observer: Anthropology, Advocacy, and Activism*. Brunswick, NJ: Rutgers U.P.

Sanjek, R. (1990). *Fieldnotes: The Makings of Anthropology*. Ithaca, NY: Cornell U.P.

Schneider, D.M. (1984). *A Critique of the Study of Kinship*. Ann Arbor: University of Michigan Press.

Scholte, B. (1972). Toward a Reflexive and Critical Anthropology. In: *Reinventing Anthropology*, (ed. D. Hymes), 430–457. New York: Pantheon.

Senft, T. (2013). Microcelebrity and the Branded Self. In: *A Companion to New Media Dynamics* (eds. J. Hartley, J. Burgess, and A. Bruns), 346–354. Oxford: Blackwell.

Sharma, U. (1989). Fieldwork in the undergraduate curriculum: Its merits. *British Association for Social Anthropology in Policy and Practice* 3: 3–4.

Sharma, U. (1991). Field research in the undergraduate curriculum. *Anthropology in Action* 10: 8–11.

Sharma, U. and Wright, S. (1989). Practical relevance of undergraduate courses. *British Association for Social Anthropology in Policy and Practice* 2: 7–9.

Sharon, D. (2015). *Wizard of the Four Winds: A Shaman's Story*, 2e. New York: Free Press.

Shell-Duncan, B. and Hernlund, Y. (2000). *Female "Circumcision" in Africa: Culture, Controversy, and Change*. Boulder, CO: Lynne Rienner.

Shostak, M. (1981). *Nisa: The Life and Words of a !Kung Woman*. Cambridge, MA: Harvard U.P.

Siegel, J.T. (2011). *Objects and Objections of Ethnography*. New York: Fordham U.P.

Sluka, J.A. and Robben, A.C.G.M. (2012). Fieldwork in Cultural Anthropology: An Introduction. In: *Ethnographic Fieldwork: An Anthropological Reader*, 2e. 1–47. Chichester: Wiley Blackwell.

Steinfield, C., Ellison, N.B., and Lampe, C. (2008). Social capital, self-esteem, and use of online social network sites: A longitudinal analysis. *Journal of Applied Developmental Psychology* 29 (6): 434–445.

Straits, K.J.E., deMaría, J., and Tafoya, N. (2019). Place of Strength: Indigenous Artists and Indigenous Knowledge is Prevention Science. *American Journal of Community Psychology* 64: 96–106.

Stoller, P. (1989). *The Taste of Ethnographic Things: The Senses in Anthropology*. Philadelphia, PA: University of Pennsylvania.

Stoller, P. (1997). *Sensuous Scholarship* 1997. University of Pennsylvania. Philadelphia, PA.

Tedlock, D. (1977). Toward an Oral Poetics. *New Literary History* 8: 507–519.

Thapan, M. (ed). (1998). *Anthropological Journeys: Reflections on Fieldwork*. New Delhi: Orient Longman.

Thorn, R. and Wright, S. (1990). Projects and placements in undergraduate anthropology. *British Association for Social Anthropology in Policy and Practice* 7: 4–5.

Tylor, E.B. (1871). *Primitive Culture*. Vol. 2 London: John Murray.

Urban, G. (1989). The 'I' of discourse. In: *Semiotics, Self and Society*, (ed. B. Lee and G. Urban), Berlin: De Gruyter.

Warner, M. (2002). Publics and Counterpublics. *Public Culture* 14 (1): 49–89.

Watson, C. W. (1995). Case study: Fieldwork in undergraduate anthropology – For and Against. *Innovations in Education and Training International* 32 (2): 153–161.

Watson, C. W. (1999). *Being There: Fieldwork in Anthropology*. London: Pluto Press.

Weston, K. (1991). *Families We Choose: Lesbians, Gays, Kinship*. New York: Columbia U. P.

Wilkin, K. (ed). (2001). *Ascending Peculiarity: Edward Gorey on Edward Gorey*. San Diego, CA: Harcourt Brace Academic.

Williams, R. (1983). *Keywords: A Vocabulary of Culture and Society*. Revised. San Diego, CA: Oxford University Press.

Williams, R. (2003). *Television: Technology and Cultural Form*. New York: Routledge. https://www.routledge.com/Television-Technology-and-Cultural-Form/Williams/p/book/9780415314565.

Zeitlyn, D. (2008). Life-history writing and the anthropological silhouette. *Social Anthropology* 16 (2): 154–171.

Index

a
activism   103, 178–179, 199–201
aesthemics   7
aesthetics   7, 25, 89, 119–122, 126, 130–131, 139, 167, 173
anonymity   31–32, 56–57, 171
applied anthropology   9–10, 200
Argentina   vi, 13, 18–19, 43, 162–163, 165
art   1, 121–122, 139, 167,
autoethnography   49, 51, 188

b
Bateson, Gregory   119, 124
bias   viii, 9–11, 13, 39–40, 120, 157, 188,
Boas, Franz   14, 103, 118

c
Cambodia   7, 48, 63, 73–75
cancel culture   176–178
community   9, 13, 100, 103, 130, 171–172
comparative approaches   69, 143, 166
cultural relativism   103–104
China   3, 73, 97–98, 150, 161, 168–169, 179
cooking   36, 70–75, 113
Curtis, Edward Sheriff   117–118

d
dance   1, 53, 102, 119, 122–123, 138–146, 168, 193
Durkheim, Émile   3, 131

e
emic   6–8, 52
engaged interviews   78–79, 104–107
ethnicity   1, 9, 18, 34, 36, 39, 43, 47–48, 78, 101, 106–107, 152, 156, 173, 179
ethnocentrism   103, 200
epistemologies   203
ethics   10–11, 17, 23, 27–32, 56, 82, 104, 107–108, 122, 124, 132, 140, 149, 197, 200–201
etic   6–8, 52
Evans-Pritchard, E.E.   5, 8

f
field notes   10–11, 13, 58, 99, 136, 142, 197–198
films   117–120, 124, 184
Flaherty, Robert   118–119
Frazer, James George   2, 6

g
gender   1, 9, 18, 37, 39, 47, 57, 69, 101, 107, 173, 176, 184

h
Hall, Edward T.   52

i
idiographic   14
Implicit Associations Test   40
indexing files   24, 77, 83, 107, 115, 150–153, 197
influencers   171, 175–176

Doing Field Projects: Methods and Practice for Social and Anthropological Research, First Edition.
John Forrest.
© 2022 John Wiley & Sons, Inc. Published 2022 by John Wiley & Sons, Inc.

informed consent   23, 27, 30–31, 56, 82, 108, 114, 122, 140, 151, 183, 195
Italy   vi, 36, 73–75, 91
iterative process   34–35, 141, 152–153

k
kinship   5–6, 12, 158–165
kitchens   36, 64, 70–75

l
London underground   60–62

m
Malinowski, Bronislaw   5–6, 8, 26, 102,
Mead, Margaret   119, 124
Morgan, Lewis Henry   3–4, 166
music   118, 132, 136, 138–146, 168, 193

n
narrative   43, 85, 87, 120, 123, 125, 147–149, 157
nomothetic   14
Nutcracker   143–144

o
objectivity   11–15, 103–104, 135, 157, 194
observation (not participant)   8, 17, 20, 37, 39, 41, 49, 51, 54–58, 70, 112, 114, 117, 122, 129–130, 135, 144, 176, 179, 188, 194–195, 198, 201
online communities   170–172
online gaming   172, 182–184
online research   25–26, 60, 64, 69, 75, 77, 195
ontologies   203
oral history   147–148

p
participant observation   6, 8, 14, 29, 31, 49–50, 76, 77, 94–109, 132–136, 142–145, 169, 182–183, 188–195, 201–202
photography   22, 25, 31, 95, 97–98, 109, 111–126, 142, 145, 168, 172–173, 189

PowerPoint   38, 116, 123, 142, 159
post-colonialism   8–10, 19, 202–203
proxemics   7, 52–58, 188

q
quantitative analysis   vii, 30

r
race   1, 118, 169–170, 184
racism   40, 105, 198, 200, 203
religion   1–3, 5, 34, 56, 96, 108, 139, 163
rituals   31, 50, 97–98, 118–119, 123, 139
reception theory   144–145
reflexivity   20–21, 26, 49–51, 188
Rivers, W.H.R   5

s
selfies   172–173
seven-day diary   40–43
smartphone   22–26, 54, 57, 66, 90, 112, 123, 125, 167, 173–175, 183, 187–188,
spelling   84–85
sports   108, 168, 172
story-telling   203
subjectivity   11–15, 50, 130, 135, 148, 157

t
Tidewater, NC   vi, 59, 125, 164
transcription   82–88, 153–155
Tylor, E. B.   2–3

u
Umwelt   130–131
unit of analysis   35–37

v
video   88–89, 119–120, 123–125
vocabulary   17–19, 92, 129–136, 167

w
Weber, Max   3
weddings   36, 97–98, 121, 125, 184